DINOSAUR HIGHWAY

Laurie E. Jasinski

DINOSAUR HIGHWAY
a history of dinosaur valley state park

LAURIE E. JASINSKI

TCU Press
Fort Worth, Texas

Opposite Page: *A park ranger sweeps sediment out of theropod tracks in the Paluxy River at Dinosaur Valley State Park.* Courtesy Somervell County Historical Museum

Library of Congress Cataloging-in-Publication Data

Jasinski, Laurie E.
  Dinosaur Highway : A History of Dinosaur Valley State Park /
by Laurie E. Jasinski.
        p. cm.
  Includes bibliographical references and index.
  ISBN 978-0-87565-375-4 (alk. paper)
  1. Dinosaur Valley State Park (Tex.)–History.
  2. Dinosaur Valley State Park (Tex.)–Biography.
  3. Natural history–Texas–Dinosaur Valley State Park.
  I. Title.
  F392.S65J37 2008
  976.4'521–dc22

                    2008003137

        Book design by Tom Martens at fusion29. www.fusion29.com

TCU Press
P.O.Box 298300
Fort Worth, Texas 76129
817.257.7822
http://www.prs.tcu.edu

To order books: 800.826.8911

TO GARY

Dappled sunlight dances on the theropod tracks that lead into the Paluxy River. These remnants of the ancient past fascinate visitors at Dinosaur Valley State Park. Photo by Gary S. Hickinbotham

TABLE OF CONTENTS

Introduction ix

Acknowledgments x

CHAPTER ONE:
The Changing Face of North Central Texas 1

CHAPTER TWO:
Fountains of Youth 13

CHAPTER THREE:
Making Tracks 29

CHAPTER FOUR:
Work and Play on Paluxy "Creek" 51

CHAPTER FIVE:
The Dinosaur Hunter and the Texas Village 61

CHAPTER SIX:
In the Footsteps of the Dinosaurs 69

CHAPTER SEVEN:
The Fight for Dinosaur Valley 91

CHAPTER EIGHT:
To Capture a Park—Landscape and Riverscape and Trailway 107

CHAPTER NINE:
Growing Pains for Dinosaur Valley State Park 121

CHAPTER TEN:
Maintaining the Dinosaur Highway 139

"The Dinosaur Waltz" 157

Notes and Other Trackways 161

Bibliography 190

Index 201

JOE AND LAURIE SANDERS

Joe and Laurie Sanders pose for a photo at the site of the dinosaur tracks in Somervell County in August 1929. Courtesy Laurie P. Sanders Collection

INTRODUCTION

Years ago, I spent countless pleasant hours recording my grandmother's stories about traveling the Texas Hill Country. My grandparents, Joe and Laurie Sanders, enjoyed many Sunday drives. During the course of poring over scads of mementos and photographs with my grandmother, a strange and amazing snapshot surfaced. A single tri-toed track evoked curiosity and wonder. The distinctive print (that I would one day know as a theropod footprint) conjured images of a giant lizard or bird.

My grandmother told me about this dinosaur souvenir and how, in the summer of 1929, she and Joe journeyed north to Glen Rose in Somervell County to see the tracks of these ancient creatures. Decades later her recollections and a few images chronicled that memorable tour. She, then a young woman of twenty-six, posed with Joe in the Somervell County countryside. They were a youthful couple of the 1920s taking part in the increasingly popular practice of the day—the scenic motor trip.

Her account of their grand adventure stayed with me and roared back to life when in 2004 I began researching and writing this book's genesis, a history report of Dinosaur Valley State Park for the Texas Parks and Wildlife Department. My husband Gary and I traveled to Glen Rose just as my grandparents had done seventy-five years earlier. We cruised through Somervell County's rugged terrain—what I call the "Northern Hill Country"—and tromped along the Paluxy River in the footsteps of the dinosaurs.

The Paluxy riverbed shares its ancient tracks with wide-eyed children and curious adults who wade the sparkling waters and skip from stone to stone in search of treasures that hint of a long-ago landscape. The fossil prints' remarkable tales have drawn international attention. The Paluxy Valley, relatively young in terms of geologic time, harbors a legacy of cedar hills, rolling prairies, and clear streams no less significant and colorful than the world of the dinosaurs.

Water sculpted this territory and attracted settlement. The earliest inhabitants camped at cool springs, and Spanish and French explorers found a region that thrived as a crossroads of trade. Pioneers homesteaded and farmed along the Paluxy. Schoolchildren played games, splashed in the local swimming hole, and traipsed down country lanes to their homes. Families nurtured a sense of community and preserved a heritage that survives today.

Many warmhearted people welcomed me in the course of my research, and they shared their stories—memories that bring the history of this land to life. Their words and photographs paint the character of Somervell County and contribute to a fascinating blend of agriculture, science, business, and recreation.

The history of the Paluxy River Valley indeed has many layers for the people who made their lives here. Memories linger in the canyons and trace the stony tracks in the stream, connecting the ancient to the present in Dinosaur Valley State Park.

ACKNOWLEDGMENTS

Many people, institutions, and archives contributed invaluable information, illustrations, and insightful anecdotes for this book. I am most grateful to everyone who provided assistance.

Thank you to the Texas Parks and Wildlife Department for the opportunity to work on this project. TPWD furnished helpful guidance, especially Cynthia Brandimarte, Historic Sites Program Director, Austin; Michael Strutt, Cultural Resources Director, Austin; Billy Paul Baker, Park Superintendent at Dinosaur Valley State Park, Glen Rose; Diane Dismukes, Cultural Resources Specialist, Whitney, Texas; David Riskind, Natural Resources Director, Austin; Mike O'Brien, Exhibits Sculptor, Austin; Aina Dodge, Marni Francell, Margaret Howard, Logan McNatt, Amy Ringstaff, and Shirley Monagas, Austin.

I also extend my deepest thanks to the paleontologists and geologist who advised me in regards to the scientific studies and terminology of this history: James O. Farlow, Department of Geosciences, Indiana University-Purdue University Fort Wayne; Louis Jacobs, Shuler Museum of Paleontology, Southern Methodist University, Dallas; James Diffily, formerly of the Fort Worth Museum of Science and History.

I am very grateful to Donald W. Olson, professor of physics at Texas State University-San Marcos, for his careful editing of my drafts as well as his scanning of illustrations.

Thanks to the staff of the following research institutions and offices: Albert B. Alkek Library, Texas State University-San Marcos; American Museum of Natural History, New York; Center for American History, University of Texas at Austin; *Dallas Morning News*; Dinosaur Valley State Park, Glen Rose; *Glen Rose Reporter*, Glen Rose; Heritage Museum of the Texas Hill Country, Canyon Lake, Texas; LDL Friends of Dinosaur Valley State Park, Glen Rose; Sinclair Oil Corporation, Salt Lake City, Utah; Somervell County Clerk's Office, Glen Rose; Somervell County Heritage Center, Glen Rose; Somervell County Historical Commission, Glen Rose; Somervell County Library, Glen Rose; Somervell County Museum, Glen Rose; Texas General Land Office, Austin; Texas Historical Commission Library, Austin; Texas Memorial Museum, University of Texas at Austin; Texas State Historical Association, Austin; Texas State Library and Archives, Austin.

A number of individuals furnished vital information and advice during this project. I want to express my sincere appreciation to everyone, especially the residents of Glen Rose: Susan Bell, Division of Paleontology, American Museum of Natural History, New York; Shawn Bengtson, Dinosaur Valley State Park, Glen Rose; Curtis Busch, Glen Rose; Donna Coates, Austin; Murray Dehtan, Glen Rose; Everett Deschner, Heritage Museum of the Texas Hill Country, Canyon Lake; Rhonda Duffie, Somervell County Heritage Center, Glen Rose; Darla Evans, Austin; Glen Evans, Austin; Ken Fry (and for his artwork), Somervell County Historical Commission, Glen Rose; Lester Galbreath, Albany, Texas; Wendy Glassmire, Image Collection/Sales, National Geographic Society, Washington, DC;

Betty Gosdin, Somervell County Heritage Center, Glen Rose; Kenneth Hopson, Glen Rose; Doug Howard, Surveying Division, Texas General Land Office, Austin; Lawrence T. Jones III, Austin; Xena Jones, Heritage Museum of the Texas Hill Country, Canyon Lake; Jean F. King, Somervell County Museum, Glen Rose; Glen Kuban, Tomball, Texas; Dorothy Leach, Somervell County Historical Commission, Glen Rose; Maxie Parker Leach, Glen Rose; Kathy Lenz, Dinosaur Valley State Park, Glen Rose; Jason Martinson, Legal Division, Texas Parks and Wildlife Department, Austin; Barbara Mathé, Special Collections, American Museum of Natural History Library, New York; Daisy Ryals May, El Paso; Geneva "Pete" May, Oakdale Park, Glen Rose; Dan McCarty, *Glen Rose Reporter*, Glen Rose; B. J. Morris, Glen Rose; Linda Newland, Austin; Mazie Parish, Dinosaur Valley State Park, Glen Rose; Collis Park, Dinosaur Valley State Park, Glen Rose; Peter Rose, Department of Geology and Geophysics, University of Minnesota, Minneapolis; Raymond Rye, Smithsonian Institution, National Museum of Natural History, Washington, DC; Jason Sanchez, Dinosaur Valley State Park, Glen Rose; Laurie P. Sanders, New Braunfels; Violet Sandlin, Dinosaur Valley State Park, Glen Rose; John Schendel, New Braunfels; Liz Sherrell, LDL Friends of Dinosaur Valley State Park, Glen Rose; Ed Theriot, Texas Memorial Museum, Austin; Charlidell Davis Wilson, Glen Rose; Doyle Wilson, Glen Rose; and especially Novella Wilson, Lanham Mill historian and artist in Glen Rose, whose stories and images capture the early history of Dinosaur Valley.

My deepest thanks for the steady support of my parents Richard Jasinski and Laurie Jo Sanders Jasinski and my brother Larry Jasinski. I am most grateful to my mother for proofreading.

My husband Gary S. Hickinbotham provided valuable service with his photography of the park, help in conducting archival searches, and assistance with conducting deed searches. He also played an integral role in this work with his support and companionship on our field trips. Most importantly, his initial encouragement made this book possible.

Lastly, I'm grateful that my grandparents made that early journey to Glen Rose—a trip that resulted in my grandfather's photograph and my grandmother's story, my first story of Glen Rose and the dinosaur tracks those years ago. "Mammam," my grandmother, gave me what turned out to be the first kernel of this book.

The Paluxy River flows past rugged cedar hills and grassy pastures in Dinosaur Valley State Park.
Photo by Gary S. Hickinbotham

CHAPTER ONE

The Changing Face of North Central Texas

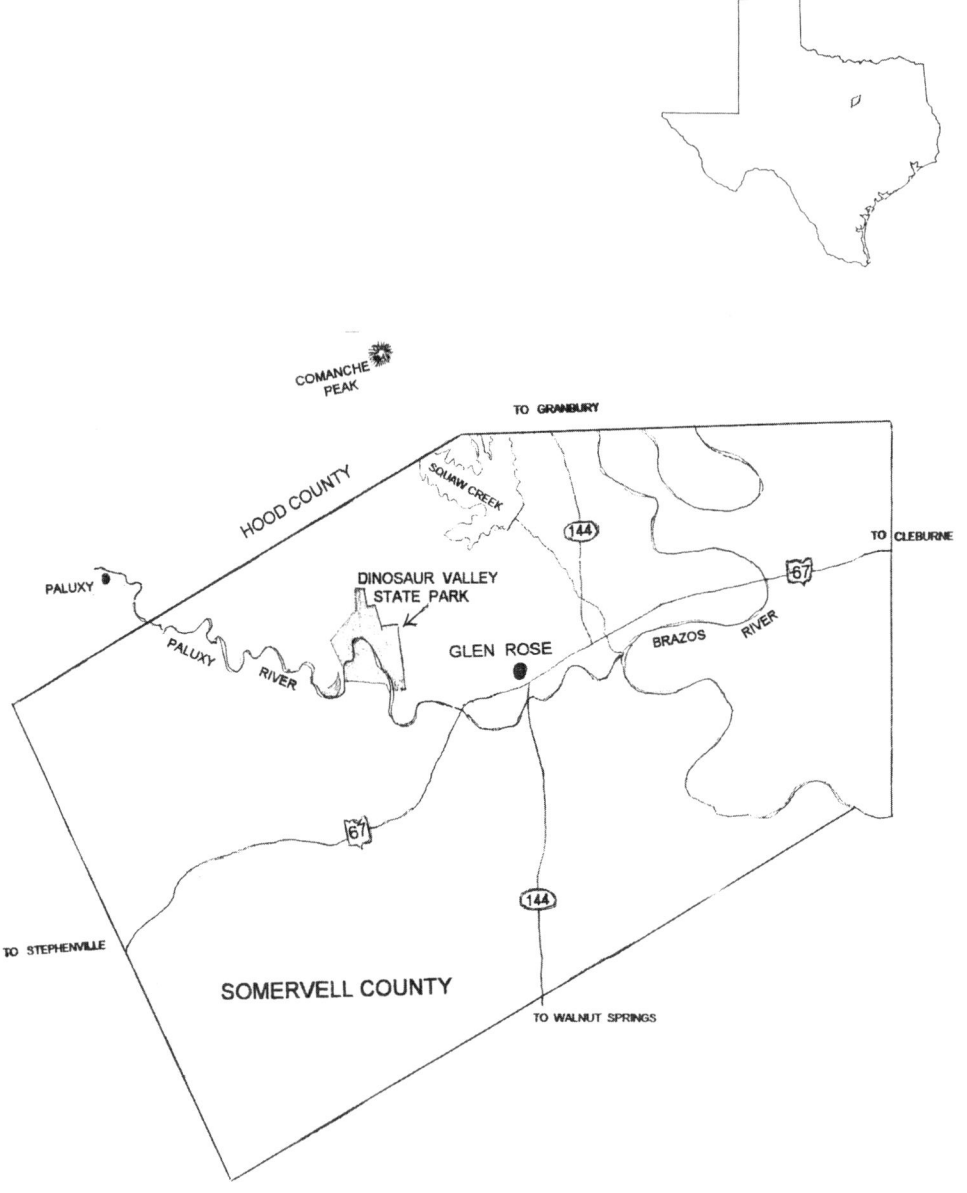

COMANCHE PEAK

TO GRANBURY

HOOD COUNTY

SQUAW CREEK

144

TO CLEBURNE

PALUXY

67

DINOSAUR VALLEY
STATE PARK

GLEN ROSE

PALUXY   RIVER

BRAZOS   RIVER

67

144

TO STEPHENVILLE

SOMERVELL COUNTY

TO WALNUT SPRINGS

DINOSAUR VALLEY STATE PARK AND VICINITY
4 MILES WEST OF GLEN ROSE

The crystal green waters of the Paluxy River dance through a carved valley of limestone cliffs that rise above the stream. In the distance, cedar-clad hills profile the rugged landscape, checkered with broad grassy pastures tossed here and there like blankets. For decades the river influenced the lives of the valley's inhabitants with its currents both peaceful and destructive. The waters also exposed the secrets of the riverbed and conjured memories of a long-ago day by revealing dinosaur footprints in the stone—tracks of time. Today visitors splash and play and marvel along this ancient Texas trail that treads through a winding curve of the Paluxy River in a place called Dinosaur Valley State Park.

The park lies on both sides of the Paluxy in Somervell County about four miles west of Glen Rose. Located in North Central Texas about fifty miles southwest of Fort Worth, this park consists of 1,588 acres of river valley and former ranchland. A mild annual average temperature of 65 degrees and rainfall of 32 inches belie extremes in weather that folks have periodically witnessed. Summers sometimes suffer lengthy droughts that greatly reduce the flow of the Paluxy, while during winters, the region may see an occasional dusting of snow.[1]

Geographically, Dinosaur Valley State Park and the Glen Rose vicinity fall within a transitional zone in the Lampasas Cut Plain, part of the Grand Prairies region of Texas. Nestled between the Eastern and Western Cross Timbers, historically the landscape held grassy prairies as well as hardwoods like oak, elm, pecan, walnut, and cottonwood along valley streams, with some groves of scrubby mountain cedar and blackjack. Rugged stairstep topography typifies the terrain, composed of layer upon layer of sedimentary rock. Much of this part of Somervell County consists of limestone of the Lower Cretaceous Glen Rose Formation.[2]

Author John Graves, describing his own "Hard Scrabble" Ranch near the Paluxy, summed up the stark beauty that the territory offers. "To a layman who cares about country," he wrote in *Hard Scrabble: Observations on a Patch of Land,* "most of Somervell regardless of what the maps call it looks like a northern counterpart of the Texas Hill Country...."[3] Indeed this Northern Hill Country, a land of transition with woods to the east and plains to the west, has served as a significant crossroads of travel and communication through the ages and ultimately a site of settlement and development.

Dinosaur Valley State Park holds a unique distinction in the Texas State Parks System. Clues to some of the ancient creatures that traversed the territory are literally set in stone here. The dinosaur tracks in the Paluxy riverbed and its tributaries tell of a very different landscape more than one hundred million years in the past, set in the Cretaceous Period of the Mesozoic Era. The Cretaceous Period stretched from approximately 144 to 65 million years ago and included the height of the reign of the dinosaurs.[4]

During the Early Cretaceous, shallow seas alternately submerged and exposed the lands of North Central Texas. As the waters marched and retreated across the flat terrain, different sediments settled in a methodical process that would be evident in the abundant marine fossils discovered by curious hillside picnickers and Sunday explorers in modern times.[5]

Somervell County artist Ken Fry's depiction of the historic landscape of North Central Texas includes rolling prairies and oak mottes. The territory supported abundant wildlife such as pronghorn antelope, buffalo, and turkeys. Art by Ken Fry

The region that would include the future park was part of a broad coastal plain whose edge advanced and receded over time to the ebb and flow of the waters as they gradually reclaimed and relinquished the shoreline. This seaside-scape offered inlet bays, offshore reefs, tidal lagoons, and salt marshes. A green prehistoric forest of conifers, ferns, and small flowering plants rose inland from the beach. And on a day, perhaps about 113 million[6] years ago, "one day not lost to the past," wrote Louis Jacobs in *Lone Star Dinosaurs*,[7] the ancient creatures walked across the coastal flats. Their feet sank into fine-grained limy mud—firm, but not too hard or too soft—and left perfect footprint impressions. The tracks were exposed long enough to dry and harden and then were quickly infilled and buried under gentle sediments, thus preserving this part of their journey. Millions of years later that "day" (or probably series of days) would live again when flooding river waters would scour away the various rock layers down to that particular stratum of Cretaceous rock, known as Glen Rose Limestone. Three-toed theropod tracks and large elephantine-like sauropod tracks formed an ancient trackway.[8]

The carnivorous theropods of Early Cretaceous North Central Texas stalked along on two three-toed feet. Though paleontologists and ichnologists (those who study footprints and other trace fossils) cannot proclaim with total certainty the specific dinosaur, based on examinations of the prints and the discovery of fossil remains in Oklahoma and Texas, the Glen Rose tracks probably belong to

Acrocanthosaurus. This intimidating meat eater left footprints up to two feet in length. Bird-like feet, tipped with sharp menacing claws, supported an imposing animal, perhaps thirty feet long nose to tail and weighing two to three tons. The mobile *Acrocanthosaurus* traveled an extensive range and used its tail as a counterweight to its large torso and head. The threatening carnosaur harbored deadly efficient serrated teeth and sported a bony ridge that covered the length of its spine. This distant relative of *Tyrannosaurus* was a formidable predator on the coastal plain.[9]

Four-legged sauropods also slogged over the ancient terrain. These animals (commonly called brontosaurs in the past) were herbivorous, and the most likely Paluxy track maker was probably *Paluxysaurus*. Paleontologists have excavated the fossilized bones of sauropods in North Central Texas, and in 2007 the new name of *Paluxysaurus* was proposed for these animals. The massive creatures, the largest of the Texas dinosaurs, could be fifty feet long and thirty tons in weight or more. The sauropod lumbered along on thickly padded shock absorbent feet—smaller, roughly horseshoe-shaped front feet and much larger, rounded, clawed hindfeet often thirty-six inches or more in length. The extended necks and large bellies of the plant eaters facilitated foraging on trees and other flora in their environment.[10]

A few of the footprints left in the Paluxy riverbed have caused some speculation that they represent a third type of dinosaur, an ornithopod. These were also plant-eating creatures in Texas during the Cretaceous Period. Some of the three-toed prints resemble the ornithopod tracks found in other parts of the world but could also be eroded or poorly-preserved theropod tracks. With the lack of positive track evidence, paleontologists and ichnologists have not identified conclusively any tracks in the park as ornithopod in origin, although bones of ornithopods have been found in parts of Texas.[11]

The sauropods and theropods traveled across the ancient plains of North Central Texas until eventually the ocean rose and claimed more territory inland. By one hundred million years ago, a great interior sea had flooded the heart of North America, essentially connecting the Gulf of Mexico to the Arctic Ocean. This vast sea remained until approximately 66 million years ago, near the close of the reign of the dinosaurs.[12]

Eventually the waters receded, and millions of years of geologic time shaped a new landscape. Layers and layers of sediment hardened. Like the tracks, trees of ancient forests had also been covered by sedimentary deposits and transformed over time into stony remnants, and the Glen Rose region would

TOP *Theropod tracks in the Paluxy streamed at Dinosaur Valley State Park were most likely made by the carnivorous* Acrocanthosaurus. **BOTTOM** *The Texas sauropod track maker was probably* Paluxysaurus. Courtesy Mike O'Brien, Sculptor, Interpretations and Exhibits, Texas Parks and Wildlife Department, Austin

come to be known for its abundance of petrified wood. As natural forces sculpted the face of North Central Texas to its modern image, streams such as the Paluxy and the neighboring Brazos carved their way through hard and soft rock strata to chisel out winding limestone valleys through Northern Hill Country and stretches of prairie.[13]

Historically seas of grasses—Big Bluestem, Little Bluestem, Indiangrass, Switchgrass, Sideoats grama, and Buffalo grass—swayed over the vast expanse, while varieties of oak, elm, cottonwood, pecan, and other hardwoods thrived in the wooded areas and along waterways. Herds of buffalo thundered south into the vicinity of Somervell County. The territory supported abundant wildlife such as turkeys, squirrels, pronghorn antelope, deer, opossums, rabbits, bobcats, wolves, raccoons, and black bears. The streams offered fish and mussels. The plentiful water and game would have been a natural attraction for human occupation and exploration.[14]

Archeological evidence indicates that human activity in the region of the Paluxy River (part of the Brazos River basin) and the surrounding vicinity of North Central Texas may date as far back as ten thousand years. Scientific surveys of the area, however, have concluded that most evidence points to human occupation from the period of about AD 700 to 1200. These early inhabitants took advantage of rugged terrain and overhangs along the river valley that offered shelter for encampments. The region furnished abundant game, and freshwater mussels of the Paluxy and area creeks also provided a year-round food source. Buffalo hunters, agriculturalists, and gatherers probably intersected paths in this land of good water.[15]

Unfortunately, no evidence or oral tradition exists to suggest that the early residents of North Central Texas observed any dinosaur tracks. Pictographs and petroglyphs are silent regarding the ancient monsters. If floodwaters scoured away the soft layers and sediments to reveal the stony footprints, Indians may have wondered at the curious giant turkey-like tracks that stretched before them. That possibility remains a mystery today.[16]

The prehistoric peoples who traveled North Central Texas and the Paluxy River Valley were probably the ancestors of the Tonkawas of the historic era. The name *tonkaweya*, meaning "they all stay together," originated from a Waco term, and these autonomous bands of hunter-gatherers journeyed throughout Central Texas. The nomadic Tonkawas hunted buffalo, deer, and small game. Their inclusive diet, however, excluded wolves and coyotes, which held religious significance. The natural resources in and around the Paluxy offered a bounty of wild game, fish, and mussels as well as other foods. Tonkawas gathered native pecans and walnuts along the creeks along with wild grapes, persimmons, plums, haws, and honey. Somervell County historian W.C. Nunn wrote that the site of Glen Rose was purportedly a favored spot for the Tonkawas, who partook of the curative properties of nearby sulphur springs.[17]

The Tonkawas fashioned crude, squat dwellings of buffalo hide and tree branches. Buffalo or deer skins made up their clothing. Men in particular adorned themselves with necklaces and earrings of bone, shells, or feathers, and both males and females practiced the art of sometimes elaborate tattooing and body painting, decorations that often drew remarks from later explorers and settlers.[18]

In North Central Texas the Tonkawas were geographically situated at a crossroads of cultures. They often bartered with the Caddos to the east, who were agriculturalists (unlike the Tonkawas) and had an extensive trade network. The Tonkawas obtained various goods including pottery from the Caddos. To the west stretched the vast Texas plains—the extensive range of the buffalo—and eventually the extreme edge of Apache country.[19]

Settlers and other Indian groups alike regarded the Tonkawas with scorn. Never large in number, the wandering Tonkawas frequently suffered hunger and destitution. Though they were often friendly with Anglos, pioneer accounts described them as filthy beggars. Their occasional practice of ritual cannibalism, designed perhaps to consume the power or soul of their enemies, evoked the ire and retaliation of other Indian groups and the disgust of frontiersmen. According to anthropology professor and author William W. Newcomb, Jr., the Tonkawas, perceived by early settlers as small and timid, did not attract the literary romanticism, savage loathing, and extensive commentary that other more formidable Native American groups engendered.[20]

Buffalo roam the rolling prairies of North Central Texas against the profile of Comanche peak in the distance. The butte served as an important landmark for Comanches and eventually explorers and settlers. Art by Ken Fry

By the early 1700s Wichita groups had begun to move southward from Kansas to the Red River and into North Texas. The southern incursion of hostile Osages and Comanches probably precipitated this gradual migration of the Wichitas, who also sought to acquire horses farther south. The Wichitas were composed of four major groups: the Wacos, Taovayas, Tawakonis, and Wichita proper. All shared a common language, Wichita, linguistically connected to a Caddoan classification. Wichitas eventually settled in the vicinity of North Central Texas. The Waco and Tawakoni (or Tehuacana) groups headed farther south, and many Wacos resided primarily along the Brazos River.[21]

Wichitas lived in villages of conical dwellings made of a framework of sturdy poles covered with grass. Though they hunted buffalo, they also practiced farming, and their gardens included corn, squash, melons, beans, pumpkins, and tobacco. The Wichitas based their division of labor on gender. The women cultivated crops and performed all the domestic chores, while the men devoted themselves to hunting and warfare. These people also practiced extensive tattooing. Their belief system attributed a soul or spirit to all things, inanimate as well as animate, and celestial bodies such as the Sun, Moon, and North Star represented gods and goddesses.[22]

In the 1700s another noteworthy group gradually swept south into the North and West Texas plains. Nomadic bands of Comanches established dominance and displaced the Apaches, driving them farther south and west. These highly-skilled horsemen based their way of life on the buffalo. With the mobility afforded by the horse, they followed the seasonal migrations of the herds. Communal hunts were proud and festive affairs. The animals served as a chief food source, and their hides provided covering for teepees and clothing. Comanches used the buffalo horns for elaborate headdresses. In addition to buffalo, they also hunted black bear and small game and collected wild fruits, nuts, and roots to supplement their diet as well as to flavor meats.[23]

Comanche society practiced the art of warfare and held its highest esteem for the young warrior who exhibited aggressiveness and bravery. In battle, they often measured success by the amount of plunder and number of scalps taken. They also attributed great prowess as a warrior to the aid of a supernatural power acquired from spirit creatures during a vision quest. Comanches engaged in frequent raids on other Indian groups and later on pioneer settlements. War parties decorated themselves and their horses with bold shades of red, yellow, black, or green paints to create colorful spectacles that evoked both fear and admiration in onlookers.[24]

The Comanches had no centralized tribal head, but rather operated in smaller individual bands. A band known as the Penatekas, translated as "Honey-Eaters" or "Wasps," was the largest and best known group and rode through the hills and valleys of present-day Somervell County and its vicinity. Author John Graves wrote:

A man I know had a Comanche grandmother, captured by whites in childhood and raised by them, who had been born at a Wasp wintering place where the

Paluxy runs into the Brazos in present Somervell County, and whose mother and grandmother had both been born there too.[25]

The grass prairies and perennial streams provided a good wintering ground for their ponies, and the limestone bluffs offered shelter from stiff northers.

A prominent butte that the Comanches named *que-tah-to-yah* ("Rocky Butte") became an important geographical landmark for the Comanches and eventually explorers and settlers in North Central Texas. Known to pioneers as Comanche Peak, this geological feature rises 1,229 feet above sea level in Hood County about nine miles north of present-day Dinosaur Valley State Park and is the closest marker to the park that cartographers first noted on early Texas maps.[26]

A Comanche descendant told Vance Maloney, author of *The Story of Comanche Peak, Landmark of Hood County, Texas,* that "Comanches held this mountain to be sacred, and some worshiped it."[27] The peak was a strategic rendezvous point before and after raids, as well as a site for the storage of supplies and plunder, a place for ceremonial dances, and a refuge. The height and expansive view the broad hill afforded made it an excellent observation post for the Comanches, who used smoke signals and, later, sun-reflecting mirrors they had acquired in trade, to communicate. A byway known as the Comanche Trail ran through the vicinity. Given the proximity of this key landmark, the Paluxy River Valley was probably a prized camping and hunting ground for various tribes.[28]

The limestone hills and flowing valley streams that set the backdrop for this crossroads of trade and travel for many Native American groups would eventually witness newcomers to the region as the age of European exploration dawned. Some county histories have credited the Spaniard Alvar Núñez Cabeza de Vaca as the first European to traverse Somervell County. Marooned with others on the Texas Coast in 1528, he chronicled an incredible trek through Texas and Mexico in his *Relación,* first published in 1542. However, most modern scholars generally support a southern route through South Texas and into Mexico for Cabeza de Vaca's journey. Though there is a remote possibility that Cabeza de Vaca may have traveled into the interior of Texas and maybe as far north as Somervell County during his years as a trader with the Indians from 1529 to 1534, it is highly unlikely.[29]

County histories have also asserted that the Moscoso Expedition, led by Luis de Moscoso Alvarado, successor to Hernando De Soto, also crossed into present-day Somervell County. This, too, is doubtful. Major studies have proposed that the explorers entered into the territory of Texas from the east or northeast in 1542 but went only as far west as the Trinity River, while an investigation in the 1990s, relying on sixteenth-century archeological sites, suggested that the party went south and west, perhaps to the Guadalupe River. Analyses have not placed Moscoso west of the Brazos or as far north as Somervell County. Catholic missionaries of the seventeenth century may have traveled through North Central Texas, but no sure evidence indicates that they reached the Paluxy River.[30]

The earliest explorers to cross the rugged terrain and clear streams of the Paluxy River Valley may have been the adept French traders and pathfinders of the eighteenth century. These dynamic adventurers were skilled communicators and merchants who took advantage of the many waterways of East Texas and also ranged west and south to the prairies and rivers of North Central Texas. With their willingness to barter furs, various novelties, and especially firearms, the French gained the support and trade of Indian groups, such as the Comanches and Wichitas, who obtained from them weapons and ammunition. The Spanish scorned the enterprising French interlopers as *contrabandistas,* but eventually were forced to acknowledge their diplomatic and navigational talents.[31]

During the 1770s the Spanish employed the French trailblazer Athanase de Mézières. Fluent in Latin, Spanish, and several Indian languages, he made several expeditions across Texas. As Lieutenant Governor of Natchitoches in western Louisiana and as Spanish agent to a number of Indian groups, de Mézières also negotiated treaties with various Wichita bands. In 1772 he toured Wichita and Tonkawan country west of the Trinity River. From the site of present-day Waco, where he stopped at two Tawakoni villages, de Mézières traveled "up the Brazos some two hundred miles"[32] where he encountered more Wichitas. With this course the Frenchman would have come upon the Paluxy where it meets the Brazos and possibly explored that countryside.

De Mézières' journeys through Texas paved the way for another French pathfinder, Pedro Vial. In 1786 Vial set out to establish a route from San Antonio to Santa Fe. Part of his course followed closely a section of the way that de Mézières had traveled up the Brazos and across the territory that would comprise Somervell County.[33]

The following year in 1787, Spanish officials ordered Corporal José Mares to improve upon the route of Vial. He set out from Santa Fe and eventually turned southwest from the Red River at the village of the Taovayas (near present-day Spanish Fort, Texas, in Montague County) and crossed the Brazos perhaps in the vicinity of Somervell County en route to San Antonio.[34]

In the 1790s the Spanish faced a new threat in the ever-growing American interest in the virgin lands of Texas. The daring mustanger Philip Nolan symbolized this threat, as he embarked on several journeys into Texas from Louisiana in search of riches in the wild horse trade. Nolan's forays brought him well into the interior to the Trinity and Brazos rivers and farther north and west, possibly to the valley of the Paluxy near the present park.[35]

These early explorations furnished the United States with important information about Texas, and historians have credited Nolan as the first American to map Texas. Unfortunately no map by him has been found. His last mustanging expedition once again took Nolan and his men well west into Texas, where they traveled extensively into both Wichita and Comanche country. At the Brazos "elk and deer were plentiful, along with a few buffalo, but wild horses numbered in the thousands!"[36] Nolan's fortunes ran out, however, when a suspicious Spanish government sent troops to intercept him, and soldiers killed him in 1801. Most historians believe that the soldiers attacked Nolan and his men in northern Hill County near present-day Blum. This location, just southeast of Somervell County, suggests that the adventurers had most likely explored the region to the northwest including Somervell County and the Paluxy on their mustanging quests.[37]

NORTH CENTRAL TEXAS WILDERNESS
(ca. 1830)

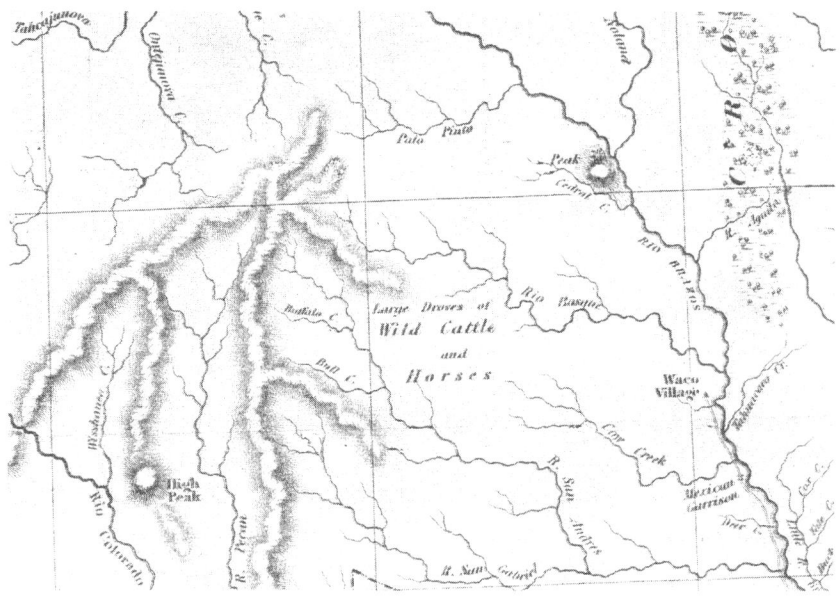

Map of Texas with Parts of the Adjoining States, Compiled by Stephen F. Austin, Published by H. S. Tanner, Philadelphia, 1830. The geographical landmark labeled "Peak" represents Comanche Peak, located about nine miles north of present-day Dinosaur Valley State Park. Cedral Creek, drawn just south of the peak, is actually located south of present Somervell County in Bosque County. Courtesy Texas General Land Office, Austin

Nolan's interest in Texas and its resources foreshadowed the American appetite for land. After Mexico won its independence from Spain in 1821, the new government sought to protect its northern territory in Texas from foreign incursion. Officials reasoned that colonists settling the region would act as a buffer to both Indian groups and foreign agents. The Mexican government's National Colonization Law of August 18, 1824, allowed individual states to form their own regulations for settlement. As a result, the State Colonization Law of March 24, 1825, provided for the colonization of the state of Coahuila and Texas.[38]

Land empresarios appealed to the Mexican government to obtain contracts to bring in homesteaders to settle sizable tracts. Moses Austin had begun negotiations as early as 1821, and after his death, his son Stephen F. Austin took over the efforts to bring in settlers. The empresario naturally took a personal interest in the vast territory of Texas. After compiling a rough map of Texas in 1822, Austin gathered additional data, conducted his own explorations and observations, and accumulated other individual accounts and surveys to compile a more accurate map of Texas. This map, published in Philadelphia in 1830, contained a remarkable record of many of the geographical landmarks of

Texas, including Comanche Peak, marked simply "Peak" out in the lonely North Central Texas wilderness. Just south and west, in the heart of the grand prairie, he noted "Large Droves of Wild Cattle and Horses."[39]

Indeed this country still belonged to the Tonkawas and Wichitas, with the mighty Comancheria to the west. But this land of transition would soon witness another crossroads of cultures, as traders, adventurers, and ultimately settlers would venture to the prairies, woodlands, and streams of the Northern Hill Country.

CHAPTER TWO

Fountains of Youth:
Settlement in the Valley of the Paluxy

In the 1830s the land of North Central Texas remained a wild country of expansive prairies and wooded streams, but as settlement marched north and west, colonizers eyed this wilderness. In 1831 Stephen F. Austin and Samuel May Williams proposed to homestead eight hundred families on a large grant. Bounded by the Colorado River to the west and the Navasota River to the east, their parcel stretched from the Old San Antonio Road well into North Texas, including present Somervell County. Even though their plans never came to fruition, this proposal helped plant the seeds for eventual colonization.[1]

When Texas gained its independence from Mexico in 1836, the vast territory that included present Somervell became part of Milam County, established from the Milam Municipality. The original Milam County covered sections of thirty-four modern counties and extended from its eastern boundary of the Brazos River, near the town of Nashville, west and north through the Cross Timbers.[2] Even though settlement stayed well south of the Waco Village, land agent Jacob De Cordova described the undying thirst for the frontier that lay beyond.

In the year 1838, the Land-Office was reopened, and a change came over this portion of the country. With the characteristic love for the acquisition of land that is so strongly developed in the American character, swarms of surveyors and locaters now filled this portion of the country, all anxious to secure the valuable lands to be found in the valleys of the Bosque, Leon, Lampases [sic], Salado, and other tributaries of the Brazos....[3]

By the early 1840s military and exploring parties increasingly traveled the territory around Comanche Peak to monitor Indian activity, wage retaliatory raids, and investigate avenues of commerce. A force of 321 men set out north of Austin in June 1841 on what became known as the Texan Santa Fe Expedition. This political/commercial outfit, supported by Texas President Mirabeau B. Lamar but not officially approved by the Texas Congress, left for Santa Fe to establish a trade route and propose participation in the Texas government. The group consisted of an assortment of merchants, teamsters, and military men and most likely tracked part of the old route established a century earlier by Pedro Vial and others.[4]

They followed a stretch of the Brazos until crossing the river in North Central Texas and heading northwest to the Western Cross Timbers. On this course, traversing "an entirely unsettled country," the men most likely passed through or edged Somervell County. Comanche Peak, already a well-known landmark at that time, drew remarks from several diarists.[5] Merchant George Wilkins Kendall, in addition to the peak, also wrote in his narrative of the awesome view of the burning prairie on their journey west of the Brazos:

... We stopped for an hour or two under the shade of some oaks that skirted the border of the valley, and here, for the first time, I saw the magnificent spectacle of a prairie on fire.... We pursued our journey in the afternoon, and reached a mud-hole ... where we encamped. All night the long and bright line of fire, which was sweeping across the prairie to our left, was plainly seen, and the next morning it was climbing the narrow chain of low hills which divided the prairie from the bottoms of the Brazos.[6]

The trip afforded a close-up view of this wilderness to ambitious trailblazers despite its ultimate ill fate. Upon reaching New Mexico, instead of a warm reception, the men faced imprisonment by Mexican authorities and a forced march to Mexico City. Two members of that expedition, however, eventually returned to that Texas frontier. Thomas Torrey and George Barnard launched enterprises in trade with the Native Americans, and these posts in the 1840s and early 1850s laid the groundwork for settlement in North Central Texas.[7]

Under the directives of President Sam Houston, the Texas Legislature enacted a series of measures to "provide for the establishment and maintenance of peace, and to regulate friendly intercourse with the Indians." This included setting up five trading houses, with Trading Post No. 2 located at or "near the Comanche Peak."[8] George Barnard went into business with the Torrey Brothers—John, Thomas, David, and James—and soon operated a post on Tehuacana Creek near present-day Waco. George Barnard's brother Charles joined him in the venture. County histories recognize Charles Barnard, born in Hartford, Connecticut, in 1823, as the first permanent settler in Somervell County and founder of Glen Rose.[9]

The early trading posts served a growing mix of Native American groups on the edge of the wilderness. Not only did Tonkawas, Wichitas, and Comanches traverse the vast Brazos River basin, but eastern tribes such as the Caddos migrated west with the increasing pressure of Anglo settlement. The trading businesses conducted an active commerce where Indians brought horses, wild mules, and all manner of pelts (buffalo, raccoon, cougar, bobcat, and gray wolf) to barter for blankets, scarlet and blue woolen cloth, calico, beads, copper wire, knives, tobacco, and other items. The post also employed a federally-appointed gunsmith who repaired the firearms of the Indians.[10]

The German scientist Dr. Ferdinand Roemer vividly described the lively exchange at the Tehuacana Trading Post and also made geological observations during his journey from there up the Brazos in 1846. He ventured just southeast of the Paluxy area and made astute comments on the characteristics of the terrain and the "dazzling white limestone walls" of the Brazos River cliffs. Roemer was the first trained scientist to write about the geology of the Lone Star State, including the Cretaceous formations, the nature of the various layers of limestone, and the numerous fossils in them. He noted the appearance of fossil wood and published the first geological map of Texas. The German made it as far as a Caddo village. Beyond, the landscape "appeared to be of a different character and much wilder" with high "sharp outlined hill formations," but before he could explore this country he took ill and was forced to turn back.[11]

Roemer's significant journey came at a time of pivotal change in North Central Texas as trade accelerated. After the annexation of Texas to the United States, in early 1846 federal representatives, Indian agents, and Native American delegates from the Indian Territory met at Comanche Peak for a preliminary

GALVESTON COUNTY SCHOOL LAND
(PATENTED MARCH 19, 1849)
(SOMERVELL COUNTY)
Courtesy Texas General Land Office, Austin

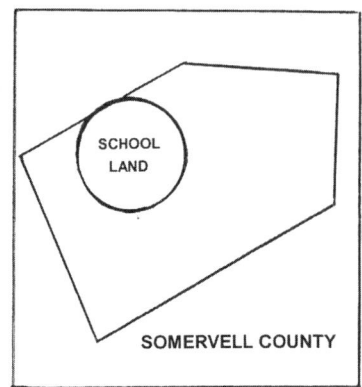

SOMERVELL COUNTY

council with a number of tribes. Participating member Elijah Hicks mentioned numerous Indian groups that held council there—Lipans, Tonkawas, Comanches, Wichitas, Wacos, Keechis, Tawakonis, Caddos, Kickapoos, and "remnants of Cherokees, Delawares, Shawnees, and Beleni." Hicks wrote:

With many Indians coming together, many of them for the first time with the wild tribes, the excitement of the occasion, feasting on the food prepared by the government, and eagerly receiving the presents of merchandise given them, a holiday spirit was manifested.[12]

A trading post, constructed by the late 1840s, stood in sight of Comanche Peak just within the boundaries of present-day Hood County. There George and Charles Barnard set up their own operation and bartered with the many and diverse Indian groups that traveled through North Central Texas.[13]

The establishment of the post signified a growing interest in the region. Roemer, in recording his visit to the Caddo settlement near the wild valley of the Brazos, included a revealing account:

When ... we looked back on the charming little plain from the hill top from which we had first seen the village, the thought involuntarily came to me how long it would remain in peaceful possession of the apparently harmless sons of nature, and if perhaps even now a land-hungry Yankee had cast his covetous looks upon it. My companion disillusioned me in a hurry, in that he assured me that not only this land, several days distant from the settlements, but also many other parts higher up on the Brazos, had been surveyed and had already been for some time the property of individuals.[14]

During the 1840s surveyors of the Milam Land District plotted the first parcels of present Somervell County. George Erath, a San Jacinto veteran and Texas Ranger who had carried out some of the earliest reconnaissance of the area as a military scout, laid out grants along the Brazos River for the Texas Land Office. His partner George Green, also a San Jacinto veteran and deputy surveyor, assisted with the arduous work. Erath later wrote, " ... we kept a section of the country west of the Brazos surveyed up for a hundred miles ahead of the forming settlements." Working on horseback, the men endeavored to match the animal's step to the length of a vara (about 33⅓ inches). Consequently many of the tracts actually contained additional acreage.[15]

All of the property of Dinosaur Valley State Park lies within the boundaries of the large Galveston County School Land Survey in Somervell County. On January 26, 1839, the Republic of Texas had approved an act "appropriating certain Lands for the Establishment of a General System of Education."[16] George Green measured this three-league grant, a total of 13,285.2 acres, for Galveston County on June 21 and 22, 1847. The large tract was "situated on the Paluxy 5 miles from its junction with the Brazos," and Green used cedars, live oaks, bur oaks, blackjacks, and elms as markers in his field notes. The school commissioners of Galveston County officially received the patent to this land on March 19, 1849.[17]

The earliest references to the Paluxy River by name appear in surveys conducted in the mid-1840s, and cartographer Robert Creuzbaur so labeled the stream on the *Map of the State of Texas* he compiled for land promoter Jacob De Cordova in 1849. The specific origins and meaning of the name Paluxy are vague, but quite possibly the term derives from an Anglo adaptation of an Indian word.[18]

Though three decades would pass before settlers would purchase eventual parkland, in the 1850s the influx of pioneers into North Central Texas on what had been Indian country began to forever change the nature of the frontier. Roemer's prophetic wonderings about the transitory circumstances of the Caddo village rang true within the span of a decade. In 1854, prompted by federal requests, authorities established two Indian reservations in Texas. They located Brazos Reservation on the Brazos River south of Fort Belknap in present-day Young County. About two thousand Caddos, various Wichita bands, Tonkawas, Shawnees, and Delawares resided there. Some four hundred and fifty Penateka Comanches settled on the Comanche Reservation located on the Clear Fork of the Brazos in present Throckmorton County. The Barnards moved their trading operation from Comanche Peak to the Brazos Reservation until it closed in 1859, when federal troops moved the Indian groups to Indian Territory.[19]

In 1859 Charles Barnard returned to his Comanche Peak Trading House. He purchased the post and surrounding land from his brother George and in 1860 also bought a sizable tract on the Paluxy River within a few miles of its mouth on the Brazos.[20] Even then the Paluxy was establishing its reputation as a temperamental stream. Thomas T. Ewell commented in his *History of Hood County*:

Among the noted events of this period, a tremendous freshet swept down the valleys of Paluxy and Squaw creeks in August, 1859, carrying away some of the early improvements in the lower valleys and drowning some stock, teaching the people caution in the matter of building their houses in the low land.[21]

Barnard, however, saw the area's tremendous potential. He built a gristmill on the Paluxy and constructed a store of cedar logs in this blossoming village known as Barnard's Mill. Ewell later observed:

Barnard's mill ... so near the confluence of the Paluxy and Squaw creeks with the Brazos, all rich in fish, deer and turkey, as well as the soils which produced the indigenous grasses and fruits in luxuriant growth, with promise of future development into farms, seemed to be the central object about which immigration converged, and then passed up these valleys.[22]

Author John Graves reflected on the pioneers that came to the Paluxy Valley:

On these purchased, usually small tracts of homestead land they put up houses of postoak logs or sometimes limestone.... The life the early whites lived was built around mixed subsistence farming and range stock raising, a pattern that had been evolving along the Texas frontier "fault line" and was both reminiscent of life in the woodlands east to the Atlantic, and prophetic of life as it would be lived on the untimbered plains west.... Most had cornfields and kitchen gardens, bees and chickens and hogs and milk cows, smokehouses and log barns and dug wells and the rest of the Eastern things. But many too were heir to the violent horseback skills of Mexico and South Texas, and ran a few or many longhorned beef animals on the open range that included the whole region except for fenced-off croplands....[23]

The terrain of Somervell County did not lend itself to large-scale plantation agriculture with slave labor. In 1860 Somervell was part of Johnson County, created in 1854. The total slave population of Johnson County numbered less than 12 percent and lived predominantly east of the Brazos. A few individuals had bondsmen. Two slaves assisted Charles Barnard, for example, with the construction of his gristmill. However, the African-American population remained small as a whole and dwindled to less than 1 percent by the late 1800s.[24]

Barnard's Mill grew significantly by 1860, but the Civil War strained the fledgling village and families along the Paluxy Valley. Here, on the edge of the wilderness, and with most men off to war or on frontier patrol, pioneers experienced periodic raids, mostly by Comanche bands from the west who sought to steal horses. In 1864 an Indian foray in Squaw Creek northeast of the Paluxy resulted in the killing of two settlers.[25] Such events alarmed the community and prompted creative safety measures. Women, left alone to tend the family farm, dressed as men in the effort to disguise themselves.

More commonly, however, Paluxy Valley families encountered the ragged remnants of the former native inhabitants, as friendly Tonkawan hunting parties who passed through the area often begged for provisions. Somervell County saw its last raid in the late 1860s, when a group of Caddos (by some accounts, though others have speculated that the raiders were Comanches) stole a number of horses.[26]

Barnard's Mill survived its first decade of existence and in fact flourished as new families arrived. By the early 1870s, Charles Barnard sold his property and mill to Major Tyler Calhoun Jordan of Dallas. Popular tradition holds that Jordan's wife, Annie R. Lewis Jordan, likened the enchanting vistas of the rugged river valley to her native Scottish homeland and proposed to rename the settlement Rose Glen. In 1872, in an informal vote, citizens instead approved the name Glen Rose.[27]

As North Central Texas filled with settlers after the war, the Texas Legislature sliced off sections of territory to create new counties. They formed Hood County from the western portion of Johnson and eastern portion of Erath counties in 1866. Increasingly pioneers in the early 1870s felt isolated from the faraway seat of government in Granbury in Hood County and clamored to demarcate a separate county of their own. Therefore, on March 13, 1875, the Texas Legislature officially established Somervell County. Named for Alexander Somervell, Texas veteran, congressman, and leader of the Somervell Expedition, this territory was lopped off the southern end of Hood County. Less than two hundred square miles in size, Somervell is the second smallest county in Texas. Glen Rose became the county seat, and T.C. Jordan and others set about the task of drawing up a proper town square and finding a suitable building in which

Early settlers William and Mary E. Lanham established a mill and cotton gin on the Paluxy, which represented the beginning of the Lanham Mill community that encompasses present-day Dinosaur Valley State Park. Courtesy Novella Wilson

to hold court. He laid out the square in a cornfield just north of the mill site. Court held sway in a store and later a log cabin until builders finally completed a separate courthouse in 1882.[28]

One of the men who had signed the petition requesting the formation of Somervell County was William Lanham. Lanham and his family came to North Central Texas from Tennessee and settled in the Paluxy Valley at the mouth of White Bluff Branch by the early 1870s. To serve a growing number of farmers moving into the valley, he established a grist and sawmill, originally known as William's Mill, on the riverbanks. By July 1877, he partnered in business with T.J. Hamick, and they added a cotton gin in 1881.[29]

The mill was a boon to area farmers who formerly drove their wagons either downstream to Glen Rose or upstream to the town of Paluxy in Hood County. The Lanham Mill, sitting about halfway between Paluxy and Glen Rose (and just upstream from present Dinosaur Valley State Park), bridged this fifteen-mile distance. An early ford on the Paluxy River became known as the Lanham crossing, and a wagon road angled through pastures eventually to join the Glen Rose–Stephenville Road.[30]

The operation of the mill represented the beginning of a dispersed country community that stretched as far as ten miles up and down the Paluxy, and this settlement included the future land of Dinosaur Valley State Park. Burials in the Lanham Mill Cemetery, located upstream from the present park, occurred as early as 1879, although that property was not formally deeded until 1893.[31]

In the heart of the Paluxy Valley and the young Lanham Mill community sat the vast acreage of the Galveston County School Survey. For three decades this land had remained unsold. In February 1878, the commissioners court of Galveston County directed that the county school lands be sold. The first sales of tracts that included future parkland took place in May 1879.[32]

Settler Samuel Adams purchased 190 acres, including frontage on the Paluxy River, on May 1, 1879. The 1870 census listed him, a Missouri native, as a 27-year-old farmer living in Hood County with his wife Ester. They had a daughter Delila and raised a lad named I.C. "Charley" Pair. After buying their Paluxy Valley property, they built a wooden dogtrot-style house with a center breezeway that allowed adequate ventilation and a cooling breeze on hot summer days. This may have been the first home constructed on the land of present-day Dinosaur Valley State Park. After the death of Samuel and Ester Adams in 1884 and 1888 and their daughter Delila in 1896, Charley Pair eventually inherited this property.[33]

Wiley Hendrix, a settler who had petitioned for the creation of Somervell County, came to the river valley with his wife Martha A. (Blackstock) Hendrix and purchased 160 acres in 1883. Wayfarers associated the Hendrix name with a well-traveled river ford used by wagons that rambled through the cedar valley. Farmers dubbed the fourth Paluxy crossing upstream from Glen Rose as the Hendrix crossing.[34]

TOP *The Lanham Mill on the Paluxy River served an important role for the farmers in the Lanham Mill community. This photograph, taken of the structure on May 12, 1896, shows a number of men most likely working to repair damage incurred to the mill and adjoining dam from flooding that had occurred the previous year. Courtesy Lawrence T. Jones III* **BOTTOM** *Historic Lanham Mill Cemetery is located just upstream from Dinosaur Valley State Park. Photo by Laurie E. Jasinski*

Since the late 1800s, Somervell County residents have enjoyed the Blue Hole, a favorite swimming spot on the Paluxy River. Photo by Gary S. Hickinbotham.

Sometime after the Hendrix family established their farm, residents constructed Lanham Mill's first schoolhouse at the south end of the Hendrix land. The log building, called Cedar Point, served a growing number of children up and down the valley by 1885. In this simple setting, pupils sat on split-log benches and learned their fundamentals. A spring above the Hendrix crossing gave forth cool drinking water. A few years later valley inhabitants built a successor to this school farther upstream across from the cemetery. This structure also served as a house of worship for both Baptist and Church of Christ congregations, and a brush arbor outside provided the site for camp meetings. Families came by wagon and horseback for many miles to attend these summer gatherings.[35]

The Wiley Hendrix farm also accessed a favored swimming and fishing spot in the valley. The shallow green waters of the Paluxy flowed over a deep hollow in the riverbed. Folks called this cool turquoise cavity the Blue Hole. Its refreshing kiss on a hot summer day would soothe generations of picnickers and gleeful children.[36]

Like Hendrix, the Abell name became very well-known in the Lanham Mill community. George Abell and his family journeyed from Indiana to Texas in 1871 and arrived at the Paluxy in October of that year. He purchased acreage upstream from the present park and moved into a log cabin. Eventually, the Abells constructed a larger home, a rock well house, and a barn. A river ford located near his home was called Abell crossing. George's son, Mathias A.

"Matt" Abell, later bought his own land along the Paluxy, sixty acres in 1893. This property was the first of several tracts that Matt would acquire into the early 1900s, and the real estate would eventually comprise more than two hundred acres of land located at the park entrance.[37]

Matt's father George, along with the original property owner E.L. Stephens, built a barn for Matt Abell, but the original house was already standing. Lanham Mill historian Novella Wilson described the unique features of this late nineteenth-century dwelling:

> Since the land was so sloping, the back of the house was almost on the ground with the cedar brake hill to its back. The front of the house was perhaps five feet from the ground.... A very convenient thing was the pitcher pump which was right beside the front porch, so the family didn't even have to leave the house for water. Later, a flowing well was drilled down under the hill.
>
> Inside, there was a large room which was used for a kitchen and bedroom. There was also a small attic room made accessible by a very steep, narrow stairway. This was one of two houses on the creek, with upstairs rooms.[38]

The Matt Abell house was built ca. the late 1800s. The Abells were longtime landowners of a portion of future Dinosaur Valley State Park. Painting by Novella Wilson, ca. 1965

Matt Abell's first wife Emma died in childbirth, leaving behind an infant, Elmer Heyman "Jack," and two small children, Ora and Tony. Matt married Cassie Florence Beck on August 18, 1900, and later that year her father James Beck purchased an adjoining forty-eight acres from Galveston County. The Beck and Abell families would retain their land throughout the twentieth century.[39]

Farmers along the Paluxy grew corn, cotton, wheat, and oats, and had vegetable gardens. Most maintained some livestock that grazed on the open range, and perhaps some adventurous cowboys drove a herd east to meet up with the Chisholm Trail during the early 1880s. From its creation in 1875, Somervell County quickly grew from sparsely-settled lands to an established agricultural and stockraising population. In 1880 the county population numbered 2,649. That total increased to 3,419 in 1890. Prices for unimproved land ranged from $1.50 to $5.00 per acre. In 1882 the county had 7,160 cattle, 1,547 horses and mules, 3,124 hogs, 314 goats, and 270 sheep.[40]

Farmers brought their shelled corn to the Lanham Mill to have it ground into meal, but cotton reigned as the cash crop. Historian Novella Wilson described the importance of the cotton harvest in *Historic Lanham Mill Community and Cemetery:*

> Sometimes, farmers would produce from one-half to a bale per acre. The men, women and children all helped to pick the cotton. It was gathered into long cotton sacks pulled with wide straps across the shoulder. Each sack full was weighed on scales hung from a tripod made of cedar posts, and emptied into a nearby wagon with tall side-boards. When 1500 to 1600 pounds were packed and tramped into the wagon, the farmer hooked up the team and took this bale to the gin.
>
> The local gin bustled at harvest time when wagon after wagon carried its crop. After the separation of the fleecy white lint from burs, trash, and seed, the remaining bale weighed about five hundred pounds:
>
> Steam power was used to operate this very early gin, burning cordwood as the fuel. After ginning the cotton was lifted to the stand in baskets. Mule power was used to press the cotton in bales. The mule, hooked to a lever, went round and round lifting the screw, which tightly pressed the cotton into bale form ready to be tied out with metal ties. The cotton bales were then hauled by wagon to Tolar or Granbury to be sold. The price of cotton was about four or five cents per pound. Money received from the crops was used to buy new shoes, coats, and other clothing for the family and the staples in groceries. Also, if any debts had been made this was about the only hope of getting them paid.
>
> Each farmer stored his cotton seed in bins to be used to feed the milch cows during the winter. The milk from cows fed with cotton seed was always very rich in butterfat. These cotton seed bins were favorite places for children to play on cold winter days.[41]

By the mid-1880s, Glen Rose had a lively business district of flour mills, gins, several stores, two saloons, two weekly newspapers, a school, and several churches.[42] Touted as a "profit and a glory to the state," the town promoted its natural wonders in its local newspaper the *Glen Rose Citizen*. "Nature terraced Glen Rose as if to afford every resident a choice in elevation. From the bed of the Paluxy to the summit of the surrounding hills the slopes are terraced with beautiful symmetry and regularity," the periodical crowed on January 22, 1885. These stairstepped "shelves" provided land "broad enough for small settlements and grounds for ornamentation and gardening." The writer proclaimed, "The healthfulness of the location cannot be surpassed ... the water abundant, pure and in great variety, and the population kind, law-abiding and hospitable."[43]

Glen Rose had a population of six hundred by 1890. One amenity that the town could not brag about was a railroad; that commercial boon bypassed the county. In 1890 Granbury, Hood County's seat eighteen miles to the north, boasted the nearest railway station. Therefore, stages, wagons, and buggies had to shoulder passenger service as they rambled people and goods down the rough byways. A hack from Cleburne carried visitors all the way to Glen Rose. The county commissioners court appointed overseers and crews to maintain the roads in the county. Matt Abell, for example, was an overseer in 1888 and as such, he assumed the responsibility of supervising the work along the winding valley trail from Lanham Mill all the way to the Hood County line. The cranky Paluxy could play havoc on the crossings and stretches of backroads that snaked along the river.[44]

Despite some inconveniences, residents of North Central Texas recognized the beauty and potential of the Paluxy Valley. They, like many citizens across Texas and the nation, advertised the benefits of their home with aggressive boosterism. The *Glen Rose Citizen* printed glowing, flowery descriptions of the river on April 2, 1885:

Here in Texas are to be found valleys of imperishable fertility, of glorious beauty, and of never failing fountains as pure as the silvery dew drops that are distilled from the skies. The Paluxy is one of these, and Glen Rose is embowered in its richest, rosiest and sweetest beneficence. All along the valley, for a distance of thirty miles or more, the creek is supplied from living fountains and flowing wells, and preserves a uniformity in the smoothness of its rock bed and bluffs.... The valley varies in width, and in places the high craggy bluffs overhang the stream on one side, and again jut down to the water's edge on the other side.[45]

In the late nineteenth century Somervell County gained the reputation as a land with abundant groundwater. Residents drilled the first flowing well in 1880,[46] and soon county guides reported on the area's gushing waters. A.W. Spaight wrote in *The Resources, Soil, and Climate of Texas* in 1882:

Somervell County's abundant artesian wells in the late 1800s and early 1900s helped advance Glen Rose's reputation as a budding health resort. Courtesy Somervell County Historical Commission

There are many good springs, and a number of artesian wells, with a large and steady flow, have been obtained at a depth ranging from 65 to 260 feet. Springs of white sulphur water, believed to possess medicinal virtues of great value, are found in several parts of the county.[47]

By 1886 the county had 130 artesian wells. Their mineral content varied from lime to freestone to yellow and white sulphur and chalybeate, depending on each well's depth and location. Additionally, many naturally flowing springs occurred along the Paluxy and its adjoining creeks.[48]

The prevalence of these mineral wells over this rugged stairstepped terrain was among many factors that attracted the first thorough and systematic study of the geology of the Paluxy and its surroundings in the late nineteenth century. This work fell to none other than Robert T. Hill, the father of Texas geology. The crusty maverick scientist had migrated to Texas after the Civil War as a teenager, settling in the town of Comanche in Comanche County. His early life included such diverse professions as cowhand, surveyor, and printer's errand boy. But his voracious curiosity about rocks and fossils led him to earn a degree in geology from Cornell University. Hill began an impressive career with the United States Geological Survey during the formative years of that agency, when the federal government assigned great significance to geological and hydrological mapping. He traveled across Texas studying rock strata, conducting surveys along the cliffs of the Big Bend, and collecting fossils in Central Texas. Modern paleontologists credit Hill as the man who first discovered dinosaur bones in Texas.[49]

Hill's studies brought him to Somervell County at various times from 1882 to 1900. In December 1890, at the meeting of the Geological Society of America in Washington, Hill, an original fellow of the organization, proposed the term "Glen Rose beds" for the Cretaceous rock beds that stretched through Central Texas, including the Paluxy Valley.[50]

Based on his investigations for the United States Geological Survey, Hill published an extensive study titled *Geography and Geology of the Black and Grand Prairies, Texas* in 1901. In the region of the Lampasas Cut Plain, Hill noted the river valleys were "occupied by the fertile soils of the Lower Cretaceous formations ... upon which is settled most of the agricultural population of the region. In some of these valleys ... are numerous shallow flowing artesian wells which have been inexpensively drilled by the farmers." Hill added, "Shallow wells of this character have been most extensively developed in the valley of Paluxy River...."[51]

By the end of the nineteenth century, almost two hundred artesian wells tapped into the underground Trinity reservoir and supplied water to practically every farm and town household. Families used well water for domestic necessities, for thirsty stock, and in some cases for irrigation. Hill recorded the well of William Lanham as an "8-inch well which discharges about 400,000 gallons of freestone water a day." Lanham irrigated thirty acres of land for cotton, corn, and Louisiana sugar cane.[52]

Hill commented that in the town of Glen Rose, "it is practically impossible to have a well there without its being an artesian one." George Abell had drilled a well in Glen Rose at a depth of 260 feet and a flow of 40 gallons a minute.[53]

Folks believed that the smelly, sulphury waters near Glen Rose had medicinal qualities, but the wells up the valley of the Paluxy were more palatable with "good, sweet, cool freestone water." Residents in and around the area of the present park often used their wells as cooling systems for drinks and food. Flowing wells kept crocks of milk and butter cool and fresh for the supper table.[54]

Hill's informative report showcased the unique and attractive geological features of Somervell County. Within two decades of the county's existence farmers had established a real sense of community in the Lanham Mill region, and Glen Rose was gaining accolades as a burgeoning health resort, despite the fact that it had no railroad. But the Paluxy and her tributaries held treasures that the citizenry did not yet know—treasures that nature would reveal in its own time.

View of Glen Rose, ca. early 1900s. The Somervell County courthouse stands prominently in the town square.

CHAPTER THREE

Making Tracks:
Moonshiners, Model Ts, and
the Lime Mud Strider

The scenic background of rugged cedar-covered hills has a quieting effect upon the taut nerves of both the mad moving city folk and the monotony mad farmer folk.[1]

Elna Martin
Glen Rose and Geo. P. Snyder:
A Texas Town, The American Coue

At the dawn of the twentieth century, Glen Rose trumpeted its Northern Hill Country to a growing flock of recreation seekers and health advocates as it entered its heyday as a resort town. With a seemingly limitless water supply and a pleasant climate, county residents utilized the natural resources the countryside had to offer.

Somervell County's 3,498 inhabitants in 1900 included 1,002 children of school age. In addition to the staples of cotton, corn, wheat, oats, and some sugar cane, farmers also produced varieties of plums, peaches, pears, melons, grapes, and berries. The value of pasturage ranged from $3 to $8 per acre, and valley tracts sold from $10 to $35 an acre.[2]

The Lanham Mill community saw new landowners move into the Paluxy Valley in the early 1900s. Like those who preceded them, these families contributed significantly to the development of the region and left their own legacies to the settlement. Houston Obediah Tidwell, for example, who purchased 179 acres in 1900, supplied a vital service to the farming community, which had been without a gin after the Lanham facility burned in 1898. When Tidwell purchased his property, he established a steam-powered gin across the creek from the old mill site. His son Percy opened a grocery store, and the Tidwell farm became a sort of community within a community. Children who could not pronounce the name Tidwell said "Tiddle" instead and dubbed this busy center of agricultural commerce "Tiddle Town."[3]

Farmers operate a horse-drawn thresher during the wheat harvest in the Lanham Mill community in 1912. Men up and down the Paluxy Valley usually came to help. Courtesy Novella Wilson

The Tidwell gin opened in 1900 and served farmers in the Paluxy Valley. Children called this center of commerce "Tiddle Town." Courtesy Novella Wilson

Unfortunately, Tidwell's short-lived gin suffered a sad fate as one of the victims of Somervell County's devastating 1902 tornado. Ominous gunmetal clouds swirled over the valley on April 28, 1902. A twister touched down and tore a deadly trail east. The cyclone damaged the Tidwell gin, uprooted trees, crumbled walls, and blew over smokehouses in its path. It finally lifted, leaving behind a frightened settlement, but thankfully no loss of life in Lanham Mill.[4]

The same funnel cloud, however, descended again and raged through downtown Glen Rose. There the tornado killed six people, destroyed thirty-six commercial buildings and twenty-five family homes, and damaged countless other structures. Determined citizens rebuilt, but the memory of that historic and tragic weather event has lingered for more than a hundred years. Locals still refer to Hereford Street, the scene of the worst destruction, as Cyclone Street. As for Lanham Mill, the twister compelled every household to dig a cellar in preparation for future storms.[5]

Though the Tidwell gin was eventually repaired, the Tidwells sold their land, and the gin was later relocated to the village of Rainbow in the eastern part of the county. Farmer Gabriel T. Daniel and his wife Mary Ann later bought the Tidwell property and probably moved into the Percy Tidwell store. Their son Joe inherited the farm which would be known as the Daniel place for several decades.[6]

Jacob T. Martin, a Civil War veteran from Illinois, had purchased real estate in the Lanham Mill area (and the present park) as early as 1893, when he bought a 110-acre parcel from V.M. Cox. In the early 1900s his farm adjoined another 110-acre tract, the land of his son Isaac Edgar Martin, who married Ollie Mae Lanham, the daughter of pioneer William Lanham. Ed and Ollie built a farmhouse on high ground within walking distance of the Blue Hole. Their farm would one day comprise the heart of Dinosaur Valley State Park inside the bend of the Paluxy and include the sites of the headquarters and playground. The Martin home sheltered many families through the years and stood near the site of the park store.[7]

Perhaps the most important contribution the Martins made to the community was the gift of land for a schoolhouse. On December 12, 1903, Ed Martin officially donated one acre "for the purpose of a school building for School Dist. No. 19...."[8] Quite possibly local farmers had already built a structure a year or two earlier. The simple, wooden one-room school sat at the southwest corner of the Martin farm near the Glen Rose–Paluxy Road. By 1905, thirty-five students attended classes. The Lanham Mill School bustled as the center of community activities with church meetings, suppers, and holiday parties.[9]

The teachers at Lanham Mill shaped their community as both educators and landowners. Early instructor James Cyrus Finley purchased the Martin land tracts in 1906. Michael T.W. Ramfield, who shared his vocal skills as a "Singing School" teacher, bought the Wiley Hendrix farm in 1904 and built a new home on the Paluxy Valley property near the Blue Hole. He and his brother Chris were active members of the country community and noted for their heavenly voices. When Lanham Mill received its first phone lines in the early 1900s, folks "tuned in" to their party line to hear Mike and Chris perform gospel songs.[10]

After Ramfield bought the Hendrix farm, residents called the river ford on their land the Hendrix–Ramfield crossing. The crossings on the Paluxy played key and sometimes troublesome roles in the lives of the farmers up and down the Lanham Mill community. Early settlers had selected the best possible places in the riverbed where a solid limestone floor provided the safest location to drive their wagons. The winding trail from Glen Rose forded a total of seven crossings through Lanham Mill and upstream to the village of Paluxy, thus connecting the valley families to important centers of social activity and commerce.[11]

Residents named the water crossings for the adjacent landowners. Other travelers simply numbered the fords from Glen Rose (i.e., first, second, etc.). But the Paluxy and its area creeks, long noted to be temperamental, played havoc with valley travel in rainy weather. Sudden flash floods swept sand and gravel downstream and flooded the banks. The high water made the fords perilous and impassable and stranded many a farmer and schoolchild. Historian Novella Wilson remembered the story of her father, Vivian May, who drove his wagon into high water at the second river crossing, known as the Hamberlin–Moss crossing. The surging water proved too powerful for his team and wagon and washed them downstream. She wrote:

MAJOR OWNERS OF FUTURE PARKLANDS
DINOSAUR VALLEY STATE PARK
(ca. early 1900s)

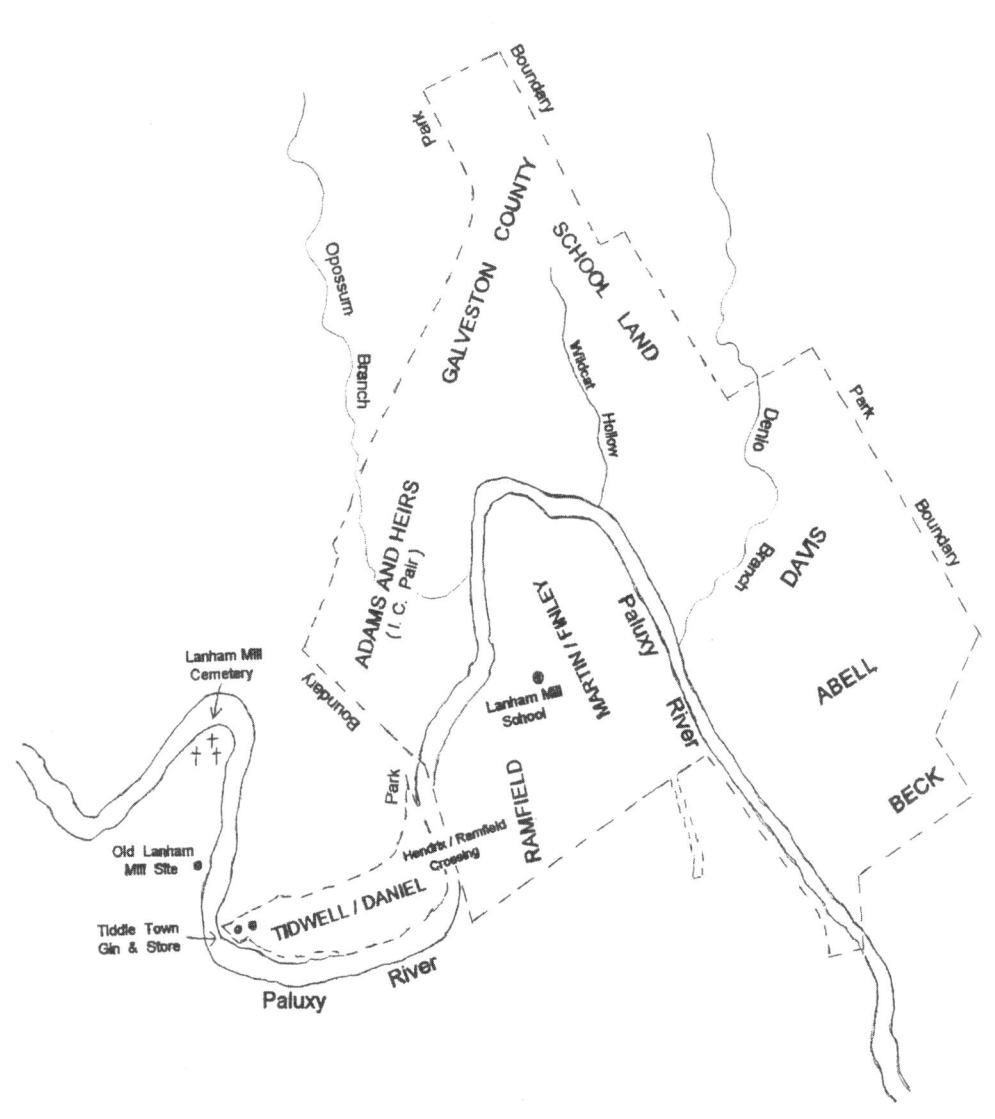

He fell downstream ahead of his wagon and team, so he had to do some fast swimming to stay in front of them. He was swimming frantically when he touched bottom and climbed to the bank and to safety. Then the team swam ashore without much damage to his wagon.[12]

Glen Rose townspeople suffered their own inconveniences fording the unpredictable Paluxy, and by 1905 they resolved to ease their traveling woes. "Off and on for years, and especially during times of high water, the question of bridging the Paluxy at Glen Rose has been discussed," the *Glen Rose Herald* reported. "The recent successive rises have again aroused our people and steps are being taken which it is hoped will result in a bridge." Citizens overwhelmingly pledged to contribute to a bridge fund. The following year the commissioners

In 1906 Glen Rose residents heralded their first bridge over the Paluxy. Courtesy Somervell County Historical Commission

court announced a contract for $2880, and soon the people of Glen Rose triumphantly opened their new bridge that led to the town square.[13]

A dramatic rise of the Paluxy sorely tested the new bridge when heavy rains in the spring of 1908 culminated in a great flood on the night of Friday, April 17. For days area newspapers reported on the rampaging rivers that ravaged the whole region of North and North Central Texas. Streams matched or surpassed their high-water marks. Washed out railroad tracks near Cleburne caused the tragic derailment of a Santa Fe passenger train, resulting in the death of the engineer and fireman.[14]

With memories of the 1902 tornado still fresh, Somervell citizens once again bowed to the power of Mother Nature. "There was a rumor here yesterday that Glen Rose was washed away," the *Weekly Enterprise* out of Cleburne commented. A correspondent in Glen Rose delivered news of the harrowing night:

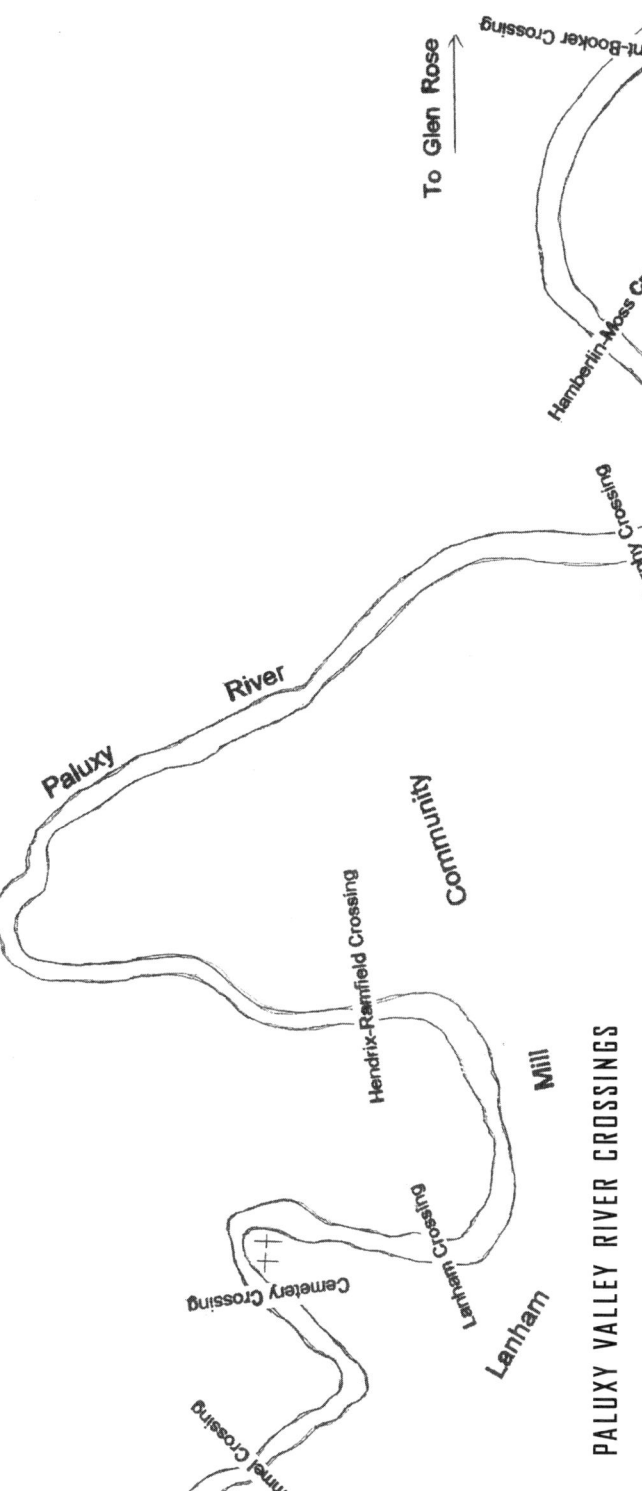

PALUXY VALLEY RIVER CROSSINGS

1. McCamant-Booker Crossing (First Crossing)
Highway 67 to Stephenville outside of Glen Rose, bridge constructed in 1923

2. Hamberlin-Moss Crossing (Second Crossing)
On County Road 1001, still used

3. Murphy Crossing (Third Crossing)
Bridge on Farm Road 205, on the way to Dinosaur Valley State Park, old crossing closed

4. Hendrix-Ramfield Crossing (Fourth Crossing)
In Dinosaur Valley State Park, closed

5. Lanham Crossing (Fifth Crossing)
Upstream from Dinosaur Valley State Park near old Lanham Mill site, closed

6. Cemetery Crossing (Sixth Crossing)
Just past Lanham Mill Cemetery, still used

7. Kimmel Crossing (Seventh Crossing)
Upstream from cemetery, closed

35

A waterspout fell on Paluxy and its tributaries Friday night, doing great damages to farms, fencing and crops. Paluxy creek was five feet higher than ever known and water was up in many houses, ten inches to three feet above the floor.[15]

Men waded three-foot-deep water in the urgent attempt to carry household items to higher ground, as cribs, stables, and an assortment of items bobbed in the rushing waters. At Lanham Mill, the Finleys stood on their kitchen table to stay dry. Nearby, Mike Ramfield and his family desperately moved personal necessities and keepsakes to safety.[16]

"The fine iron bridge that spanned the river here was washed away," the newspaper correspondent at Glen Rose sadly reported, "leaving only two spans of the west abutment." The waters also destroyed the iron bridge at the village of Paluxy upstream of Lanham Mill. In fact, the deluge packed sufficient force to damage or wash away every bridge and culvert in the county. Financial losses in crops and fencing totaled as high as $1 million.[17]

The various creeks, branches, and gullies had been transformed into angry torrents, washing everything in their paths into the swift currents of the Paluxy that scoured the canyons. It was a flood for the ages and a flood that revealed the ages.

In 1909 a youngster traipsed about the rocky bed of Wheeler Branch. This Paluxy tributary just northeast of Glen Rose had the characteristics of many of the creeks in the area. During wet years, gentle springs fed the stream that flowed over a solid limestone bottom. Down the branch, a swimming hole or two delighted area kids. Artesian wells flowed on farms here too, just as in Glen Rose and Lanham Mill. In times of flood, however, Wheeler Branch was as cranky as the Paluxy.

Young George Adams was probably not concerned with any of that on this day in late winter. He simply wanted to explore. As he kicked over stones and tramped through the creekbed, something caught his eye—something he'd never seen before. There in the limestone were the huge tracks of some strange animal. Time and erosion were finally revealing that long-ago "day" written in the now-exposed layer of Cretaceous rock.[18]

Though George Adams may not have been precisely sure about the nature of his amazing discovery, he must have felt nonetheless that it was amazing. He soon told of his find to his Glen Rose School principal, Robert E. McDonald, who lived on Wheeler Branch.

McDonald recounted the boy's revelation and the exciting events that followed:

One day he waited after school to tell me something that he had found to interest him. On this occassion [sic] he went to the black board and drew some tracks. I was impressed and we set out immediately for Wheeler Branch. About one mile up stream George stopped and pointed them out. There they were! No doubt about it—dinosaur tracks!

Next morning at school it was announced that George Adams had discovered dinosaur tracks up Wheeler Branch. There was much excitement among the students—the result—<u>field day</u> was declared and away went the entire student body to view those amazing tracks that had remained hidden throughout the ages.

Wheeler Branch, a tributary of the Paluxy, was the site of the first known discovery of dinosaur tracks in Somervell County. Photo by Laurie E. Jasinski

George was a true naturalist—able to read, all alone, as he wandered in the hills, along the streams or in the depth of the forest, the secrets and wonders that Nature reveals to a chosen few.

Fortunately in the instance of the finding of the dinosaur tracks along Wheeler Branch a spring flood had cleared the sand and gravel sufficiently to partially expose the tracks—thus making the find possible.[19]

At the time the discovery raised quite a stir in Somervell County, and area newspapers reported on the strange and magnificent tracks in the weeks that followed. Cleburne's *Weekly Enterprise* published a lengthy article on April 8, 1909, about the fossil footprints and the assessment of the Smithsonian Institute:

A REMARKABLE FIND
Furthr [*sic*] Particulars of a Huge Dinosaur
Which Was Discovered Near Glen Rose.

The *Glen Rose Herald* has the following to say of the strange discovery made at Glen Rose, of which *The Enterprise* spoke of yesterday, and also gives the report of the Smithsonian Institute at Washington:

Some weeks since, George Adams, while rambling on Wheeler branch near town, discovered tracks of some large animal, in the solid rock in the bed of the creek, evidently made many thousands of years ago. There were four or five of the tracks first discovered, and others have since been uncovered, and now there are twelve to be seen. The tracks are 4 feet 2 inches apart and the depth of the impressions in the rock are at least three inches. They are directly in line with each other, showing they were made by a large biped of some description. There are two branches, which form a junction just below where the tracks cross both branches. They first emerge from underneath an embankment some twelve feet high. The track of this huge, but extinct bipedal dinosaur that once roamed over this section before the hills and creeks were formed, and before uncivilized or civilized man ever saw it, have attracted much attention, and people are pouring in from other counties to view them.

Geo. P. Bessant sent a sketch of the tracks to the Smithsonian Institute, and has received the following reply:

Smithsonian Institute,
United States National Museum,
Washington, D. C., March 22.

Mr. Geo. P. Bessant, Glen Rose, Tex.

Dear Sir: The sketch transmitted with your letter recently received has been examined by C.W. Gilmore, Custodian of the Reptilian Collection of the Division of Vertebrate Paleontology, who has furnished the following information concerning the footprints which it represents:

"The sketch undoubtedly represents a footprint of one of the large bipedal dinosaurs. Since the formation containing the footprints is unknown it would be hazardous to even suggest the particular reptile which made the impressions. Fossil footprints are commonly found in the Triassic rocks of Connecticut, and those of one slab figured by March [O.C. Marsh] in Part I of the 16th Annual Report of the U.S. Geological Survey, plate V, figure 3, appear quite like the footprints shown in the sketch. Another very interesting article relating to footprints, by R.S. Lull, was published in the *Popular Science Monthly*, for December 1904."

The Museum will be glad to accept your kind offer to send a photograph of the footprints, and a frank is enclosed for its transmittal by mail.

W.A.C. Ravenel
Administrative Assistant[20]

For a little while, Glen Rose merited at least a small footnote in dinosaur paleontology's first "Golden Age," a time from the 1890s until 1920 when North American dinosaur exploration and research enjoyed its heyday. The American Museum of Natural History in New York, the Smithsonian Institution, the Carnegie Museum of Pittsburgh, and other institutions sent dinosaur hunters into the field. Paleontologists, including Charles Gilmore and Richard Swann Lull, made immense discoveries and contributions to the study, while museums added significant fossils to their collections.[21]

At this time gigantic skeletons were the desired prize for exhibition and research. Though dinosaur tracks did not generate the same excitement as huge bones, fossilized footprints nevertheless had a history that stretched back over a hundred years. The first tracks were discovered by another boy, Pliny Moody, as he explored the rocks of the Connecticut River Valley near South Hadley, Massachusetts, in 1802. People thought that large birds made these stony prints. Not until 1841 did British scientist Richard Owen propose the term "dinosaurs" (Greek for "fearfully great lizards") for the fossil reptilian creatures. In 1858 American geologist Edward Hitchcock published a book on the tracks of the Connecticut River Valley and concluded that bipedal "reptilian birds" had made the three-toed tracks. By the late 1800s, the real dinosaur hunting had begun, when every season, field paleontologists tried to best their previous endeavors.[22]

As for the Glen Rose tracks, once the excitement of the initial discovery settled down, locals relegated the footprints to curious objects of stony oddity, but eventually at least one paleontologist came calling. In October 1917 Ellis Shuler of Southern Methodist University in Dallas published his studies in *The American Journal of Science* as an article titled "Dinosaur Tracks in the Glen Rose Limestone near Glen Rose, Texas."

Early postcard (ca. late 1910s to early 1920s) of the first dinosaur tracks discovered near Glen Rose. These theropod prints in Wheeler Branch evoked curiosity from local residents and studies by paleontologist Ellis Shuler of SMU.

"The dinosaur tracks," he wrote, "are exposed in the flat bottom of a ravine near Glen Rose, Texas, where they are locally known as the 'bird tracks.'" He said that the waters of Wheeler Branch had "stripped back to steep banks a flat bottom more than fifty feet wide, one side of which is covered by stream gravel and sand." Five tracks were exposed and three more covered by stream gravel. Shuler observed footprints ten inches wide and sixteen inches "from the anterior end of the middle toe to the heel...." He also noted imprints of claws, and, based on his observations, he concluded, "The dinosaur was moving N.E. and the tracks are directly in line, each step following consecutively, and not alternately from side to side."[23]

Fascinated by these prints set in the "hard white limestone," Shuler painted a picture of an ancient landscape:

First of all, the dinosaur was walking on a mud surface, lime mud to be sure, but mud.... The mud was sufficiently plastic to hold the form when the foot was withdrawn.

The tracks were probably made while the mud was underneath the water. There are neither sun-cracks as evidence of desiccation or emergence of the muds; nor ripple marks or other evidence of current action. The limy clays immediately above the limestone, which were deposited after the passing of the dinosaur, show little stratification and were evidently laid down by very gentle currents.

That the dinosaur was a land animal seems highly probable from the character of the foot. That it was wading also seems probable....

If the dinosaur was wading near shore then, since the dip of the beds is very gentle it would be necessary to think of the seas of Glen Rose time as very shallow, extending over many square miles but only a few feet deep, perhaps not more than five to ten feet deep....

Finally he proposed a name for the footprint—*Eubrontes* (?) *titanopelopatidus*—"the lime mud strider." Shuler's use of the question mark in the name indicated his uncertainty as to whether his species was correctly attributed to Eubrontes.[24]

Though no reports from that time period have as yet surfaced about dinosaur tracks in the Paluxy, it is highly probable that the same 1908 flood scoured sedimentary layers away to reveal tracks in that streambed as well. Later accounts by Lanham Mill resident Charles Moss recall his exploration of the Paluxy with his brother William Boone "Grandy" Moss throughout the 1910s and 1920s. He included in his accounts descriptions of strange elongated tracks that he suggested were possibly the "footprints of apparent giant human beings." High waters in a 1918 flood, however, washed those rock slabs and their tracks away.[25]

For Paluxy Valley farmers, the revelations in the rock may have elicited an interesting comment or two, but beyond this novelty, the daily business of agriculture and commerce continued as usual in the Lanham Mill community. By the 1920s, some of the Paluxy lands of the future park had changed owners.

William Edgeworth Muse, a prominent and wealthy judge in Glen Rose, bought the Mike Ramfield farm and part of the old Martin/Finley place—two tracts that were components of a large country estate comprising over 1,200 acres that Muse amassed. He employed several men of the Lanham Mill area to build a system of impressive fences on his property near Murphy crossing.[26] Muse lived the life of a country gentleman with his wife, and friends remembered his exotic collection of souvenirs. One visitor wrote:

26   GLEN ROSE AND GEO. P. SNYDER

ingly unimportant cottage. Yes, inside are
seen the most unusual things from the far
away foreign ports. Curios is not a word
comprehensive enough in its meaning and yet
that is what the average person would term
these objects Judge W. E. Muse has bought
at the initial cost of three trips around the
world and approximately $150,000 in money
and brought to this secluded farm house on
the banks of the Puluxy.

Judge Muse

The judge himself is the country gentleman one pictures in his gallery of ideals. He
makes a picturesque figure dressed in a
white linen suit, black tie and white shoes,
sitting in a low rocking chair placed in the
doorway at the north end of the living room.
On either side of him is an $1800 artistically
carved marble vase resting on marble pedes-
tals. His white hair, his intellectual face and
his silver tongue cast a peculiar quieting
power over his eager listeners as they drink
in his lecture on these rare embroideries,
forty oriental rugs, pictures, marble replicas

Judge William Edgeworth Muse

Landowner–Judge William E. Muse

A fairy with her most mysterious of wands must have created the interior of this humble appearing house by the open road. One can't imagine what is in the interior of that seemingly unimportant cottage. Yes, inside are seen the most unusual things from the far away foreign ports. Curios is not a word comprehensive enough in its meaning....

The judge himself is the country gentleman one pictures in his gallery of ideals. He makes a picturesque figure dressed in a white linen suit, black tie and white shoes, sitting in a low rocking chair placed in the doorway at the north end of the living room.[27]

In 1920 Christopher Columbus Rowland purchased the old Adams farm of 190 acres from Charley Pair. Like some of the other owners in the valley of the Paluxy, Rowland never actually lived on the 190-acre tract but rented it out instead, and in late 1920 or early 1921, the Wilson family moved onto the Rowland land. Jerdon Dillard Bismark Wilson, known as Dillard, was born on March 22, 1887, in Blairsville, Georgia, and came to Somervell County with his family in the mid-1890s. He married Ora Helen Abell, the daughter of Matt Abell, in 1910. Five of their twelve children had been born by the time they came to the Rowland land, and for thirty-two years the Wilson family would make the farm their own.[28]

The family set up housekeeping in the old Adams dogtrot cabin, and while a cool zephyr through the breezeway eased the summer heat, that same passage

MAJOR OWNERS OF FUTURE PARKLANDS
DINOSAUR VALLEY STATE PARK
(ca. 1920s and 1930s)

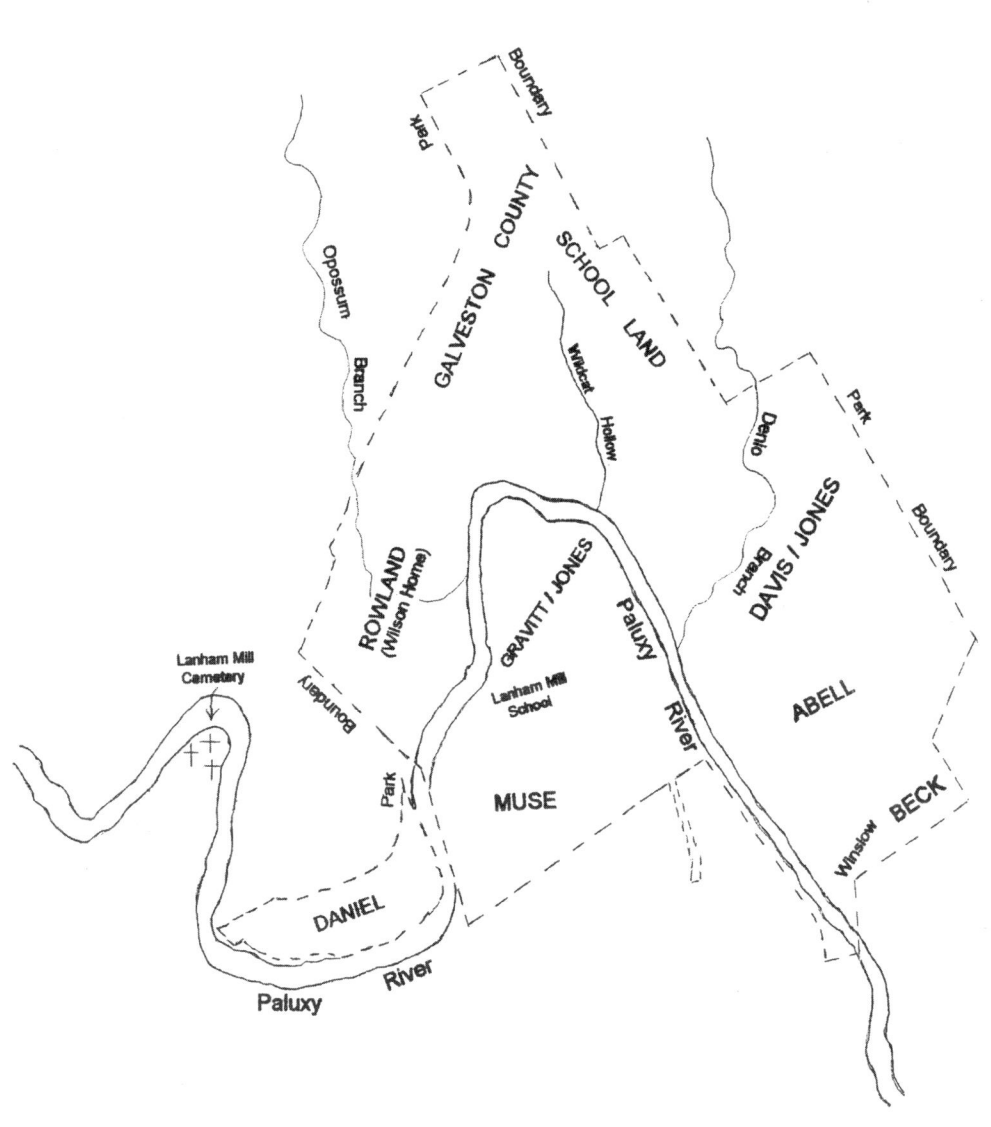

funneled bracing gusts in the winters. Young John Wilson, a mere five years old when they arrived, recalled that the gaping cracks between the wood of the house provided so much ventilation that snow blew through them![29]

The Wilsons raised the crops typical of many of the farms in the Paluxy Valley. Corn, maize, wheat, and oats swayed in the fields. Corn fed their teams through the winter, but cotton was still the money crop. In fact, the dawn of the 1920s saw for a time the rise of cotton from five cents to forty cents a pound, promising significant profits for enterprising growers. For the children, this life on the Paluxy, though filled with all the hard work required on a farm, offered rewards with the Blue Hole in short walking distance and acres of cedar brake country to explore.[30]

While contemporary write-ups of the early twentieth century heralded the perceived bounties of Somervell's valley farms, perennially quenched by artesian springs, the wells of Glen Rose propelled that city's claim to outsiders as a resort. The mineral waters attracted considerable attention and established the town as a destination for health seekers and health givers. Throughout the 1910s and 1920s, an assortment of doctors, osteopaths, chiropractors, and magnetic healers came to town. Commonly known as "rubbin' doctors," these healers blended water therapy, magnetic massage, and even clairvoyance to ease their patients' complaints. Their practices at that time reflected some of the more creative notions in vogue among some members of the psychotherapy community in the United States and Europe.[31]

In Glen Rose, the "rubbin' doctors" set up camp resorts and built sanitariums to accommodate a growing number of visitors. George Snyder, one of the best known healers, opened the Snyder Sanitarium in 1915 and by the 1920s had constructed an impressive two-story building as well as cottages and surrounding grounds called the Snyder Hotel.[32]

"The hotel is a concrete expression of one magnetic personality," wrote Elna Martin, a visitor to the hotel and author of *Glen Rose and Geo. P. Snyder: A Texas Town, The American Coue*. "A mental vibration with all the force of a great electric dynamo is felt the instant a person comes in the same atmosphere with George P. Snyder, a psychic and healer of many mental and physical ailments."[33]

Thousands came to Glen Rose to seek health and calm renewal. Martin described, "It is the soothingly restful little quiet town hidden away in a county where not even a railway engine's shrill whistle breaks the stillness as there is not a railroad in the whole county."[34]

It seemed that every yard and resort in Glen Rose had the constant gurgle of flowing wells that exuded their thick sulphurous odor. "Speaking of water, the sulphur water served with the ice cream at the local soda fountains makes one feel as if all things are queer in general in this village," Martin commented. "And for a distinct shock just taste the strong sulphur water at the horse trough directly in front of the court house."[35] For some, the stinkier the well, the better, especially for those who relied on the cleansing effect of these medicinal waters.

Others imbibed different "medicines" for well-being. With the onset of Prohibition, the springs, rugged hills, and thick cedar brakes of the Paluxy Valley became an ideal setting for the production of bootleg whiskey. The saloons of Glen Rose had long closed after citizens voted the county dry in 1906, but in the 1920s, the ready black market of customers in Dallas and Fort Worth inspired bootleggers to perfect their art. The land of the present park and environs harbored numerous stills, as producers needed both the seclusion of brush or limestone overhangs along with easy access to fresh water to make the corn mash and set up their barrels. Constantly on the lookout for revenuers, the moonshiners did not stay in one place for long but continually stole from hiding place to hiding place.[36]

Ora Wilson warned her children to avoid a still if they stumbled onto one. Once her son John suffered a close call when he had taken his horse on a shortcut to town for his dad's smoking tobacco. As his horse stumbled along a bluff, the boy slid off an embankment and right on top of a still. The startled lad suddenly faced a real live bootlegger who commented, "That's a good way to get hurt son."[37]

All of the farming families generally understood that some residents bootlegged for survival. When the farming income fell short, families still needed money for food and other essentials. Folks quietly recognized Charlie Moss as the biggest moonshiner in the vicinity of the present park. He and his brother "Grandy" learned of their great-grandfather's North Carolina whiskey recipe from their grandmother Hamberlin. The Hamberlin and Moss families were among the pioneers of the Lanham Mill community in the 1870s, and Hamberlin–Moss crossing (second crossing) on the Paluxy was named for them. They also carried on their family legacy, however, through a lucrative bootlegging business.[38]

Somervell County became a "Little Appalachia" of sorts with the prevalence of the white lightning trade. "Hooch" makers kept their senses keen to stay ahead of the law. Spies monitored the main roads into town to watch for authorities, and eventually communication advanced to the telephone age.[39]

The area's dubious reputation earned Glen Rose the label as the "Moonshine Capital of Texas." The bootleg liquor temporarily stopped, however, in August 1923 when Texas Rangers raided the county. They dumped their spoils on the courthouse lawn—66 gallons of whiskey, 84 gallons of hoe beer, 8 gallons of wine, 550 pounds of sugar, and 7 stills. This

The Charlie Moss moonshine still is displayed in the Somervell County Museum. Photo by Gary S. Hickinbotham

Texas Rangers show off their spoils after a raid on Somervell County bootleggers in August 1923. The bust caused a temporary setback in the area's white lightning business. Courtesy Somervell County Historical Commission

did not include the 9,750 gallons of mash destroyed. A shocked citizenry saw the arrest of thirty-one residents, including the county attorney and the sheriff.[40]

The raid made a bold statement, but only temporarily slowed the production of "mountain dew"—a practice that remained a noteworthy part of the underground economy especially into the Depression years. Even in the modern day, the art of moonshining is not entirely lost in Somervell County.[41]

Somervell County looked to shed its shadier claim as a "hooch haven" and capitalize on the growing phenomenon of the touring motorist. "This is the day of autos," one mid-1920s Glen Rose brochure proclaimed:

Ninety percent of the recreations or summer vacations are now taken by auto. It does not matter whether you are within 25 or 200 miles of Glen Rose, a few hours drive will land you in Glen Rose.[42]

The town advertised jitney service from the area burgs of Cleburne, Granbury, Stephenville, and Walnut Springs,[43] but the touring cars of the 1920s had to contend with the wagon trails and byways of old.

Folks who lived up and down the Paluxy "Creek," as they called it, all agreed that the roads were terrible. The Paluxy's periodic angry rises just exacerbated the troublesome travel. High water usually covered the river fords with a new layer of sand and gravel and caused headaches for those farmers who proudly negotiated their first Model Ts along the Lanham Mill Road. Residents and later road workers had to take teams out in the Paluxy to scrape the limestone bed clear of sand and gravel. Storms also caused erosion along the bluffs of the hill-side road and created dangerous obstacles. And, of course, many vehicles bogged down in the muddy byways.[44]

Crews did some of the first paving in the county in Glen Rose in 1922. Somervell County, like other counties across Texas, sought its share of state and federal funds for highway improvement, a concept long lobbied by the Good Roads Movement across the Lone Star State and the nation, as the growing use of the automobile exposed the drawbacks of the antiquated wagon roads.[45]

In 1923 workers built a concrete and steel bridge over the Paluxy on the Cleburne–Glen Rose Road—Highway 68 (the forerunner of present-day U.S.

LEFT *In the early 1920s highway improvement in Somervell County helped open the area to motoring tourists. A Model T tools down the Cleburne–Glen Rose Road, Highway 68 (today's U.S. Highway 67), amidst the scenic Paluxy River Valley* **RIGHT** *In the 1920s, Glen Rose gained a reputation as "The Petrified City" because of numerous buildings constructed with petrified wood, such as the former Lane's Ford Agency and Garage, still standing in 2008.* Photo by Gary S. Hickinbotham

Highway 67).[46] Here drivers cruised through to behold the town that maximized its natural resources. The phenomenon of tourism gave a kind of freedom for folks to explore. Writer Elna Martin asserted:

The poor man with his tiny fliver [*sic*] full of family and fun can see just as much as the big fat millionaire lolling in his expensive upholstered limousine in which may be his lovely wife and her latest poodle dog.[47]

Advertisements dubbed Glen Rose the "Petrified City." Farmers plowed up petrified wood in abundance. Eventually the sale of these geological souvenirs developed into an unexpected industry with the shipment of 1,000 to 1,500 tons annually to other parts of the country. A ton of petrified wood sold for up to twenty dollars. The construction of petrified homes and businesses became the fashionable trend. Sanitariums used the materials, as did service stations and cafes. The stones' rich sienna and ivory-blended tones glowed intense hues in the setting sun as drivers tooled past.[48]

Motorists heading down Highway 68 could choose from a variety of parks and tourist camps where families splashed in Paluxy Creek, sipped from a cool

artesian well, or napped in a shaded glen. Apparently, the "lime mud strider" tracks on Wheeler Branch merited the attention of curious travelers and local families alike.

Dorothy Leach of the Somervell County Historical Commission told of the reminiscences of her mother, Maxie Parker Leach, who grew up on Wheeler Branch. During the 1920s, the dry rock bed of the creek provided great fun for friends and family who picnicked, played games, made bonfires, and held wiener roasts. Children frolicked up and down the stream and dug for fool's gold along the banks. Sometimes they ventured on expeditions to the fork of the branch to see the dinosaur tracks. "My old home place is up there close to Wheeler Branch," Dorothy Leach recalled. "My mother talked about that a lot—going to see the dinosaur tracks, taking people up there, relatives, visitors—something to do."[49]

In 1927, in her book *Glen Rose and Geo. P. Snyder: A Texas Town, The American Coue,* Elna Martin lauded the ancient tri-toed trackmaker as the original tourist. Though she estimated the tracks to be quite a bit younger than their true age, she was, nevertheless, following the conventional thinking of geologists of the time:

Five million years ago the first visitor to Glen Rose left his calling cards in the form of foot tracks in the bed of a creek. His name, as his size indicates, was Dinosaur....[50]

The tracks invited both admiration and fanciful whimsy, and Martin cheerfully described both viewpoints regarding the fossil footprints:

Mystery appeals to the human heart today with as much force as it did to superstitious people of other lands centuries ago. One tale found floating in Glen Rose about the dinosaur tracks must have been created by a vivid imagination of one loving mystery. This is it. An old man saw the strange

TOP *In addition to sporting a trail of dinosaur tracks, Wheeler Branch also held Lane's swimming hole–a fun and cool haven for youngsters. Maxie Parker Leach (center) recalled family picnics and dinosaur track expeditions on the branch in the 1920s. Somervell County Historical Commission* **BOTTOM** *"One of Glen Rose's First Visitors." Artist Ralph S. Rowntree of Dallas sketched this portrait of the "Dinosaur," for author Elna Martin in Glen Rose and Geo. P. Snyder..., published in 1927.*

imprints in the rocks. He decided immediately that they were signs leading to a hidden treasure so he spent much time and energy digging thereabouts to unearth the much spoken of but seldom seen pot of gold. Robbers buried their spoil here years and years ago when Texas was indeed all that the modern movies depict the wild and woolly west or so reasoned this dear old man still clinging to his boyish adventurous nature.

Another man with another mental background saw these little traces of Glen Rose's first callers and he was delighted. But he was a New York geologist, consequently he recognized these foot prints as would the interpreter of finger prints at police headquarters recognize the criminal's imprints.

The slice or imprint hewed out in the creek bed was sent to Texas A. and M. College for the museum. And some local citizens say $30 was paid for it. That must be where we get the saying "stepping high."[51]

In her book Elna Martin also presented to the reader a description of the private park that held the dinosaur tracks:

Detour to Dinosaur Tracks

... You cross the creek and follow the branch to the first house on the left of the road. In fact, to be exact, it is one mile to the farm gate, through which you enter to see the dinosaur tracks, from the point on the state highway where the road leads up the hill there by Martin's Park. Twenty-five cents entrance fee is given to the enterprising farmer at his gate. One-half mile from that gate into the farmer's pasture are the tracks. The road is rough, though, and along a rather scarey [sic] looking cliff. It winds in and around, as some people do in trying to discover for what they are here on earth.

The two tracks of the dinosaur are in a trough-shaped affair with a wooden door over them. One poor track is left on the outside as if it were a step-child left out in the cold bleak world unwanted. Really and truly this artificial arrangement may be symbolic for as the steps of a personality ascending the ladder of success so the steps of that animal, so long gone, might each have had a different effect on its future.[52]

In 1929 Glen Rose held a contest to select a town slogan. The winning catchphrase was more than fitting: "Glen Rose for Health and Pleasure."[53] In

In 1929 Joe and Laurie Sanders took a road trip to Glen Rose. Their adventures included an excursion to see the dinosaur tracks. Courtesy Laurie P. Sanders Collection

August of that year a young couple journeyed north to Glen Rose. Joe and Laurie Sanders lived in New Braunfels. Joe, a mechanic who loved to motor the open roads, had made a hobby of exploring the scenic byways and out-of-the-way parks around his Hill Country home. Now they ventured to this Northern Hill Country. Laurie Sanders recalled, "We went up to Glen Rose. That's where the dinosaur tracks are." In their black Model T coupé, they crisscrossed narrow dirt and gravel roads through the countryside for most of the way.[54]

The trip illustrated both the elegant and seamier side of Somervell County and Glen Rose. They stayed at the Glen Hotel, a new establishment built in 1928 just off the town square. It offered fine rooms and family dining, but in the sweltering heat of August, the stifling night air kept Laurie from sleep. As she sat in the window fanning herself, she heard the endless negotiations of bootleggers in the alley below. All night various characters would come and go, dealing and squabbling over the sales of their home brews.[55]

Days, however, brought sun and sights, and Joe, ever interested in scenic and geological oddities, headed out to view the fossil footprints. Typically, many scenic attractions in Texas at that time were located on private property, and folks asked permission to traipse about and picnic. Laurie, of course, had learned to be prepared for such outings and slipped her house shoes over her silk stockings. She remembered the effort required to see the dinosaur tracks:

At that time they were doing nothing about that. You had to go through a barbed wire fence and weeds up to here, and hunt around in there in a creek bed. You could find it, but they had nothing about it. They didn't think anything of it. We took pictures of it.[56]

Joe snapped a picture of one of the three-toed dinosaur tracks. Clad in their typical 1920s fashions, Joe and Laurie posed for photos at the site as well, thereby memorializing one couple's trip to Somervell County.

And so Glen Rose and its Northern Hill Country had come of age for travelers during the high times of the early twentieth century. It was home to both the notable and notorious. Visitors could heal their weary spirits amongst the gushing mineral waters and scenic countryside. Others perhaps lifted themselves with the homemade spirits of the bootleggers! All came in the wake of the area's earliest tourist—"Dinosaur."

Joe Sanders photographed this theropod track, probably on Wheeler Branch, in August 1929. Photo by Joe Sanders, Courtesy Laurie P. Sanders Collection

CHAPTER FOUR
Work and Play on Paluxy "Creek"

As the effects of the stock market crash in October 1929 settled upon Somervell County, to residents, the slogan "For Health and Pleasure" didn't ring so true as "for survival." Crop markets and decent prices dried up. Cotton that had sold for as high as forty cents a pound in 1920 brought only five cents a decade later. The price of beef fell as well, spelling a disastrous combination for a little county that depended on farming and stock raising. Somervell was limited in its amount of acreage for crops and livestock because of the sizable areas of unusable rocky hills and cedar brakes. Harvested cropland decreased from a total of 22,894 acres in 1909 to 16,906 acres by the mid-1930s. Total population began to drop, with 3,016 in 1930 compared to 3,931 in 1910.[1]

For the Dillard Wilson family in the Paluxy Valley, the 1930s literally blew in with a vengeance. The clouds didn't look so threatening that summer day in 1930, but in a flash the winds whipped as rain and debris slapped the old dogtrot home. Dillard and his son Murry were across the breezeway by the fireplace when the twister dipped down. Most of the family was in the kitchen. The house shifted on its foundation, and the porch blew away as everyone struggled to get to safety. By the time they reached the storm cellar, the tornado was gone, but its fury had exacted a terrible toll. The damage to the old home-stead was irreparable. Fortunately, no lives were lost, but John Wilson would never forget the sight of his three-year-old sister Fern, perched on a rain-soaked mattress. "Where are we going to sleep?" she asked.[2]

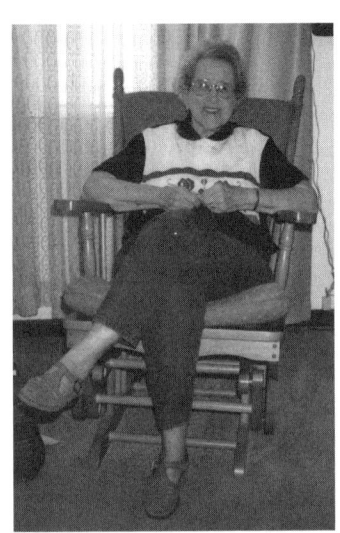

For a time the whole family endured days of miserably wet weather in a tent, while landowner Chris Rowland helped Dillard Wilson build a new home. This wooden structure sported a bungalow-style roof that dropped down from a central point to four evenly-proportioned walls. Though modest, the newly-completed box house was a welcome sight![3]

Folks up and down the Lanham Mill community came together in good times and in bad. A stubborn self-suffi-ciency pervaded. Agriculture, so economically fickle, was also their saving grace. Families grew their own food, fed their own stock, mended their own fences, and made their own fun.

Novella Wilson, the daughter of Vivian and Dora Ramfield May, fondly reminisced about the simple pleasures of life along the Paluxy. She was born on her grandfather Chris Ramfield's farm near Murphy crossing, the third river ford. Soon, her parents took their baby Novella back home about a mile away to the May farm. Her father Vivian had been born and raised there on the home place, which was in sight of the Abell house.[4]

Novella and the other valley children walked the country lanes to the Lanham Mill School. Their treks brought occasional excitement. Novella and her brothers,

Lanham Mill historian and artist Novella Wilson recalled her childhood days in the Paluxy Valley. Photo by Laurie E. Jasinski

George and Marvin, were frightened to stumble across fifty gallon barrels, presumably for moonshine, one day as they took a shortcut through the cedar from school. She remembered another adventure:

Another time, a man was parked ... in his open Model T while a buddy of his was out there trying to steal our turkeys. Our turkeys had wandered off.... They were going to catch those turkeys. My brothers and I were on our way home from school. When he saw us, he went on down the hill in his car, and we piled our book satchels on little Billie Jean Rhodes, who was too little to carry them, but she did. She walked ... all the way down to our house carrying all of our books, while we chased the turkeys home. But we were determined the man wouldn't steal our turkeys!

LEFT *Student Olive Fay Trimble holds a garland of roses. Plays were presented at the close of each school year. Local men constructed an outdoor stage, equipped with a miniature log cabin and a picket fence. The schoolhouse was the scene of holiday celebrations and community gatherings.* Courtesy Novella Wilson
RIGHT *Children play baseball in the Lanham Mill schoolyard (ca. early 1940s).* Courtesy Novella Wilson

The one-room school served eight grades, and often the teacher lived with a family in the area. The schoolhouse not only fulfilled an educational function but also represented the heart and soul of the Lanham Mill community (in the heart of present Dinosaur Valley State Park).[5] "There were plays at the end of school," Novella Wilson recalled, "and ... revivals in the summertime, and that would be outdoors at the schoolhouse."

Folks attended church every Sunday and celebrated any special event or holiday that came along at the school, with assemblies, box suppers, Easter egg hunts, and parties. The Lanham Mill schoolhouse was the Lanham Mill community. Novella's brother-in-law Doyle Wilson confirmed, "You had a Christmas gathering of the community there. I guess all my life the Christmas presents I got from home were given at the schoolhouse."[6]

Though sometimes families made a trip into town to see a picture show, many youngsters created their own fun in the valley neighborhood. Novella commented:

We had parties and we'd ... go to somebody's house. They'd have a party, and we'd play things like Snap and Ring Games and stuff like that. We'd have ice cream suppers. We'd all get together ... on Saturday night. Somebody'd put the money together to buy ice. I don't remember what ice cost, but each person would hand in a few cents, and they'd go to town and buy the ice.... The ladies would each make an ice cream...and we would meet at the schoolhouse.[7]

She explained the art of playing Snap:

Well, it's like you choose partners, a boy and a girl, who stand holding hands. Another boy "snaps" [his fingers at] a girl to catch him, and she chases him around and around the couple until she "tags" him. At that time, the boy exchanges places with the boy of the first couple, while she "snaps" another boy to catch her. This was a very active game, and it continued until everyone was tired and decided it was time to play Ring Games or some other game.

Playing Ring Games cleverly disguised a way for the youngsters to dance. "That's like square dancing only it was singing," she smiled. "We'd sing the songs instead of using the music."

Music did ring out through the Paluxy Valley from time to time with the sweet sounds of country when the Wilson family showed up at get-togethers. Novella commented that their humble ways but powerful talents made for an irresistible charm:

[Dillard Wilson] was one of the best fiddlers in the business. He was a wonderful fiddler, and he had four sons that played guitars ... and [Dillard's] sister ... played the accordion, and when they got together they had very good music.... The Wilsons though were very modest about their abilities. They didn't want to just push themselves on you. They wanted to make sure everybody would want to hear them if they played music. So usually they'd come to all the parties or whatever went on and leave their musical instruments at home. Everybody'd start saying, "Where's y'all's instruments? Go back home and get your instruments." Here they'd have to go back home to get their instruments.

With the setting up and tuning of the instruments, the melodies might not kick off until midnight. But Dillard's old mountain tunes, inspired by his Georgia roots, resounded until dawn!

Paluxy Creek itself supplied a main playground for the kids who splashed and swam in its green waters. By the 1930s that stream had also revealed its bed's secrets as people stumbled across more and more dinosaur tracks. Perhaps children dreamed of their prehistoric counterparts thundering at play in ancient tidal pools.

The three-toed oddities inspired imagination and wonder, and the community of Glen Rose capitalized on its unique treasures by featuring an excavated theropod track set into the petrified wood of the bandstand on the town square.

Somervell County residents excavated this excellent theropod track at the Hendrix–Ramfield crossing (fourth crossing) on the Paluxy River and placed it in the bandstand on the courthouse square at Glen Rose in 1933. The print still attracted tourists in the twenty-first century. Photo by Laurie E. Jasinski

This "perfect" print came from an impressive trackway located at the Hendrix–Ramfield crossing.[8]

Once again Ellis Shuler of Southern Methodist University came to study, just as he had investigated the footprints on Wheeler Branch years before. By the mid-1930s, folks had located eight or more dinosaur track sites in Somervell County. Shuler first saw the excavated track in 1934. He wrote:

Recently a superb dinosaur track was taken from the "fourth crossing" of the Paluxy River about six miles west of the town of Glen Rose and placed by the citizens of the community in the base of the bandstand located in the court house yard. This track is one of the largest known from the area and is remarkably well preserved.[9]

Shuler made a cast and mold of the track. Dr. Barnum Brown, an eminent paleontologist of the day from the American Museum of Natural History, New York, eventually viewed the cast and mold and rated the original dinosaur's size as "medium to large," but he declared that the American Museum had a larger one. Shuler proposed the name *Eubrontes (?) glenrosensis* for the track of this flesh-eater and concluded that he had "seen nothing to conflict with his views expressed in 1917, that the Glen Rose limestone is a near shore phase, deposited as lime mud, the conditions of deposition probably being lagoonal."[10]

In August 1934 Shuler made a field trip to examine and admire the twenty-six tracks exposed just below the fourth crossing. Paluxy Creek, unusually low that season, offered excellent viewing. Among those who accompanied Shuler was Dr. Robert T. Hill, whose study of the geology of the area before the turn of the century had set the standard for those who followed. The expedition inspired Hill to comment on the work in his *Dallas Morning News* column titled "Open Season for Dinosaur Hunting."[11]

He referred to recent, more-publicized discoveries in the field of paleontology as signaling the "open season for finding remains of the great dinosaur lizards that roamed parts of the United States." A "great war whoop" reverberated from the 115-degree heat of Arizona, "as compared with our own little 100," Hill interjected, about the uncovering of some fifty or more ancient tracks. Another "publicity yelp" lauded the discovery of at least twenty-five "ancient lizards" at one Wyoming site by Professor [Barnum] Brown.

"But why all of this noise about the dinosaurs in foreign countries?" Hill growled. "Just take a three hours' drive out to Glen Rose and see what Dr. E.W. Shuler of our own village showed me ... while these Arizona and Wyoming folks were making so much noise about their finds."

Hill and others counted numerous theropod tracks in the bed of the Paluxy. One small spot alone held twenty-five fossil footprints and spurred the ornery geologist to write, "No doubt but hundreds of them could be found in Somervell County if one-tenth the effort and means could be devoted to the search that Professor Brown has at his command in Wyoming...."[12]

The men measured each track and mapped them with excited plans to return and conduct further study. However, as was typical of the Paluxy's whims, a flood swept through the canyon in the spring of 1935. Shuler wrote two years later:

It is with keen regret, that this article records the disappearance of ... the well known track locality at the fourth crossing of the Paluxy River.... Stream erosion, which brought to view there a superb collection of tracks, continued its work too well and wiped out the exhibit as an eraser wipes out a schoolboy's blackboard drawing....

The whole incident emphasized the fact that tracks exposed in streams and to open weathering are ephemeral exhibits and should be studied at the earliest possible time.[13]

Farmers along the Paluxy were accustomed to seeing the appearance of "bird tracks" in the creekbed, but in the early 1930s, the Moss brothers discovered the most unusual set of tracks of all. They were quite different from the tri-toed specimens. These footprints sank broad and deep, and the brothers wondered if Somervell County had once been home to some kind of prehistoric elephant. Their mystery would not be solved for several more years,[14] but farmers did occasionally discover that the potholed impressions harbored fish, serendipitous finds for the supper table.

Throughout the Great Depression residents tried to make the most out of Somervell County's natural resources. Water, one of the region's greatest assets, was allowed to flow unchecked from artesian wells that had no control valves. In fact, in his report to the Department of the Interior, geologist Albert G. Fiedler stated that users had dug more than five hundred wells since 1880 for "domestic supply and for watering stock," but actually only utilized a small amount for irrigation purposes. Many of the early wells were already abandoned because they "ceased to yield water by natural flow."[15]

Fiedler warned about water waste, underground leakage, and possible pollution:

The 360,000 gallons a day permitted to flow from wells without being used for any beneficial purposes is an unnecessary drain upon the artesian reservoir. The head of many of the flowing wells in Glen Rose and vicinity is already low, and a further decline of only a few feet will greatly reduce their flow or cause them to stop flowing.

In August 1934, Lanham Mill resident Charlie Moss photographed these strange "elephant-like" tracks on the Paluxy. This is the earliest known image of sauropod footprints in the riverbed. Courtesy Novella Wilson, Photo by Charlie Moss

Fiedler recommended repairing defective wells and installing valves to control flow. A large quantity of the water went to the supply of outdoor swimming pools and for recreational use for tourist camps.[16]

In the hills, fresh springs and flowing wells still facilitated the production of moonshine, which appeared more economically important than ever, even after the end of Prohibition. But most farmers looked for more aboveboard means to earn extra dollars. Some collected and sold petrified wood. Others hunted game both for food and for the pelts. Bobcat, raccoon, fox, and skunk hides sold fairly well. The Wilson family mailed hides to a buyer, though occasionally pelt merchants passed through town.[17] "I think skunk hides would bring nearly more than

Vivian May (left) sits beside his son Alton and son-in-law John Wilson (behind the wheel) with Buster the dog in their trusty 1924–25 Model T truck. For years they used the work-horse vehicle to haul cedar posts. Cedar chopping provided good supplementary income to farmers in the Paluxy Valley, especially during the Depression. Photo by Novella Wilson

anything," Doyle Wilson commented. "But back then, growing up in this country, anything you could do to make a dollar you nearly had to do it."

The thick cedar brakes also supplied a growing local industry of cedar chopping. According to Novella Wilson:

My Dad [Vivian May] and John's Dad [Dillard Wilson] and John and his brothers and everybody would cut cedar posts, and you know ... still ... I can't keep from looking at them. What a good post that would make, and like any of these good straight posts, you could sell those for five cents a piece. If you cut a hundred, you could have all that much money—five dollars. And John could cut a hundred posts in one day. And that was a pretty good day's work.

... And then there were buyers that would come. They stacked the posts in [rows] of ten and then crossways a row of ten, and that way ... they could count them.... There were buyers that would come in and buy them and take them to other places like Fort Worth or around where they didn't have cedar posts.[18]

Even the dinosaur prints themselves encouraged a unique cottage industry. Some farmers quarried tracks in the streambed. "My Daddy dug one out too one time," Novella said. They displayed it in their yard. For others these stony oddities helped supplement the household income. Jim Ryals, who rented the old Mike Ramfield place at Blue Hole from owner Judge William Muse, capitalized on this unusual enterprise. Ryals dug out tracks and sold them to universities around the country. "He worked with just his wife and his children," Novella recalled. "One of his children was my sister-in-law, Daisy [Ryals] May. She helped to dig out a number of tracks with him."[19]

Young Daisy had to help in the hard labor as her daddy painstakingly worked to free a print from its limestone prison. He held a chisel while one of the children hit it with a sledgehammer, or they would alternate and the father pounded with the sledgehammer. He fashioned a metal rim, a big wagon wheel, to encircle the track.

His daughter Daisy recalled, "He was the one that could take out a track without breaking it." The band helped to keep the print and surrounding limestone intact as they chipped a wide circle around it. This backbreaking work took hour after hour, but for a price of up to twenty-five dollars, it helped to feed his family. A few others also dug up tracks, and some took to carving them. George Adams, who as a boy first discovered Somervell County's illustrious fossil footprints, became very skilled at carving both dinosaur traces and giant human footprints. Ryals, however, was the best-known track collector in the county and later estimated that he may have quarried dozens of tracks.[20]

"John [Wilson] hauled one track to Southern Methodist University in Dallas one time," Novella remembered, "and I went along."

As the 1930s progressed and families of the Paluxy Valley discovered their own inventive strategies to survive the Great Depression, the joys of life and rites of passage marched on for the children of Lanham Mill. Novella May and John Wilson grew up. They married in 1936 and lived near his father's farm.[21]

By this time John's baby brother, Doyle, the youngest son in the family, spent his days exploring the rugged landscape. For young Doyle the wonders of his surroundings were enough. "I traipsed up and down the creek. I had all my fun doing that I guess."[22] Often he would peer out over the bluff above the Paluxy to see the paths of the dinosaurs. As the clear green water sparkled over the trackways, he could imagine that a pack had just traveled through the night before. He could spy the ferocious creatures, teeth gleaming, roars echoing through the canyons, stalking through the stream. It was a great place to grow up. A great place to explore.

"One of Glen Rose's First Visitors." Artist Ralph S. Rowntree of Dallas sketched this portrait of the "Dinosaur," for author Elna Martin in Glen Rose and Geo. P. Snyder…, published in 1927.

CHAPTER FIVE

The Dinosaur Hunter and the Texas Village

The November sun angled golden ribbons across Dillard Wilson's field. The air breathed crisp, with a whiff of smokiness that fingered through the cedar hills and down the valley. Thanksgiving was coming, and Christmas would follow. Doyle Wilson busied himself with chores, but his thoughts strayed to the coming holiday and drifted further to presents at the schoolhouse. The familiar lull of the day was broken by an engine vibration growing ever stronger. Folks knew everybody along Paluxy Creek, so the sight of a well-worn light green touring Buick with a cloth top rambling up to the Wilson house announced the arrival of a stranger to these parts.

A thoughtful-looking man, a bit wiry and with a mustache, stepped out and knocked on the door. Roland T. Bird introduced himself to Dillard Wilson and explained his quest for the dinosaur footprints. "Mr. Bird, he just appeared at the house one day," Doyle Wilson remembered. Here stood someone who had journeyed from far away to see the tracks Doyle had known all of his life. The family went outside and gathered around the Buick. This was probably the biggest, nicest car Doyle had ever seen. He noticed Mr. Bird's twinkle of pride as he told of his motoring adventures across the country, as if the vehicle was the most faithful traveling companion he had.[1]

"[He] asked Dad if he could stay down there [on the river], and he stayed down there—I don't really remember how long—two or three days," Doyle said.[2] Dillard Wilson smiled at the request. He was a fair-minded soul who appreciated someone willing to work hard and get dirty.

•   ●   ◦

Roland Thaxter Bird had led a varied life by the time he arrived at the Paluxy Valley. He was born in Rye, New York, on December 29, 1899, and was the eldest of four children of Henry and Harriet Bird. His young life, filled with reading and play, was saddened by the death of his mother from tuberculosis when he was just fifteen. R.T. himself was pestered with colds and various respiratory maladies, and his father sent him to an uncle's farm in the Catskills with presumably a healthier climate. The lad's budding interest in cattle eventually took him to Florida, where he worked on a Jersey ranch and traveled the national livestock exhibition circuit. His investment in the boom of the Florida real estate market went bust with the onslaught of the Depression.[3]

R.T. found himself a wanderer. With his Harley motorcycle and a unique sidecar camper that he fashioned, he drove about the nation and performed various odd jobs to get by. Perhaps he relied on his years of cowboying to make a dollar or put his one-time apprenticeship to a plumber to good use. But as he motored the open roads, undoubtedly his "Pater" Henry Bird's respect for learning and scientific curiosity also influenced R.T. He developed keen observational skills that served him well when he made a chance discovery of a fossilized jaw in the desert of northern Arizona in 1932, an event that changed his life and broke wide open his career as a dinosaur hunter. The find earned Bird the opportunity to work with Barnum Brown and scout potential sites for bones for the American Museum of Natural History in New York.[4]

Barnum Brown, reportedly named for the great showman P.T. Barnum, had shone as one of the stars of paleontology's first golden age. By his early twenties, he was already working for the American Museum of Natural History. He traveled North America and the world gathering fossils, and his finds helped establish the core of the museum's significant paleontological collections. Colleagues and protégés rightly lauded him as one of the great dinosaur hunters of the day. The titles of books written by his second wife colorfully attest to Brown's intense dedication to his field—*I Married a Dinosaur* and *Bring 'em Back Petrified*. In 1927 he became Curator of Vertebrate Paleontology at the American Museum. In this capacity, Brown, impressed by R.T. Bird's eagerness and tenacity, hired him in 1933 to conduct field reconnaissance and excavations for the museum.[5] Thus began a close professional relationship between two like-minded adventurers. But unlike Brown's boom days of dinosaur hunting, Bird's work during the 1930s and 1940s coincided with a period that modern scientists have dubbed the "Dark Age" of dinosaur exploration, signifying a "lull in the pursuit of dinosaur studies...."[6] Perhaps this makes Bird's contributions to paleontology during these years all the more noteworthy.

By November 1938 Bird had worked as Brown's field collector for more than five years. Brown assigned him the task of traveling to New Mexico to crate and ship a fossil plant to New York.[7] Excerpts from Bird's letters vividly describe the tale of his remarkable journey from New Mexico to the Paluxy Valley and the historic work done there. Interestingly, the trail that led Bird to Glen Rose began at an Indian trading post—a fitting place, considering the important role trading posts played in the development and settlement of North Central Texas and Somervell County. "It all began in Gallup, New Mexico," Bird wrote to Brown. "But for a chance remark while crating Mrs. Seymour's cycad, I would have returned east in a few days from Pueblo. I was told I ought to see some strange tracks in an Indian trader's store."[8]

When R.T. Bird walked into Jack Hill's post, he spied a most peculiar set of tracks. They were giant human-like footprints, about fifteen inches long and perfectly imprinted in stone. The store clerk informed him that the proprietor Hill had recently purchased them along with dinosaur tracks displayed at a branch store in Lupten, New Mexico, nearby.[9] Bird's investigation of that post revealed several carnivore footprints:

> The tracks were surprising to say the least. Some of them had been made by dinosaurs, and were most remarkably perfect; others were of a type I even hesitated to venture a guess about. My first reaction was that they were <u>all</u> fictitious....[10]

They all recently came from a Texas village—Glen Rose. When Bird realized the town's connection to the Lower Cretaceous rock formation, he considered his options. "Going back to the traders I did everything but smell of the tracks," he wrote to Hans Christian Adamson, Chairman of Public and Press Information at the American Museum. Fake or not, maybe the tracks symbolized something greater. Maybe the Texas village did hold paleontological promise. He would detour via a southern route east through Glen Rose.[11]

A few days later, Bird's chartreuse Buick wheeled into downtown Glen Rose. "I arrived with the hunch still strong and healthy, though was relieved to think it hadn't cost me many extra miles," he recalled. "I didn't want to feel too encouraged, but the fact also remained this was a region never worked by the American Museum before."[12] A pass around the square quickly confirmed his instincts:

I hadn't been in Glen Rose thirty minutes when I spotted two of the very same things the trader had. One lay out in front of a curio store and the other—a big one—was inserted promenently in a bit of stonework in front of their little courthouse. Yes, the natives said, looking me over carefully, there were lots of them up along the Paluxy River.[13]

Bird, of course, had not been aware of Glen Rose's reputation as a resort town. Maybe if he'd seen the *Dallas Morning News* article the previous year he would have rushed to the area much sooner. In an effort to bring back the annual 250,000 to 300,000 visitors the village had hosted prior to 1929, the Glen Rose Chamber of Commerce launched a renewed effort to attract city dwellers from the Dallas/Fort Worth region. The dinosaurs made for a unique gimmick. The Dallas paper's headline of July 25, 1937, declared:

Glen Rose Claims Original Tourists Of 10,000,000 B.C.
Noted Resort Town Says Even Dinosaurs Chose It as Vacation Spot.

One of the oldest resorts in the Southwest, Glen Rose claims it was first visited by tourists 10,000,000 years ago—and offers to submit proof of its claims. The earliest tourists were dinosaurs that roamed this part of the country when the world was still young....[14]

The town still advertised its mineral waters, health resorts, scenic hills, and unique petrified wood homes. Bird discovered all of this for himself. "Some of the houses here have been very tastefully decorated...," he wrote regarding the fossil wood structures.[15]

Residents suggested that he contact Jim Ryals. As the main track excavator in the area, Ryals knew the riverbed. Bird motored to the Lanham Mill community and forded the river up to the Ryals place near the fourth crossing. The farmer explained that his side business of quarrying dinosaur tracks was certainly a more novel enterprise than cedar chopping or bootlegging, though the work was difficult. They walked the Paluxy a bit as Ryals recalled the many three-toed tracks and some that the locals described as "man tracks." He came across one curious print. "Ryals sloshed a shovel back and forth and then stood back while the current washed the surface clean," Bird later described. "I watched closely as

Jim Ryals (wearing hat) displays some of his Paluxy quarry for sale. His son-in-law Johnny Holder, a descendant of the Holder family (area landowners), looks on. Ryals sold the tracks near the front gate of his house, located just down the county road from the Lanham Mill School and within the boundaries of present Dinosaur Valley State Park. Courtesy Paluxy Valley Archives and Genealogy Society and Somervell County Heritage Center, Photo by Roland T. Bird

the outline of a foot took form, something about 15 inches long with a curious elongated heel."[16]

Then Ryals talked about another type of footprint he had encountered in the riverbed—large rounded tracks with claws. For Bird the description cried out the name sauropod, but the possibility seemed too remote. "I questioned him at length, hesitating to believe the man," he later wrote. "A sudden desire to dig into the gravel bar almost overcame my better judgment."[17]

These intriguing descriptions piqued Bird's curiosity even more. His conversations with locals made clear to him that for them, the dinosaur prints had become just another aspect of the changing landscape, since the early discoveries of George Adams and the Moss brothers. The whims of the river revealed trails of stony tracks and then scoured the bed clean.

Folks made another point clear to Bird—he should talk to "Bull" Adams, considered to be the smartest man in town. Ernest Tolbert "Bull" Adams was the brother of George Adams. As youths they had marveled at the tracks of Wheeler Branch and the Paluxy. "Bull" Adams was a Rhodes scholar, Oxford University graduate, and a brilliant attorney. Though he had achieved many professional and academic accolades, he still loved best exploring the country-side of Somervell County.[18]

Bird wrote to Brown:

He is a graduate of Oxford, practices law when the spirit moves him, but spends a great deal of his time just out in the hills of this region.... He is a big burly heavyset man; never wears a hat or a tie; he lives alone in a room cluttered with indian relics, bows, arrows and whatnot. He is considered the leading authority on the indian lore of this region and the one day I spent out with him soon realized he knew it too.[19]

Like his brother George, "Bull" Adams was an adept carver who could flake out arrowheads with ease. He was of course familiar with the various tracks up and down the river, including those large rounded prints that Bird suspected could be some type of heavy quadruped. He encouraged Bird's search along the Paluxy.[20]

　　　　•　　　●　　　•

The Wilsons were long-established residents of the Paluxy Valley when R.T. Bird drove up to their farm. Like other residents in the Lanham Mill community they weathered the Depression the best they could. Farmers grew staples of corn, wheat, and oats, and most ran ten to fifteen head of cattle on the available pastureland. Peanuts were becoming the next big crop as cotton production declined, but Dillard Wilson still cultivated the formerly king harvest. "My Dad, he couldn't stand it if he didn't have a cotton crop somewhere," Doyle exclaimed.[21]

Dillard Wilson knew the comings and goings of the Lanham Mill residents and was always willing to lend a hand—whether it be with a plow, an ax, or a fiddle. The same courtesy he extended to his neighbors he also extended to R.T. Bird when Bird asked to stay on the river. "Dad told him then he could do whatever he wanted to. There would be no charge," Doyle said.[22]

For several days the Buick sat parked above the riverbank on the Wilson property, while Bird made camp and systematically sloshed up and down the stream. Only for a brief time did he let his imagination wander and fancy that his footsteps followed where a great sauropod had sludged millions of years before. No one had ever found verifiably well-defined sauropod tracks and put to rest the debate over the movements of the four-footed giants.[23]

The longtime controversy divided paleontologists into opposing camps. Some argued that the sauropods were much too big and heavy to ever have walked on dry land. Their weight and massive frames required water to buoy them up, thereby strictly relegating them to an aquatic environment. A second debate had emerged regarding how the large creatures walked. American paleontologists had concluded that sauropods walked in an erect fashion, based on bone studies. German paleontologists, on the other hand, believed that the animals were more semi-erect and moved in a sprawling manner.[24]

In Bird's mind the debate would have to wait. There was no real reason to believe that the Paluxy could reveal such a find, especially in light of the numerous accounts of destroyed tracks—victims of the river's rises. However, the streambed did hold superb theropod prints, some of them almost perfect. Bird worked his way upstream and stopped about a mile above the third crossing. Several excellent carnivore trails there would present good candidates for a slab exhibited at the American Museum. They were remarkable examples in a streambed obviously tested by the surging currents of past floods, as evidenced by other furrows, eroded ledges, and washed-out potholes.[25]

The morning sun sparkled on the Paluxy as Bird set about with shovel and whisk broom cleaning out the tridactyl trails. The work, though routine, was pleasant enough on this mild day. By lunch time, a marching line of slate clouds announced the coming norther.[26] Bird went about to complete his job for the day when it took an amazing turn.

His own words, written to Mr. Adamson just days later, paint a vivid picture:

... I had cleared a series of carnivore footprints for a photograph. And while I was still engaged in washing the last of the mud off I noticed a large pothole not far away that seemed oddly out of place. Could anything as big possibly be a track? Could it be .... and a wild thought occurred .... possibly sauropod?

Almost in idle curiosity but with very little hope I began to shovel a wheelbarrow load of mud out of it. The depression <u>did</u> have the general contour of a foot. Finally the shovel grated bottom; I got down into the thing; dug with my fingers where possibilities seemed best for a toe and a claw. Three or four handfulls o[f] dirt came loose and a large stone that was wedged in a crack— there was something there. Next to it was another ... next to that another.

Suddenly filled with a wild thrill that I hardly dared to accept, I got up and looked around. A full twelve feet away was another pothole. I could hardly throw the mud out it fast enough. It too, was a gigantic footprint.

There come rare moments in the lives of all of us when we see things we do not actually believe. I had two tracks alright but they were undoubtably both rights—and there was no sign of a left between. But as my imagination painfully accepted the great bulk of the creature that had left the tracks ...... and as I looked on the <u>double</u> row of potholes that now were very apparent under the mud in the river ahead ... bolstered up by the still further discoveries each one had a forefoot impressed just in front of them ... I began to think in terms of what I knew it must be—could only be in fact ... a giant sauropod.

The rest of the afternoon was spent in the chill waters of the river. When my bare feet became so numb I couldn't feel and explore down in the mud with my toes, I would come ashore, warm them by a fire, and go plunging in again. Track after track was churned out for correlating evidence.[27]

Bird was fighting against time and the weather. The day would soon fade, and the foreboding clouds threatened rain. A flood on the Paluxy might ruin it all! He resolved to at least make plaster casts of a forefoot and a hindfoot track imprinted on the rock ledge peeking above the water line. With only a limited amount of plaster in the Buick, he made a mad dash to a lumberyard to purchase a hundred-pound bag of plaster along with two gallons of thin oil that would function as a separator between the porous rock and setting plaster.

He labored into the darkness, determined to finish the task before possible disaster from the cruel clouds. At ten o'clock he ran out of oil, but the trusty Buick helped him finish the job. He drained just enough oil out of the crankcase to complete the molds and by morning lugged them up the thirty-foot embankment.[28] Now in his mind's eye he could picture a mighty sauropod—standing erect—his giant feet plunging into the mud.

With the largest cast strapped on the top of the car, Bird rolled away along the edge of the field. He later chuckled, "Mr. J.D. Wilson, owner of the adjacent farm, watched me drive into his yard in open-mouthed amazement."[29] The family gathered around to gape at the casts. They were thin and light, but cumbersome at the same time. Dillard expressed his utter surprise, and Doyle gazed wide-eyed at the impression of the huge clawed foot. Bird extended his thanks and enthused over the possibilities and implications of such a remarkable find. Doyle stared and followed the outline of the monstrous track as Bird motored out of sight. He would be back.[30]

CHAPTER SIX
In the Footsteps of the Dinosaurs

The quoted passages from R.T. Bird's correspondence are faithful to the original typescript and handwritten letters, including misspellings.

R.T. Bird drove into Glen Rose to the astonishment of all, his Buick's roof adorned with a most unusual ornament—the giant cast of the sauropod track. Residents had recognized the county's acclaimed theropod prints as items of curiosity and commerce that boosted the area's tourist appeal, however, most farmers who had seen the "potholes" thought they were only useful for trapping catfish when the river was low. But Bird knew the true importance of the tracks. Once he crated and shipped the molds from nearby Cleburne off to New York, the resulting buzz would reverberate throughout the scientific community.

Bird wrote to Barnum Brown on Thanksgiving Day 1938 and told the whole amazing story. His specific details about the sauropod tracks no doubt made Brown proud.

The fore foot is wider than it is long, being 24x20 inches in size. It is heavily padded and while no claws are in evidence there is a scar that may indicate the tip of one as indicated in the drawing. Of the three other fore feet I have seen above water, one has been superimposed on the print of a carnivore, and the other badly waterworn, so this is the best of them.

The hind foot measures a full yard in length not counting a possible bit of slipage, and is 26 inches wide at its greatest point. There are three large claws arranged typical sauropod fashion and still another mark suggesting a small nail. The mud bulges up in front of the foot as it does with all the tracks—rather spectacularly—proving these great beasts did, occasionally at least, move about where the buoyancy of their native element, water, was partially if not entirely lacking. That small carnivore tracks are found at the same levil would indicate this also.

As for the trail itself it measures about six feet across its lateral margins. I saw no conclusive evidence of a tail having been dragged (the rocks are too waterworn) but there were suggestions and I have had it from others that tail furrows have been seen. The strides (measurements taken from corresponding rights and lefts) run from 11 feet 5 inches to 12 feet 10 inches—which of course strikes an average a little over 12 feet.

Regarding still future possibilities here I believe one could come here in late summer or early fall (low water) and construct a coffer dam to hold the river back (not a difficult job at all) and clean the track area. Then with a multiple of prints exposed one could tell excatly what he had. As it would seem almost prohibitive to take up a large slab because of the expense, it would readily be possible to make a series of impressions and reconstruct a very convincing composite trail—prehaps much better than the hit and miss quality of their natural arrangement. Under the ledge, as the tracks disapear, they are at their poorest.

So it goes, and after one or two more prospecting excursions I still would like to do, will be headed north. Of the large casts I will have to take them to Cleburne for crating and shipping. They are large and clumsy but not heavy—I used about one hundred and fifty pounds of plaster and the bracing is all dry and seasoned cedar. The big one just goes on the Buick truck rack, with not a bit to spare.

Bird also made special mention of his faithful mechanical steed:

The dear old Buick, God bless her, still retains her almost unfailing vitality and I begin to feel that nothing will ever really wear the old girl down. Have treated her with all the care possible on some of the roads she has had to negotiate this year—so as yet had none of the old trouble with springs.[1]

R.T. Bird included this sketch of sauropod tracks in his letter to Barnum Brown on Thanksgiving Day, 1938 (November 24, 1938). Courtesy of the Division of Paleontology, American Museum of Natural History.

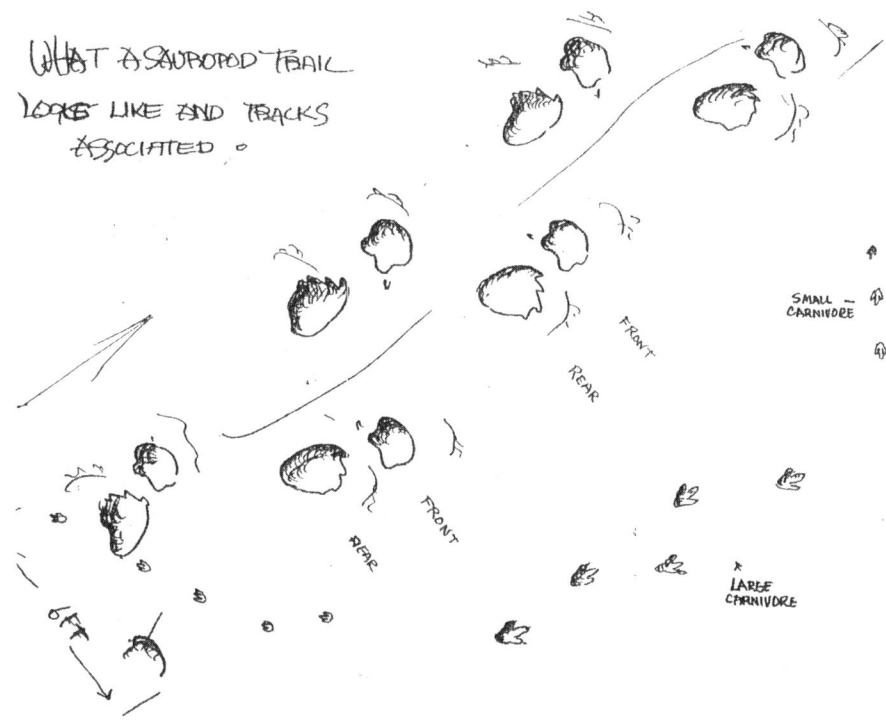

R.T. Bird drew this sketch of the Paluxy trackways and included it in his press release to area newspapers on November 29, 1938. Courtesy of the Division of Paleontology, American Museum of Natural History

Within a week the proverbial dinosaur was out of the bag, so to speak. The *Dallas Morning News* published an article on November 30, 1938. An accompanying photo showed Bird with the sauropod cast, and the headlines and quotes echoed its significance:

Tub-Sized Prints of Dinosaur 100,000,000 Years Old Found
Glen Rose Discovery Thrills Explorer Of American Museum

... The 100-yard trail imprinted more than a hundred million years ago by a gigantic sauropod dinosaur, the greatest of all known land vertebrates of the Age of Reptiles, clears up one of the mysteries in fossil science, Mr. Bird said. It ends a long textbook battle over whether the aquatic sauropods ever walked on land and a long dispute among scientists over how the leg bones were mounted.

"I've been around dinosaur remains long enough to know I have made a find," Bird announced enthusiastically....[2]

Bird's "find" was so extraordinary that the Society of Vertebrate Paleontology voted it discovery of the year.[3] He published the article "Thunder in His Footsteps" in *Natural History* in May 1939. Bird and Brown were both eager to get to work at Glen Rose, and in the months following the wondrous disclosure, they determined that an excavated slab of a sauropod trackway would fit in perfectly as the base of the American Museum's enormous *Apatosaurus* (called *Brontosaurus* at the time) skeleton.[4] A year passed and other projects continued as Brown procured the necessary funding for their ambitious plans.

Much of Brown's financial backing had come from his association with Sinclair Oil. Since 1930 the Sinclair Refining Company had used dinosaurs in their ad campaigns, relating the age of their crudes with the ancient creatures that inhabited the earth. The gentle giant, *Apatosaurus*, emerged as the most popular representative, thus giving rise to Sinclair's "Dino." The Sinclair Company

DALLAS, TEXAS, WEDNESDAY, NOVEMBER 30, 1938

Tub-Sized Prints of Dinosaur 100,000,000 Years Old Found

Glen Rose Discovery Thrills Explorer Of American Museum

Roland T. Bird of the department f vertebrate paleontology at the American Museum of Natural History, New York, announced in Dallas Monday he had stumbled on a trail of dinosaur footprints entirely new to science at Glen Rose last week.

The 100-yard trail imprinted more than a hundred million years ago by gigantic sauropod dinosaur, the greatest of all known land vertebrates of the Age of Reptiles, clears up one of the mysteries in fossil science, Mr. Bird said. It ends a long textbook battle over whether aquatic sauropods ever walked on land and a long dispute among scientists over how the leg bones were mounted.

"I've been around dinosaur remains long enough to know I have made a find," Bird announced enthusiastically as he reached Dallas on his way back to New York.

Mr. Bird was studying other fossil footprints about a week ago when he matically uncovered the first sauropod track.

It Crosses River.

About five miles from Glen Rose along the Paluxy River bed he had sharply defined footprints of other beasts. He was raking away debris to make photographs. Suddenly, he saw outlined a depression large as a washtub. Excitedly, he started digging. After unearthing the first print, he dug out a trail six across which followed a shelf of the river, crossed the river bed, came up on the other side.

Ordinarily the footprints become filled with sand which hardens into so that it is impossible to dig the finer details," he said, "but were filled with soft silt which would wash out."

the place of the discovery the

Roland T. Bird, American Museum of Natural History field worker, stands beside a cast of the important sauropod footprints he found near Glen Rose last week. The cast represents

—News Staff Photo.

roughly how the bottom of the huge dinosaur's foot looked. There are four toes at the left side. The foot print was nearly a yard long.

R.T. Bird poses with his almost yard-long sauropod track cast for a Dallas Morning News *photographer.* Reprinted with permission of *The Dallas Morning News*

In the 1930s Sinclair Refining Company's "Dino" emerged as the popular symbol for its oil and gasoline products. The gentle giant brontosaur, the Apatosaurus, represented power and stamina, and advertisements and cartoons of the day capitalized on the dinosaur's appeal. Sinclair also provided funding for the expeditions of paleontologist Barnum Brown. Courtesy Sinclair Oil Corporation

registered the brontosaur as their trademark in 1932. Consumers loved the friendly dinosaur symbol on its oil and gasoline products. Sinclair's dinosaur stamp album and weekly stamps issued at service stations in 1935 resulted in enormous sales and the distribution of forty-eight million stamps. The company increased the stature of its promotions by financing the "Sinclair Dinosaur Expeditions" of Barnum Brown. Brown turned to his familiar patron to secure field money for the track excavation.[5]

Funding also surfaced from two other notable sources. The Texas State-wide Paleontological Survey came on board under the direction of Dr. E.H. Sellards of the University of Texas at Austin. The federal government provided laborers under the Works Projects Administration (WPA). Ironically, when it seemed like every bureaucratic piece had fallen into place, Bird found that he was returning to Texas by way of Bandera, not Glen Rose—Sellards' geologists had come across a sauropod location in Bandera County![6]

Sellards' assistant Glen Evans had actually negotiated the agreement between the American Museum and the Texas State-wide Paleontological Survey at the University of Texas. He was a bright, young geologist who had earned his way into the field through grit and persistence. Born in North Texas near Henrietta in Clay County, as a youth he drove a four-horse team with a guide

mule moving dirt for highway construction. The work was brutally hot and tedious, but Evans focused beyond all that on his dreams.

"Well, I worked on those roads and kept them up. And then I saved three hundred and eighty-something dollars," he recalled. "I'd been wanting to go to college. I wanted to go to the University of Texas, and I put my check in the bank one day, and the next morning the bank went broke."[7]

Two-and-a-half years of toil went down the drain, and back to his four-horse team with its guide mule "Old Blue" he went. "So I had to go through the whole damn business again.... It went on hour after miserable hour in those days, when it was hot and dry, and everybody was broke!"

But Evans' spirit was not broken. Eventually he made it to Austin and the University of Texas, where his hard work earned him a place as E.H. Sellards' right-hand man. Evans entered into the world of field geologist and fossil hunter. He supervised geological and paleontological expeditions and arranged projects that included WPA assistance:

It involved getting fossil hunters, whether they were professional or otherwise, in different parts of the state.... I was pretty good at it—good in the field. I

Geologist Glen Evans fondly recalled his field work for the Texas State-wide Paleontological Survey at the University of Texas and his involvement in surveying dinosaur trackways near Bandera and Glen Rose.
Photo by Laurie E. Jasinski

spent so much time out there, and I soon had charge of a whole bunch of it.... Oh I thought it was heaven. My God did I work.... I spent the night out where I was hunting places for excavations to go and things to do, and I took a little bed roll that I carried on my back.

Sometimes his work epitomized the romanticized image of an intrepid rock and dinosaur hunter camping in the wild and sleeping under the stars. Evans assisted Sellards, director of the new Texas Memorial Museum at the University of Texas, with researching and acquiring specimens for exhibits.[8]

In early 1940 Evans met his counterpart R.T. Bird at Bandera as they investigated what ranchers called "them old hoof prints" in the creekbeds. They surveyed several sites on ranches in Bandera County (and on the boundary of adjacent Medina County) which involved extensive work. The tracks appeared to be those of a large wandering herd. The impressive footprints, however, did not bear quite the detail and distinctiveness of those of the original discovery on the Paluxy. Bird felt that river's streambed still held the perfect trackway slab for the museum's brontosaur.[9]

By spring, the Glen Rose project was finally coming together. Bird excitedly wrote his father Henry Bird, his dear "Pater," on March 26, 1940:

And now the powers that be are about to grant me a new fund to work with—in Sommerville County. Back in dear old Glen Rose. The old Paluxy River is certainly going to see a lot of digging take place along her shores. I'm going to build a dam to partially divert the stream. I'm going to quarry a lot of rock. And when I start to really collect a lot of those gigantic sauropod footprints.....

To reach his Paluxy trackway, Bird had to motor across several river fords, including Murphy crossing (third crossing), in the Lanham Mill community. Photo by Novella Wilson

I made a trip up there over the week end to look this situation over. It looked better than ever before. I really had to restrain myself over the prospects.

He reiterated his eagerness on March 29th:

Dear Pater:

I don't know whether I told you or not, but a new fund has been alloted to me to work Sommerville County, the Glen Rose locality. I think I did. But what I didn't tell you was the starting date. I had offical word of that today. It will be April the 8th....

I am mighty glad to have the opportunity to have a crack at this particular project, now coming up at Glen Rose. I have learned the rather lavish advantages of having the government finance things, this way. It is one way to put money to good use, if the government has it to spend. I had over three thousand dollars here in Bandera county—all of which I did not spend. And as for the disadvantages of handling this sort of good old government gravy—well, I've learned about that too..... in Glen Rose one of the first things I am going to do will be to hire a capable girl to take the paper work off my hands. A secretary in other words. As I make altogether around ten dollars a day, I can afford to do so, and it will take a load off my mind. The nights I have set up swearing at this sort of a thing here haven't been pleasant ones.[10]

Early April brought rain that swelled the Paluxy for a few days, but by April 9, 1940, Bird was able to get work underway officially. He rolled into Glen Rose to assemble the WPA crew of young men, many from Cleburne. The hands jumped at the chance to earn a dollar a day. Those with special rock-working skills might pull in $1.25.[11]

In his old Buick, laden with tools, shovels, buckets, and other items, Bird enthusiastically led a parade of cars out of town to the Paluxy Valley and Lanham Mill. The hum of the vehicles filled the canyon as they splashed through each crossing, and soon all the valley farmers, the Abells, Becks, Mays, Ryals, and of course the Wilsons, and others, knew what the commotion heralded. Bird had come back.[12]

Bird set about outlining his ambitious plans for the crew. To expose the tracks, they would have to build a coffer dam and scoop out the silt, sand, and water. "There was an expanse of yellow, muddy water some seventy-five yards long by twenty wide swirling over the track ledge," he wrote to Brown. Immediately they stuffed burlap sacks with the mud and sand.[13]

"It really went like clockwork," Bird reported. "I had three men filling sacks, another sewing them up, still another man getting them overboard, and two others in the water dragging them in position." When they ran low on burlap bags, Bird scavenged and purchased all the available sacks he could from area farmers.[14]

Those early days of the project went smoothly as the streambed buzzed with activity. Men bailed water with buckets, shoveled mud, and methodically cleaned out the area. Within a few days the workers were comfortably ensconced at the site.

Bird described:

My new crew of men just camp out on the banks of the Paluxy, not far from the quarry site, do their own cooking and are generally self-reliant. So far I have had seven men—and they are all good ones. I stay in town myself, as I'd have to go in daily anyhow for mail. Have been most fortunate in finding a very nice room at a very moderate rate (the Lane Hotel) and the food is good and equally moderate in price....[15]

His lodging was a convenient fifteen-minute drive from the excavation site. The downtown Lane's Hotel, a fashionable two-story building appropriately adorned in petrified wood, advertised "Home Like Service."[16]

Though it was a comfortable stay, Bird's heart would have preferred to be with his crew "roughing it" on the Paluxy and living a hardy existence out in the field. Some of the men even brought their families to live at the camp. The mild April weather was glorious, the air sweet. Perhaps, as Bird smiled at the rambunctious children laughing and playing, he floated back to his own childhood games with his sister Alice and the brave plans they made for their Teddy Bears. He had constructed boats, cars, airships, and a house for their original Teddies.[17] Now he could only wonder how the kiddos regarded this work of quarrying the tracks. What brave plans might they make one day?

As the workers soldiered on, he may have noticed another youngster perched on the bank above and eyeing intently all of the goings on. "I sat up there on that bank hour after hour and watched them," Doyle Wilson remembered. "When I had free time and Dad didn't have me doing something, I was over there watching them."[18]

During the course of the excavation the men uncovered two more sauropod trails and could distinguish at least six other trails farther out in the water. Bird reasoned that a migrating herd of the mighty "Thunder Lizards" had lumbered through that ancient landscape. He reported to Barnum Brown "at least two suggestive slabs in view" that would be marvelous exhibits for the American Museum and the University of Texas. He assured Brown that he would obtain "one of the most

Doyle Wilson, ca. early 1940s. For young Doyle, the Paluxy Valley was his backyard to explore. The work of a dinosaur hunter (R.T. Bird) and his crew in the riverbed provided hours of entertainment for the boy.
Photo by Novella Wilson

ambitious track slabs ever collected ... worth the effort in every way." The streambed was also rife with three-toed carnivore tracks that, he observed, seemed to follow the sauropod footprints. "A big carnivore was (as it might seem) hot on his trail, and came clumping along right through it."[19]

He wrote to Brown on April 17, 1940, "The bed of the Paluxy River seems to be a regular footprint treasure trove."[20] The first couple of weeks produced remarkable results. The crew cleared out gravel and upper rock layers (sometimes with dynamite) to expose even more tracks that were under the ledge. Bird began to look ahead to the next phase of the project—cutting out the slabs of rock.

Weekend rains to the west in late April caused a temporary setback with a rise on the Paluxy that submerged the homemade dam. In his report to Barnum Brown on April 29, Bird acknowledged that factors such as the weather introduced considerable variables in his timeline. In ideal conditions, however, he might be bold enough to predict completion in three weeks. Bird confidently reassured Brown that his (now eight) workers would resume the "spectacular undertaking" quickly. "The stone isn't going to be hard to cut, trim or even saw, and the natural fractures thru the rock here and there should expedite removal of sections that can be handled and crated."[21]

Ever mindful of the goal of the task at hand, he also remarked on a specimen for the University of Texas' Memorial Museum. "The third trail, also excellent material, will more than satisfy Sellards' wants here...."

By mid-May Sellards' assistant Glen Evans had visited the Paluxy site twice as the quarrying began. He enthused over securing an impressive section of trackway for the Texas Memorial Museum.[22] The Paluxy prints were perfectly preserved:

They were made in a calcareous, highly limy mud. This mud, when it gets dry, it solidifies very quick.... In that limestone, if it's viscous enough to retain the footprint as it goes by, and if it stays there a few days, it'll harden.... But it's sitting there and some more mud washes over it, and it fills it up, and when that hardens, it gets filled up by something else. That's why they're preserved. These tracks were made in mud and more mud came over them.[23]

He was also amused at the curious observations of some of the locals and the growing number of visitors attracted to the project site. Seeing the myriad of footprints of a dinosaur herd apparently sloshing across the river made it difficult for some to picture the ancient terrain as a broad coastal plain. The tracks disappearing under a rock ledge caused special bewilderment.

"You mean them things go under the bluff?" Glen Evans repeated the exclamations of one onlooker. "That's what they told me when I was doing the digging. You mean them tracks go under? How did the son-of-a-bitch get under there?! I remember them saying that, and it shook me up a little."

Each morning the Wilsons saw the old Buick roll past the house, along the field towards the river, and each evening Bird motored past back to town. "I know Dad and Mr. Bird got to be real good friends," Doyle Wilson recalled. Dillard

R.T. Bird's Magnificent Trackway. During the spring of 1940, Bird and his WPA crew labored to uncover dinosaur tracks in the Paluxy riverbed. They exposed a mother lode of sauropod and theropod trails. Courtesy Paluxy Valley Archives and Genealogy Society and Somervell County Heritage Center, Photo by Roland T. Bird

Wilson knew the Paluxy well enough to respect her cantankerous moods. The work crew had been fortunate up to now, but typically spring could be rainy, and he warned Bird about the river's sudden rises. Heavy downpours could send it on a rampage until the dry season set in, normally in June. The warning remained with Bird and bothered him like a worrisome mosquito. Raging torrents that originally scoured the Paluxy to reveal the footprints could also obliterate the stony traces. He remembered the farmers' recollections of whole trackway slabs torn up and washed downstream.[24]

Dillard Wilson was right. The rains came, prompting Bird to comment to Brown, "I've seen it rain harder in the tropics sometimes but not much." On May 23, 1940, Bird wrote of his personal encounter with the Paluxy's whims:

I guess I was growing a little too optomistic about this Paluxy River. Or at least I thought that rain on Friday missed upper watershed. It Didn't. The rise came along Saturday night. It was only a minor one, but I was well aware of it trying to get to the quarry Sunday morning.

That wouldn't have been so bad if it hadn't rained again last night.... The local run off was gone by morning however, so I left for the quarry and was about to drive the Buick through the first crossing when the mail carrier stopped me. He said there was a "wave" coming. My crew were there with the same idea.

It came in about an hour. The water rose and made the crossing a churning, impassable torrent in almost the flicker of an eyelash. It was still rising slowly at eleven o'clock when I returned to Glen Rose. It doesn't look as if we might get the quarry drained now until the end of the week; and the skies are still so threating it is difficult to say whether we might return to work even then.[25]

So followed a tedious ritual that would repeat itself well into June. Doyle watched the men bail out bucket after bucket of mud and muck to clean off and dry out the tracks:

They'd fill these sacks full of sand and they'd get the water all out and get a nice place to work and then there'd come the rain and it wash it all out. And then the creek would be up so much that they couldn't do nothing for a little while, and then it go back down. Then they'd put their sandbags around it and keep all the water out and clean it up.[26]

Bird faced another challenge. Increasingly, a flood of onlookers poured into the site. From his vantage point young Doyle Wilson often saw Bird's "audience" lined up on the other bank. They marveled at the massive undertaking and asked questions. E.H. Sellards had publicized the work of the WPA and the state's role in the project through news releases to the media. Bird had patiently answered the inquiries of a *Dallas Morning News* reporter one day, and the resulting coverage brought more people. "Of course visitors from all over began descending on me in droves," Bird wrote Brown.[27]

One day the visitors included little eight-year-old Charlidell Davis (the future wife of Doyle Wilson). "See we didn't live in this area, but the Becks lived up there on the Jones [farm], and then we had gone up there to visit them," she said. Charlidell and her family drove through the Paluxy Valley and forded, what seemed to Charlidell, an endless number of river crossings to reach the Jones farm nestled in the bend of the river. Though owner W.D. Jones had purchased the old Martin/Finley property in 1936, Johnny Beck, son of nearby farmer Charlie Walton "Buck" Beck, rented the land and lived there in the homestead. Charlidell and her family had heard about the exciting goings-on in the riverbed, and so they arrived at the farm eager to watch. "Then we walked down there to see them taking these tracks out," she exclaimed.[28]

Novella Wilson, who had made her home with Doyle's big brother John just up the road from Dillard Wilson's place, was not so lucky. "John wouldn't let me down there," she sighed. "We lived right up there a little ways from it, and John didn't think it was appropriate for a lady to be down there much, so he never took me down there." Likewise, Daisy Ryals, the daughter of James Ryals, never went to the site. Ironically, after helping her father quarry a number of the dinosaur tracks herself, her family thought it inappropriate for the ladies to be in the presence of a work crew.[29]

The track site certainly saw its share of the fairer sex however. One Saturday a YWCA camp of three hundred girls descended upon the place as part of an all-day picnic. "Feminine charm overflowed the bank above the quarry," Bird later wrote in his memoir, *Bones for Barnum Brown*. "Beauty threatened to fill the excavation itself."[30]

Between dodging the bad weather and dealing with the crowds, Bird had his hands full trying to advance the project. The situation threatened to grow more complicated. Knowing that Bird would have to load and transport his quarry across the Wilson land, some area farmers approached Dillard Wilson about a deal. With all the publicity, the growing number of tourists, and the importance of the enterprise, it made sense to them to make a profit from the whole affair. They offered Dillard $500, a king's ransom, if he would sign a contract that would keep R.T. Bird from moving specimens over his land. The men eyed a greater prize, a larger sum of $1,500 to be secured from Bird for the privilege of crossing their own property. Talk of other schemes also surfaced about charging visitors admission to traverse adjoining land and enforcing tolls over the river.[31]

It was an awful fix, pitting farmer against farmer, with Dillard Wilson caught in the middle. Doyle witnessed the trouble, but along with it he saw his dad's resolve—the kind of resolve and the kind of memory that stays with you the rest of your life. Dillard's word to R.T. Bird on that very first day, a day that now seemed quite awhile ago, meant something. Doyle Wilson repeated:

Dad told him then he could do whatever he wanted to. There would be no charge. He'd have died before he went back on his word.[32]

That was that. Dillard went to Bird and told him of the proposed scheme. Though Bird was alarmed by it all, he was also reassured to hear his friend both reaffirm their original arrangement and acknowledge the scientific significance of the whole project.[33]

R.T. Bird addresses his audience. Increasingly, the publicity of the track excavation brought crowds of curious onlookers. Courtesy Paluxy Valley Archives and Genealogy Society and Somervell County Heritage Center

(Onlookers from left to right: [standing] Johnny Beck, Coll and Lois Davis [Charlidell's parents], Tennie Davis, Charlidell Davis, [sitting] Carl Beck, Nip Beck, Larry Davis, and Charles Styron.) Young Charlidell and her family and friends watch R.T. Bird (front center) hard at work in his quarry. This scene also shows some common tools of the trade for the dinosaur hunter, such as a whisk broom, plaster strips, and a box of Kleenex. Courtesy Charlidell Wilson

Dillard Wilson pumps cool water for R.T. Bird after a hard day's work. During the course of the track excavation, Bird often relied on Wilson's knowledge of the Paluxy Valley, and the two men became good friends. Courtesy Novella Wilson, Photo by Roland T. Bird

By June 1940 the quarrying of the tracks was well underway. E.H. Sellards had visited the site in late May and also pronounced his delight. A long section of the third sauropod trail would go to the American Museum of Natural History and an adjoining slab would go to the University of Texas. The crew also mined smaller blocks of specimen tracks for Baylor University, Southern Methodist University, Brooklyn College, and the National Museum of Natural History at the Smithsonian Institution.[34]

Throughout the course of the excavation Bird formulated in his mind what he observed to be the major revelations of the tracks. Beyond the scientific break-through that the sauropods could walk erect and on dry land if necessary, these traces showed that these sauropods traveled in a herd of different-sized animals. He was also convinced that a predatory pack of theropods followed them. As the mammoth sauropod prints turned, so did a set of pesky three-toed tracks. Looking at the footprints—the impressions of the living creatures frozen in a moment in time—Bird envisioned an epic struggle as the flesh-eater finally caught up with a lumbering sauropod. The appearance of a theropod track imprinted upon a sauropod track told him that the predator had reached his prey and lunged upon the massive brontosaur, as the carnivore hopped on his right foot and sliced the claws of his left foot into the lizardly skin of the retreating sauropod. It was a fascinating scenario.[35]

The Tommy Pendley Photo

During the course of his Paluxy tracks excavation, R.T. Bird took many photographs to document the progress of the project. But one of his most beloved and often-used pictures was the image of little Tommy Pendley splashing in a huge sauropod footprint. The boy's father Tom Pendley, "a dark haired, slender man of medium stature" in his early 20's, was one of the WPA workers at the quarry. The occasion of shooting the picture proved memorable for Bird, who recalled the event for Novella Wilson years later in 1973:

His wife ... often appeared at the quarry, for the family camped in a tent and an old car up on that level ground under the pecans and liveoaks just below the Jim Ryals farm house. She always kept quietly in the background however, a slender girl of about her husband's age, moving gracefully along the shady bank above the quarry. I could not help noticing she was very pretty, a reminder at the time that I was still unmarried at the ancient age of 40, and wishing this was not so.

I well remember the afternoon she allowed me to take five photographs with my big 5x7 camera of the then small boy, Tommy. He had been playing in the nearby water with the Mathews children and was already pretty well soaked. So I said to Mrs. Pendley, "Let's have him sit in this big track filled with water, just as if he were taking a bath, and I'll get his picture."[36]

The huge footprint took fully eighteen gallons of water to fill, and timid Tommy at first toddled up to the track and dangled his feet over the edge. With the coaxing of his mother and Bird, the boy slid into the footprint bathtub, content with the full blessing of Bird and his mother that he could "take a bath" with all his clothes on and splash to his heart's delight. Of the five pictures taken, one turned out to be a gem. There sat Tommy in this monstrous left hind-foot track as he looked up at his mother with a twinkle in his eye. The photograph later appeared in *National Geographic* and became one of the most-used illustrations relating to dinosaur tracks. The image won numerous photographic honors and captured a unique and pleasant moment in time.[37]

Courtesy American Museum of Natural History Library, Photo by Roland T. Bird

The crew worked diligently to break up the rock as sledgehammers and chisels clanged throughout the days. The monotonous symphony of sound stretched on as Doyle Wilson watched from his perch. "They sat down there with a drill and a hammer and drilled them holes in them rocks to bust them apart," he observed. "Everything was 'armstrong.' There was no power ... he took it out and busted that track up and numbered each piece so he could set it back together right."

After numbering each block and coating the edges with plaster-dipped burlap sacks for protection, the men manually lugged each chunk on a fashioned cradle up the steep embankment to Wilson's field above. "Back then everything was done the hard way," Doyle Wilson summed.[38]

Many a time the old Buick, loaded with a precious few pieces of the quarry, huffed through the pasture on its way to the lumberyard in Glen Rose where Bird crated the specimens and then hauled them to Walnut Springs, the nearest railroad station, for shipment to New York.[39]

Though Novella Wilson never went to the quarry, she saw the Buick motor by her house on numerous occasions:

He [Bird] was dedicated to it. That's the way he did it, because he had to pass our house, where Doyle's folks lived, down over Opossum Branch, and up through the field to go over to the track site. Came back that same way. He came up the hill past our house where John and I lived every day.

With the unstable weather, the work went painfully slow. "When it isn't raining, you are afraid it will before the day is over—and between bailing water and repairing dikes from the last drencher it usually does," Bird lamented to Brown. "I was told the month of June here was supposed to be dry—but I've failed to note any arid state of affairs thus far."[40]

Men toted each piece of quarried trackway up the riverbank to load on Bird's Buick. Courtesy Paluxy Valley Archives and Genealogy Society and Somervell County Heritage Center, Photo by Roland T. Bird

So it was on June 12, 1940, when the men once again faced ominous weather and struggled to protect the tracks from encroaching water. Suddenly a streak of lightning flashed, and the skies cracked open. Bird and the crew labored as the distant cries of a little voice drew closer to the riverbank. The young daughter of one of the workers raced through the rain as the news was now becoming painfully clear. The Buick! For years the car had served him well. The girl cried out, "The lightning hit Mr. Bird's Buick, and it's afire!" The men all scrambled up the bank. Glen Evans, who was at the site that day, witnessed the whole incident. The bolt struck the back of the old auto that was filled with steel bars and tools. A portion of the cloth top ignited. But this time the rain, so long a tormentor, helped save the day. The falling drops, along with the quick-thinking women in camp who beat the flames, helped put out the fire.[41]

He was glad to have the excitement behind him when he wrote Barnum Brown that day:

Even the lightning has been playing cute tricks toward hampering the business. Today the Buick was hit.

It was a wonder she didn't burn up on the spot.... I thought to myself; well at last she comes to a noble end ..... but her nine lives seems to have once more stood her in good stead.... Her top is almost a wreck, and she looks amusing

Bird's "dear old Buick" weathered years of cross-country fossil hunting and even a lightning strike, evidenced in the vehicle's tattered top. Daily, the faithful car hauled track specimens from the Paluxy Valley. Courtesy Roland T. Bird Collection, Somervell County Historical Commission Archives

enough—as if she had been a target for one of Hitler's bombs—but she still runs and functions.

So goes. I guess we've been lucky in a way....[42]

A Timely Moment of Flooding Captured on Film

Bird's letter to Brown on June 28, 1940, vividly described the temper of the river and its effect on the work. His account is particularly of interest because he captured this event on film for posterity.

Dear Dr. Brown:

For the first time since early in the month the old Buick returned to Glen Rose tonight with sections of the track slab riding her trunk carriage. Trail No. 3, well garnished, has taken three days to resurrect from the mud. Even at that, on Monday, when it seemed this freak wet spell was about at an end, we had a final rise in the river that put us out of business.

It rained the night before but not very hard at Glen Rose. The river was down again to normal. We didn't know a much heavier downpour had occured west of here, or we never would have gone to work, but such are the uncertainies of the old Paluxy. As it was I only got an on-the-spot version of what this sort of thing is like on motion picture film, but it's a graphic illustration caught in a timely moment when I so happened to have a borrowed camera handy.

I had taken the camera along to get some ordinary shots of removing mud from the quarry when the flash flood came. I had just secured thirty or forty feet of general action & mud slinging and was in a position for a final panorama when it happened.

It was on us almost without warning. In a twinkling of an eye the river rose and sloshed over the entire length of the outer dike. It made a sound like a wave does slaping the side of a boat. No one knew what was going on until we heard it and noticed the water pouring in. Almost instantly the inner (and higher) dike around Trail 3 seemed inadequate. The water continued to rise with a rush. It poured over the lower end of the inner dike and swirled along the track ledge.

From my vantage point at the end of the quarry there seemed no reason why I shouldn't make the best of a disheartening situation. An old story, yes, but one that will show why any sandbag dike I might construct will not stem these floods.

I started the camera grinding film. Men splashed futilly about until I had them drag sandbags over the best tracks to later protect them from rolling rocks, a procedure followed always with the threat of swift currents. Water was cascading in over the...dike now. I got a good angle shot of that. It was all over in a moment. That is, all but a final touch of humor, furnished inadvertantly by old man McCoy, the old clown that he is, who fell overboard off a flooded dike in an unhappy moment (for him) right in front o[f] the lens. Such are vicissitudes and otherwise concurrent happenings akin to the collection of track slabs below the levil of an occasional rampant river.[43]

July finally brought blessed dry weather, but the favorable conditions also invited back droves of visitors. "The fourth, in fact this whole week-end holiday, has sent hundreds from Fort Worth and Dallas vacationing in this region, and we have had our share of them...," Bird wrote. At this time, he also had to requisition for a couple of new workers:

During the recent uncertain weather, devious and sundry things left me with but three after the fourth.... Jail claimed one for writing checks he had no business doing; another for knocking down officers when he was, I presume, drunk; still another joined the C.C.C.; a veteran's pension came to another, and old man Matthews, one of my best (a ruptured man) just worked himself down at the start of the week.[44]

In spite of all the setbacks, the work neared completion. The gorgeous track slab would be twenty-eight feet long with a double stride that would "match steps with the way the skeleton is mounted...." He wrote, "I have cut, squared, and dressed it to fractions of an inch...," and estimated a shipping weight of twelve thousand to fifteen thousand pounds.[45] Bird also proposed the possibility of making the Paluxy site a National Monument under the protection of the National Park Service and stated that he had the cooperation and support of many of the farmers in the valley and leading citizens of the county.[46]

By late July, with the American Museum slab squared away, the men finished the Texas Memorial Museum section. They finally completed the job in August, and Brown himself came to visit the site.[47] It had been a long spring and summer when the men packed up their tools, and the Buick drove through the Wilsons' pasture for the final time. The Paluxy Valley would never be quite the same, but then neither would Bird, for this field work had been like no other, and from start to finish he could call it his own.

It was the high point of a brief but shining career. Within a few short years, Bird's health got the better of him and forced an early retirement. Brown himself had reached mandatory retirement in 1942. Unlike the Texas Memorial Museum slab, which was reassembled and displayed in its own little building adjacent to the museum in Austin in 1941, the broken-up trackway for the American Museum sat for years—a confused pile in rotting crates in the museum yard in New York. A decade passed until E.H. Colbert, the museum's Curator and Chairman of the Department of Vertebrate Paleontology, resolved to save the tracks and coaxed Bird out of retirement as the only man who could make sense of the puzzle. The plaster was crumbling, labels were missing, but after six months of toil, Bird had succeeded in carefully reconstructing a magnificent trackway under Brown's beloved brontosaur.[48]

The *National Geographic Magazine* had encouraged Bird to tell his story in their prestigious publication since 1941.[49] The story of the Paluxy Valley and its ancient and wondrous tracks finally reached the world in May 1954 in R.T. Bird's extensive feature titled, "We Captured a 'Live' Brontosaur."

The tracks had trudged a long way from that first discovery on Wheeler Branch to the submerged trails through the Paluxy. Now Roland Thaxter Bird brought them to the world. His discovery had shed new light on the significance of fossil footprints in scientific study, and ultimately, the sauropod prints were named *Brontopodus birdi* in Bird's honor.[50] The long journey of those ancient tracks from their limy mud beginnings came to its rightful destination under a museum spotlight because of Bird's determination, but also because of those in Lanham Mill who recognized the importance of the work simply because it was the right thing to do. Glen Rose too had earned its place in history. Not bad for a town with no railroad.

R.T. Bird's Paluxy trackway in all its glory at the American Museum of National History. Courtesy Robert Sisson / National Geographic Image Collection

CHAPTER SEVEN
The Fight for Dinosaur Valley

You know you stand where they walked.
It is that knowing and looking that shakes your earth and turns your sky old.

Ed Syers[1]

The quoted passages from R.T. Bird's correspondence are faithful to the original typescript and handwritten letters, including misspellings.

Around the Lanham Mill community, the hoopla of the dinosaur track quarry in 1940 soon died down on the eve of great upheavals in the world and on the homefront as well. World War II took many Somervell County sons away, including several of the Wilson boys who served in the army. When Novella May Wilson's husband John was drafted, they gave up their little home, and she lived with her parents. Up and down the Paluxy Valley, farmers coped with the manpower shortage. It was only the beginning of changing times.[2]

In 1947 Lanham Mill consolidated with the Glen Rose educational district. Lanham Mill School, the heart of the community, closed forever. Dillard Wilson and Vivian May were two of the last trustees. The land reverted back to the Martin family, and the one-room schoolhouse sat vacant amidst an empty silent yard flanked by encroaching cedar.[3]

In the wake of the war, Texas implemented an extensive system of Farm-to-Market roads across the state. In Somervell County the new Farm Road 205 curved through the Paluxy Valley. This route bypassed the Hendrix–Ramfield and the Lanham crossings and saved motorists the headache of driving some of these troublesome river fords. The Lanham ford, washed out by flood in the late 1940s, never saw traffic again. Ironically, the farm road afforded easier travel at a time when the valley saw fewer and fewer residents.[4]

Somervell County's population fell from 3,071 in 1940 to 2,542 in 1950, a loss of approximately 17 percent. Glen Rose, with 1,248 residents, had almost half of the county population. After the war, many servicemen did not return to the family farm. Like other rural Texas counties, Somervell County witnessed a gradual exodus as a portion of its younger generation migrated to larger cities such as Fort Worth and Dallas to work in the professional and manufacturing sectors.[5]

Farmers who stayed behind struggled with limited resources and with fickle Mother Nature. Peanuts had replaced cotton as the main crop, supplemented with corn and other grains, hay, and some garden produce. Families still earned part of their income from stock raising—mostly beef cattle. The relentless cedar in the valley at least provided good posts to sell, and the limestone constituted road building materials. But the lengthy drought of the 1950s dealt a cruel blow. The Paluxy withered down to a trickle, and most of its tributaries went dry, thereby putting an exclamation point on the warnings about water waste and a declining water table by geologist Albert Fiedler years earlier. Many of Somervell's famed artesian wells stopped their natural flow. Some had gushed and bubbled freely upon the ground until they simply ran out. Other wells now had to be pumped, thereby hurting Glen Rose's claim as a health resort.[6]

Author John Graves deftly described the "Big Drouth of the early 1950's— the worst in at least two centuries":

It was a fierce time when the climate gods wrinkled their noses at men's and beasts' demands, rolled back the "semi-arid" twenty-inch rainfall line far to the east of where it belongs, and left it sitting there for five or six years running. That drouth probably had as much to do with the destruction of old ways of

LANHAM MILL COMMUNITY AND VICINITY
(ca. 1947)

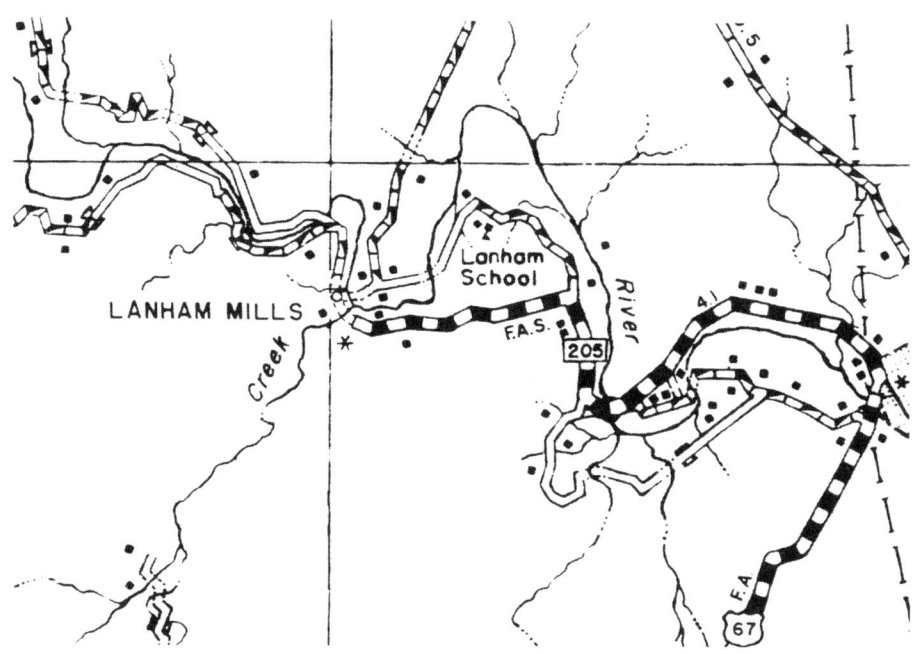

A highway map of Somervell County shows the new Farm Road 205 that winds through Lanham Mill community and the Paluxy Valley. Sections of the old county road are depicted, including the byway that curves past Lanham Mill School in the heart of present-day Dinosaur Valley State Park. The school closed in 1947. From: General Highway Map–Hood County, Somervell County, Texas, Texas State Highway Department, Austin (1936, completely revised to July 1947)

farming and ranching in our part of the world as did World War II with its social dislocations and technological changes. Operations that were marginal on overworked land, as most of the old ones were, collapsed.[7]

As families moved to town or out of the county, some of the larger rural areas along the Paluxy increasingly fell to absentee ownership, "a fact," as Graves put it, "productive of certain sadnesses inherent in the death of any old way of being...."[8]

Much of the land that would become Dinosaur Valley State Park changed hands during the 1950s. In 1951 W.D. Jones sold his farm of 347 acres to Esquire Whitaker. This included the property located within the bend of the Paluxy where sat the old Martin home. By the end of the decade Esquire's widow Julia and their only son Earnest had sold the real estate to Esquire's grandson Earnest Winston Whitaker. W.D. Jones did retain a small tract of eighteen acres that still served as a pasture for Abell stock.[9]

The Abell family continued to farm their land. After the deaths of Matt Abell in 1943 and his wife Cassie in 1950, their son J.B. received the acreage from his sister Zula Dismukes in 1953. A parcel of forty-eight acres adjoining the Abell place remained in the Beck family.[10]

After the wealthy country gentleman William E. Muse passed away, 258 acres were sold out of his estate to J.O. Pruitt in 1951. This land, formerly part of the old Mike Ramfield place, which included the Hendrix–Ramfield crossing and access to the Blue Hole, went through several buyers and investors until purchased by Doyle and Ella West in 1961.[11]

Just upstream near the site of old Tiddle Town, the Daniel heirs sold their respective interests in their farm in the mid-1940s. The property went through a succession of buyers in the 1950s until finally purchased by John Kerr in 1961.[12]

Dillard Wilson and his family continued to live and farm on the Chris Rowland land until the early 1950s. Rowland's daughter, Era Mae Helton of McLennan County, sold the property to the Veterans' Land Board. By early 1952 Dwight McDonald had purchased the real estate, along with an adjacent 451.82 acres that had remained available as a remnant of the original Galveston County School Land Grant until the mid-1940s.[13]

In 1952 Dillard Wilson faced what many of the Paluxy Valley farmers faced. The new landowner raised the rent. The Wilson children were busy with their own lives. (Doyle, the youngest son, married Charlidell Davis in July 1950.) A big farm was simply too much to handle alone. After thirty-two years, through floods, a tornado, endless musical shindigs, and even a dinosaur hunter, it was time to leave. Dillard and his wife Ora moved to a small home in Glen Rose. Of the Paluxy farm they left behind and all its memories, Novella Wilson later wrote: "While living there, they enjoyed the most relaxed and happy time of their lives."[14]

The Paluxy Valley was becoming a mix of old families that hung on to their farms, new investors and absentee owners, and urban retirees who looked for a picturesque place to settle. One of the newcomers, author John Graves, purchased land just upstream of Lanham Mill on White Bluff Creek, a Paluxy tributary, in 1960. In *Hard Scrabble: Observations on a Patch of Land,* Graves' observations of his "Hard Scrabble" Ranch, a part of what he called the "Tonk Nation" (recalling the region's early inhabitants, the Tonkawas), described the outsiders' fascination and old-timers' love for this land of scrubby cedar hills that stairstepped to streams that ran clear over limestone beds.[15]

The drought of the '50s finally broke, with a flood of course. Sediment carried by the Paluxy covered some dinosaur prints and exposed others. Bird's article in *National Geographic* in 1954 had introduced the tracks to the world, and from time to time, scientists, tourists, and other curious visitors trekked the riverbed in search of them.

Bird's track work resulted in another interesting consequence—the growing fascination with the human-like footprints that he had reported in his initial feature story, "Thunder in His Footsteps," published in *Natural History* in May 1939. Finding the large man-like tracks "of questionable origin" in Jack Hill's trading post had begun the saga of the sauropod tracks discovery.[16] But during the course of his exploration, he also observed a "mystery print" on the Paluxy. Bird wrote about the footprint with the elongated heel:

Apparently it had been made by some hitherto unknown dinosaur or reptile. The original mud had been very soft at this point, and the rock had preserved faithfully this element of softness, but the track lacked definition on which to base conclusions.[17]

Bird's description of the curious trace certainly added a touch of mystery intended for his readers, including Harry Sinclair, whose oil company was the chief patron of Barnum Brown's funded expeditions.[18] This mention of the unknown track also caught the attention of another audience.

Over time, creationists had expanded upon the "man track" claims in the effort to advance their belief in the literal interpretation of the chronology of the Bible. Advocates of this view assert that Earth's age is measured in thousands of years, as opposed to the much longer time span required by the theory of evolution and standard conclusions of geology.

In the 1950s creationist Clifford Burdick, one of the earliest proponents of the alleged "man tracks," attempted to prove that man and dinosaurs coexisted. He eventually located the pair of human-like footprints that Bird had seen in the trading post and suggested that they were authentic giant human tracks. His article, published in the religious magazine *Signs of the Times*, and his public

This human-like footprint is actually a fabrication formed in concrete that for many years was located on the grounds of the Snyder Sanitarium in Glen Rose. Other carved "man-like" tracks, elongated natural prints, and vague erosional features in rock have fueled speculation about human tracks since the 1950s. Courtesy Dinosaur Valley State Park, Photo by Collis Park

support of the traces attracted other creationist groups in search of man tracks on the Paluxy. A creationist book, *The Genesis Flood,* published in 1961, further publicized the mystery tracks, and periodically creationists visited the Paluxy River.[19]

R.T. Bird regretted his inadvertent instigation of the "man track" debate and the subsequent selective quotes mined from his dinosaur articles to suggest that he had actually found human fossil footprints. He later wrote about the erosional features that mimicked footprints:

These are nothing more than simple depressions or eroded flaws in a rock surface with an accidental (and very slight) resemblance of human footprints ... in the minds of these beholders.

He also presented a probable scenario for the making of a featureless elongated dinosaur track:

... Let us consider a large predatory carnosaur wading in deep, almost fluid mud that also rises well above this animal's ankle. The feet sink deeply; as each foot is withdrawn with all three toes compressed together for easy extraction, muds that were extruded outward and upward on penetration, slump partially back, leaving only this character-less, oblong cavity.

How did I ever get caught up in these persistent arguments (based on these and other "tracks") that hold that men and dinosaurs existed on earth at the same time together?[20]

With the continued interest in the dinosaur footprints by tourists and other groups, the business of quarrying tracks remained a steady and somewhat worrisome enterprise. In 1958 *Dallas Morning News* columnist Frank Tolbert commented on his run-in with the Glen Rose "courthouse senate," a motley assortment of old-timers, town ambassadors, and Monday-morning quarterbacks, who often gathered and jawed on the courthouse square. Tolbert wrote, "We heard talk ... that scientists have been coming in and carting off so many dinosaur tracks out of the Paluxy that Somervell County may soon be out of one of its most famous tourist attractions."[21]

Tolbert consulted one of the track "experts" in the Paluxy Valley, Charlie Moss, who reported that storms had covered a lot of the traces with silt but washed clean others. The four-toed sauropod footprints were the preferred prizes of the riverbed, but they were harder to find than the more prevalent three-toed "dragon tracks."

"Mr. Moss said that he recently helped a visitor from New York City get a fine, 4-toed specimen," Tolbert continued. "They had to break it up in getting it. However, Charley [*sic*] numbered the pieces for better ease in re-assembling."

Next Tolbert visited the McFall farm, located just upstream from present-day Dinosaur Valley State Park. The McFall family operated their own private park to welcome tourists in search of the Paluxy's dinosaur tracks. Tolbert found Jacob McFall, who offered theropod prints for sale from fifteen dollars to thirty dollars. At that time, only two tracks remained out of more than a dozen previously for sale.

Several years later in Dallas, Tolbert ran into a man from Connecticut. A Connecticut newspaper had reprinted the column on the Paluxy's dinosaur prints, and this man was traveling to the Paluxy to add a sauropod track to his collection.[22]

The removal of tracks had become problematic. People who tried to "steal" prints from the riverbed often badly damaged the traces instead in the effort to quarry them. In 1963 Texas passed a law forbidding the removal, disturbance, and damage of fossilized footprints and artifacts from another person's land or state property, including a public waterway. Violators faced a $50 to $500 fine and up to thirty days in jail.[23] On paper, the measure represented a major break-through in the protection of the tracks; actual enforcement was another matter, because authorities had to catch someone in the act of quarrying the prints.

Travel writer Ed Syers, who published his pieces in a series of collections titled *Off the Beaten Trail*, eloquently posed the question for Glen Rose and Somervell County about the future of the dinosaur trail in early 1964. His essay painted a vivid portrait of the town, its river, and the ancient treasures held there:

The old resort, with its mineral baths and iron-sulfury drinking wells, bends south with its stream and, bypassed now, leisurely waits rediscovery. It will come. Secluded about are dozens of excellent campsites where you can fish, swim, rockhound it, or just look lazy at beauty.

The beauty is one way to travel far from city tumult.

Another is to look very closely along the wooded Paluxy bottoms.

This—as few sights anywhere—will put man's metropolis in focus: a minute dust speck this side of a bottomless chasm of time.

Footprints are in the stream's rock bed—scores of them—many, clear as though imprinted just yesterday. Their size is awesome. But it is their "yester-day"—the truly old Glen Rose—that staggers the senses....

Eugene Connally, graying and soft-spoken Glen Rose historian, and Charlie Moss, who has farmed Paluxy bottoms and known its tracks most of his 67 years, showed me the spoor of Somervell County's monster herd....

Over the years, Glen Rose has been prodigal with its prehistoric treas-ure. They cut biscuits with single tracks and gave them away, ruined others try-ing. There was defacement and always weathering as new tracks were flood-upturned. They helped quarry the Paluxy bottom to send to New York and to Texas Memorial Museum in Austin....

I've seen both Austin's and New York's excellent exhibits. At both, you are quite aware that is what they are—exhibits.

Not so with these stone footsteps. You need pretend nothing. You know you stand where they walked. It is that knowing and looking that shakes your earth and turns your sky old.

What will Glen Rose do with its Dinosaur Valley?

With Texas waking to tourism, and the Paluxy hills superlative for outdoor families, Historian Connally believes his town must do something, get help somewhere.[24]

Residents of Somervell County took to heart the question of the fate of their special Dinosaur Valley. By the mid-1960s a growing movement spearheaded by local citizens sought to gain recognition and protection for the tracks. Glen Rose looked to an old friend—tourism—to help revitalize the local economy.

By the summer of 1965 the Somervell County Historical Society and the Glen Rose–Somervell County Chamber of Commerce had marked out a "Dinosaur Trail" for touring motorists to enjoy the beauty of the Paluxy Valley and its tracks. This action reflected a greater interest across Texas in the travel trade as a viable method to generate both publicity and revenue for the Lone Star State. In fact, during this same time U.S. Congressman W.R. "Bob" Poage of Waco proposed the construction of a scenic parkway to run from Fort Worth south to San Antonio in order to showcase some of the state's most picturesque places, including the Paluxy River Valley.[25]

The "Dinosaur Trail" snaked off Farm Road 205 and followed the county road that wound along the Paluxy and through the old Lanham Mill community past the Blue Hole, still one of the favorite swimming spots in the county. In October 1964 the Wests sold their farm of 258 acres, the old Ramfield place that accessed the Blue Hole, to Oliver W. Fannin, Jr., a Fort Worth attorney. By the following July, Fannin met with the Somervell County Commissioners Court and asked that the road be closed.[26]

Generations had enjoyed the Blue Hole, and no one had ever publicly objected to the free access to this recreation spot. County Judge Temple Summers advised that Fannin would have to present a petition with the signatures of all the landowners along the road requesting the closure. The threat of the loss of a popular picnicking area brought many local citizens out against the road closure. People debated over whether the Paluxy was actually a river or just a creek which would further define its status regarding public entry.[27]

By late July the county commissioners denied the request. The *Glen Rose Reporter* printed:

County Judge Temple Summers said this week that public response against the closing of the road on the Dinosaur Trail route via the "Blue Hole" on the Paluxy River had been so great since publication of a story in the *Reporter* concerning the request for closure that closure would be impossible.[28]

In September 1965 good Samaritans came forward to further ensure public access to the Blue Hole. Winston and Martha Whitaker, owners of the old Martin farm in the bend of the Paluxy, donated a small tract of land adjacent to the Blue Hole for use as a county park.[29]

The events of the summer of 1965 illustrated both the importance of the dinosaur tracks to the heritage of Somervell County and the need to protect them. So began the push to secure some of the land of the Paluxy Valley for a state park. Many individuals championed this effort of preservation and economic renewal.

"The community was very well-grounded in unification of trying to get something in here that would stimulate the economy," Dorothy Leach of the Somervell County Historical Commission recalled. "Chamber of Commerce was real strong—didn't have any money—but was very strong!" Jack McCarty, president of the Chamber of Commerce at that time, was also publisher of the *Glen Rose Reporter*, "published in the land of the dinosaur." He and his son Dan strongly supported a park, along with county historian Eugene Connally, Mayor Walter Ernst, Earl Jackson (chairman of the chamber's parks committee), County Judge Temple Summers, State Senator J.P. Word, Representative J.E. Ward, Congressman W.R. "Bob" Poage, and others.[30]

The idea of a park on the Paluxy had two other notable proponents—Mr. and Mrs. Winston Whitaker. In the spring of 1966 they offered an option on their property of 347 acres for this purpose, and on May 4, 1966, the Glen Rose–Somervell County Chamber of Commerce signed the option on the land. The *Glen Rose Reporter* described the momentous occasion:

A dream of many present and deceased Somervell Countains [sic] took a long stride forward here Wednesday morning when an option was taken by the Glen Rose–Somervell County Chamber of Commerce on a 347-acre tract of land on the Paluxy River, owned by Winston Whittaker [sic] of this city, for a park to preserve the famous dinosaur tracks of the Paluxy River Valley.

The option gives the local organization 18 months to sell the tract to private capital with the stipulation that it be given to the State of Texas for development as a State Park....[31]

Tom Roden, a Glen Rose native, temporarily provided the option money of $2,500 until the chamber could get sufficient signatures on a note through the First National Bank. Representative J.E. Ward and Senator J.P. Word volunteered to sign. The various town and political representatives, along with John Ben Sheppard, president of the West Texas Chamber of Commerce, had already met with Will Odom, the chairman of the State Parks and Wildlife Commission, in

Dorothy Leach of the Somervell County Historical Commission recalled the overwhelming support for a state park in the Paluxy Valley. Photo by Laurie E. Jasinski

Austin to devise the option plan and lay the groundwork for a private entity to purchase the land and donate it to the State.

The *Glen Rose Reporter* concluded:

If you are interested in a state park to preserve the famous dinosaur tracks for future generations and at the same time, improve the tourist attractiveness of the Glen Rose area, you are invited to sign the note to provide option money. Each signature will be obligated for only $100.[32]

There was no shortage of takers. Twenty-five men each put up $100 in about two hours. They had eighteen months to raise $80,000 for the land.[33]

By the end of May 1966, the drive for a dinosaur park gained even more momentum but from an unexpected source. U.S. Representatives Bob Poage of Waco and Jim Wright of Fort Worth announced their plans to propose that the "Dinosaur Trail" be recognized as a national monument. This designation would secure Dinosaur Trail National Monument under the protection of the National Park Service.[34]

The congressmen contended, "If these remaining marks are not preserved, a treasure of untold historic worth will be lost to future generations." The proposal garnered widespread area coverage and even national media attention in support of the measure.[35]

Glen Rose citizens welcomed the possibility that their dinosaur valley might become a national park. Newspaper editor Jack McCarty commented:

If the federal government comes in there will be some fine facilities. No one in town has registered a single complaint about making it a park. And I would have heard about it if they had. We're willing to turn over the land option to the federal or state governments or to private enterprise if they'll make a park out of it.[36]

State Representative J.E. Ward agreed:

We'd rather see it a national park than a state park because there will be more money for it that way. We've been working for something like this for a long time and this is the best opportunity we've ever had.[37]

The potential promise of a park, national or state, brought visions of a return to the boom years when folks celebrated Glen Rose as a popular resort. The *Fort Worth Press* on June 5, 1966, painted a rosy scenario:

A ride down a bumpy, unpaved road may become a trip down a smooth parkway.

The ruined gate may become a stone park entrance; the abandoned house, a museum; the plank and pile of rocks, a bridge.

The backroad farmer may become a professional, uniformed guide, and the rocky river bed a scientific exhibit. Perhaps a replica of a tyrannosaur or brontosaur may rise from the water.

For this to happen, a quiet land where dinosaurs walked must become a national park—the long-awaited answer to the dreams of the old-timers in the area.

With the progress and grand plans however, also came a downside. The feature continued:

But with tourists, protection and the park will come some loss. No longer will one be able to drive down a dirt road ... through ramshackle gates, by abandoned houses, with dove and red-winged blackbirds beside the road.

The summer bustled with interested visitors and dignitaries, and the local chamber made certain that a visit to Glen Rose included a tour of the dinosaur trails. Associate Supreme Court Justice William O. Douglas made a special stop on his way to the LBJ Ranch. Lady Bird Johnson had also expressed her support to preserve the tracks. The Somervell County Historical Society conducted tours regularly on Sundays. "The historical society began giving tours out there with permission of the landowners," Dorothy Leach recalled. Visitors also stopped off at the McFall farm and paid about a dollar to see the fossil footprints.[38]

Glen Rose proudly proclaimed its dinosaur heritage on the courthouse square with the large steel silhouette of one of the creatures, in this case, a

Postcard of Somervell County Courthouse Square, ca. late 1950s to early 1960s. Glen Rose's courthouse dinosaur, named "Tex," was erected on the square in the 1950s. The steel reptile remained there until the late 1980s, when courthouse renovation took place. Courtesy Somervell County Historical Commission

Dinosaur Hunting License

SPECIAL PERMIT NO. 86-U2869

ISSUED TO:

Name _____

Street _____

City _____ State _____

ISSUED BY AUTHORITY OF THE TEXAS REPTILE CONTROL COMMISSION
Restricted to Somervell County, Texas

This license entitles the holder to hunt for, pursue, shoot, kill and remove from the area known as Dinosaur Valley in Somervell County, Texas, which is along the Paluxy River in the vicinity of Glen Rose, Texas, the following types of reptilian wild game:

1. **BRONTOSAURUS** - one only (adult male).

2. **TRACHODON** - one only (either sex) and weighing not less than 2,000 lbs., live weight.

3. **ALLOSAURUS** - two only (without young).

Holder of this license agrees to remove all such game, legally bagged by him under the proper restrictions, properly preserved and in sanitary condition within five (5) days of time of reptile's death, and further agrees to have said game inspected by the Texas Game Warden before removal.

Signed _____
Deputy Lizard Warden

---

duckbilled dinosaur. (Many still believed at this time that duckbilled dinosaurs had made some of the tri-toed fossilized prints.) A new historical museum on the square also exhibited artifacts of the county's interesting past.[39]

Groups had fun with whimsical gimmicks. The Somervell County Historical Society, along with the Glen Rose Future Farmers of America and the Young Farmers, printed dinosaur hunting licenses, "issued by the authority of the Texas Reptile Control Commission," for those who wanted to bag their very own "reptilian wild game." This was restricted to Somervell County, of course![40]

In the fall of 1966 the Glen Rose dinosaur publicity campaign received a boost by riding the coattails of the Sinclair Dinosaur Show. The Sinclair dinosaurs were nine life-size dinosaur replicas commissioned by Sinclair Oil Corporation for its "Dinoland" exhibit at the 1964 New York World's Fair. Animal sculptor Louis Paul Jonas constructed these mammoth figures, and Barnum Brown had served as a technical consultant before his death in 1963.[41] R.T. Bird later recalled the spectacle of these dramatic models as he watched them make their journey to the World's Fair:

They were made at a small town up the Hudson River, blown up from small models made in dinosaur hall at the museum by an artist commissioned by the Sinclair Oil people.... These models were first pictured in Sinclair advertizing; and later when the giant replicas were made, they were eventually transported down the Hudson River on a train of barges, and were towed around Manhattan Island for all who wished to come to the waterfronts to watch, as people did in hundreds of thousands. Quite a stunt.[42]

"Dinoland" was one of the highlights of the New York World's Fair, and Sinclair looked to capitalize on its popularity. Dan McCarty of the *Glen Rose Reporter* recalled, "After the fair they had hauled them all over the United States. Set them up in shopping center parking lots." The dinosaur exhibit traveled to thirty-seven cities at a cost of approximately $500,000.[43]

In September 1966 the dinosaurs came to Fort Worth, the thirty-second stop on the tour, and the caravan of flatbed trucks hauling the monstrous models rolled into Seminary South, a local shopping center. The Glen Rose–Somervell County Chamber of Commerce had a booth at the show. Among those who

Novella Wilson snapped this picture of her niece, Connie May, daughter of Mr. And Mrs. Alton May, when Sinclair's "Dinoland" came to Fort Worth's Seminary South Shopping Center. Connie is astride a baby Bronto, one of Sinclair's green promotional models. The large Bronto of "Dinoland" towers in the background. Photo by Novella Wilson

Dinosaurs Come to Big Town!

One Sunday in early October 1966, the Mask family made a special trip from their home in Paris, Texas, to Big Town just east of Dallas. Big Town, heralded as the first indoor shopping mall in Texas, played host to the Sinclair Dinosaur Show. With her parents, Bernard and Joyce, and older sister Carol, nine-year-old Linda Mask gazed up at the monstrous figures of "Rex" the *Tyrannosaurus* and "Bronto" the *Brontosaurus*.

"I remember ... how wonderful they were—these huge models!" Awestruck children wandered around the large open trailers that held the dinosaurs "direct from the New York World's Fair."

Linda commented, "It was also neat to me that they were from the World's Fair, because I didn't go to the World's Fair." Her sentiment echoed those of many who were excited that a little part of "Dinoland" had traveled to them.

Sinclair's long-lasting and brilliantly-conceived trademark appealed especially to children. Linda had often begged her father to stop at the Sinclair service station because they had the dinosaur, and the gentle vegetarian brontosaur was her favorite of the ancient creatures.

The Sinclair plastic model souvenirs delighted young and old alike at Big Town. "One thing I remember ... specifically," Linda smiled, "is they had these machines that you put quarters in, and then they put the liquid plastic [in] somehow. After you put the quarters in, it would do the liquid plastic into a *Brontosaurus* mold."

Her older sister captured Rex and Bronto with her Polaroid Swinger camera and preserved a memory of that exciting day at Big Town when the Mask family, like many families, enjoyed a close-up meeting with the dinosaurs![44]

TOP *"Rex," Sinclair's Tyrannosaurus, wowed visitors at Big Town shopping mall just east of Dallas in the fall of 1966.* **BOTTOM** *"Bronto," the Brontosaurus, impressed viewers as part of the traveling "Dinoland" exhibit that rolled through Big Town in the fall of 1966. The Dallas media reported that dinomania had struck "Big D."* Courtesy Linda Newland, Photos by Carol Farrell

helped staff the kiosk was Mrs. Alton May, Novella Wilson's sister-in-law, who recalled the long hot days out on the mall parking lot. "Several of us went up there, and I stayed five days and nights with the dinosaurs." Even then, Mrs. May and others wondered about the ultimate fate of the big models, and she chatted about the prospects of retiring them to the Dinosaur Valley.[45]

More than 365,000 people visited the display at Seminary South in Fort Worth over its five-day run, before the caravan headed east for Dallas, and volunteers at the Glen Rose booth handed out 40,000 dinosaur hunting licenses. Jack McCarty and the chamber expressed their gratitude to officials of the Seminary South Shopping Center for inviting them to "tell the Glen Rose Dinosaur Story."[46]

Though park proponents endeavored to promote their mission to preserve the Dinosaur Valley, precious time was ebbing away. More than six months had passed since Glen Rose citizens had taken the option to buy the Whitakers' property, and as 1966 slipped into 1967, no firm action had occurred even though state and national officials had toured the Paluxy Valley. Earl Jackson, chairman of the Parks and Recreation Committee of the Chamber of Commerce, pushed for a state feasibility study in late 1966. In January, Parks and Wildlife personnel conducted a field investigation of the area. At this same time Congressman Bob Poage officially proposed a bill to establish Dinosaur Trail National Monument, and the proposal went to a House Committee for consideration.[47]

In March 1967 the Texas Parks and Wildlife Department (TPWD) published their preliminary report of the proposed Glen Rose Dinosaur Tracks State Park. The study presented several reasons for securing part of the Paluxy Valley for a park. It stressed the importance of protecting the dinosaur tracks, which were certainly of statewide "geological significance." Dr. Wann Langston, vertebrate paleontologist at the University of Texas, had likewise viewed the site several times and advocated preservation of the footprints.[48]

The examination also reported that part of the property constituted "good habitat for the endangered species, the golden-cheeked warbler." The region's accessibility to several major highways and population centers, including the Dallas/Fort Worth area, also played in its favor. TPWD agreed to help supply materials for a brochure for local officials at Glen Rose to submit to possible benefactors.[49] Some speculated that Sinclair Oil Corporation might be an appropriate target for securing grant money or as a buyer.

The spring and summer of 1967 both fired and dashed the hopes of park supporters. The proposal to declare the area a National Monument was still mired in the Committee on Interior and Insular Affairs. Finally, Representative J.E. Ward and Senator J.P. Word persuaded the Texas Legislature to pass a bill providing for the creation of a state park. Dan McCarty of the *Glen Rose Reporter* remembered, "Politics what it is, appropriations were delayed, and then [Gov.] John Connally line-item vetoed the thing out of the appropriations."[50]

Here Glen Rose sat with the State's blessing for a park but no money to follow through with it. "There for awhile it looked like it was going to really come to a screeching halt," Dorothy Leach recalled.

The *Fort Worth Star-Telegram* sympathized:

Glen Rose's frustrating perplexity began 20 years ago. Today, it com-
mutes from New York's glittering lights to the hallowed halls of our national
Congress to Austin's political showrooms to a placid horseshoe bend of the oak-
lined Paluxy River.

Impaled on the dilemma's horns are a much-yearned-for $80,000....[51]

For a poor county like Somervell, an $80,000 tab seemed insurmountable!
Time was running out on the option. Governor Connally favored a $75 million
bond issue to be put forth to the voters in mid-November. If passed, funds would
be available for purchase of the park, but this would be too late for the option
deadline of November 3, 1967. The eighteen months that had seemed like so
much time were dwindling down to nothing. Meanwhile, the local sheriff periodically caught souvenir seekers trying to chisel out tracks.[52]

CHAPTER EIGHT

To Capture a Park—
Landscape and Riverscape and Trailway

November 1967 loomed over Somervell County's dreams of preserving its dinosaur tracks as part of a park. While the option deadline for purchasing the land marched closer, residents looked for a champion to come forward. They would find two.

Landowners Mr. and Mrs. Whitaker extended the Chamber of Commerce's option, just before its expiration date of November 3, 1967, to January 3, 1968. Citizens collectively breathed a sigh of relief. The following week, Texas voters passed the bond issue. With the hope of future funding on the way, in January 1968 the Whitakers extended the land option on a month-to-month basis, and park supporters donated money to a Dinosaur Park Option Fund to make the monthly payments.[1]

A final option date was set for October 3, 1968, but as the bonds that would enable the State to buy the real estate remained unsold through much of 1968, Chamber of Commerce members recognized that they could not hang on to the option forever. Somehow, they would have to act on the now $88,000 price tag if state funds did not come through.[2]

"Where is the fiscal cavalry? It's crisis time again for the dinosaurs," wrote Jerry Flemmons, travel writer for the *Fort Worth Star-Telegram*:

What will happen if the Chamber committee fails to acquire the land[?] One of two things may occur. The property may be sold to a person who will rope off the existing tracks and be more interested in charging admission to all comers than preserving that horseshoe treasure for everyone to enjoy.

Or a land speculator will buy the acreage, and inflate the cost, guessing that the state will pay a high price for the tracks. The taxpayers are the losers if this happens.

Anyway, a rescue is needed before Oct. 3. If you know of any U.S. Cavalry troops with $88,000 tell them to make tracks for Glen Rose.[3]

The fiscal cavalry did finally come to the rescue. On September 27, 1968, Texas Parks and Wildlife Deputy Director Robert G. Mauermann executed a sales contract with the Whitakers to buy their property for Dinosaur Valley State Park. Money from more than $5 million in sold park bonds had finally enabled the State to make this purchase. Local residents were elated. The *Glen Rose Reporter* triumphantly announced the happy event and thanked the many supporters, especially the Chamber of Commerce and its park committee:

This group spent endless hours of their time and their own personal finances and maintained a "never-say-die" spirit to keep the movement going when everything appeared to be lost.[4]

Another hero of the hour was Winston Whitaker himself. "Winston Whitaker is probably as responsible as anyone anywhere for that park," Dan McCarty commented. Dorothy Leach agreed, "He could have sold the land to somebody else, maybe even made more money, but Whitaker was interested in seeing that it became a park."[5]

Mr. and Mrs. Winston Whitaker (second and third from left) accept payment for their land from Robert G. Mauermann, Texas Parks and Wildlife Deputy Director. Onlookers (fourth through sixth from left) are County Attorney Sam Freas, Chairman of the Dinosaur Park Committee Early Johnson, and State Representative J.E. Ward. This was the first real estate transaction for Dinosaur Valley State Park. Courtesy Eugene Connally Collection, Somervell County Historical Commission Archives

On December 31, 1968, the State of Texas officially bought the Whitaker land. A resurvey showed that the "347 acres" actually totaled 383.35 acres. The sale included the tract tucked inside the bend of the river, with the old Martin homestead, now abandoned, as well as acreage across the river that the Whitakers had leased to local rancher Andy Wood on which to run cattle. This was the State's first purchase of parkland with money out of the passed bond issue. The federal government supplied matching funds for the acquisition under the Federal Land and Water Conservation Act.[6]

The Texas Parks and Wildlife Department quickly conducted hiring for the park. Local citizen Ed West became the first paid employee at Dinosaur Valley State Park in February 1969. As a guide and seasonal worker, he oversaw fencing the area. Lanham Mill resident Charlie Moss and other local men, Zollie Wilkins and Roy "Bummy" Garner, continued to keep an eye on the place and serve as informal guides. During those early days the regional game warden periodically checked on things and secured the area.[7]

In March 1969 the U.S. Department of the Interior approved the dinosaur tracks of the Paluxy River for recognition as a registered Natural Landmark. Though this status acknowledged the great significance of the footprints as natural features, it did not place them under the direction of the National Park Service. Texas Senator Ralph Yarborough and Representative Jim Wright both introduced bills in the U.S. Senate and House of Representatives, respectively, to "authorize the establishment of the Dinosaur Trail National Monument in the State of Texas," but this legislation never went through.[8]

TPWD purchased additional property in the spring and summer of 1969. In May the agency secured more than 612 acres of the land that had been owned

Lanham Mill resident Charlie Moss cleans out one of Dinosaur Valley's impressive sauropod tracks in March 1969. Moss served as a guide during the park's early days. Courtesy Novella Wilson and Somervell County Historical Commission Archives

by Roland Ball. This large tract encompassed the other side of the horseshoe of the river across from the former Whitaker land. Two creeks, Wildcat Hollow and Opossum Branch, ran through the property. Part of the real estate included the former 190-acre Chris Rowland farm where the Wilsons made their home for many years. The house still sat there.[9]

More parcels for the park sold in August 1969. The daughter of W.D. Jones, Euella Marie Jones Nix, sold the small tract of eighteen acres adjacent to the Abell place. Likewise, J.B. Abell and Elmer Abell sold their farm, 209 acres. The homestead and barn were torn down, and Abell hauled off some of the lumber to build another barn. Eventually, J.B. Abell also purchased the adjoining land of some forty-eight acres from Walter Beck and sold it to the State early in the following year.[10]

Many of the present and past residents of the Paluxy Valley rejoiced to see the creation of a park. "I was pleased myself," Doyle Wilson commented. But, not knowing how the Parks Department might change the area or the tracksite, Novella Wilson, an accomplished artist, set out to preserve the scene for her own memory. "I wanted to try to capture it like I saw it at that time, before anything was done, because at that time, we had no idea what the State would do with the area—what changes might be made."[11]

Day after day she sat on the river bank and painted the Paluxy and its tracks that had seen so much scientific activity almost thirty years earlier. Her mother, Dora May, accompanied her and quietly sat as Novella painted each detail. One day a crowd interrupted their serene afternoon:

Here comes this big busload of people, and they were a church group from Red Oak, Texas. Came down there to see the tracks....Word was getting around, and here they went down there and crossed the stones to walk over there and everything.[12]

Not everyone was impressed. Novella recalled one woman, who seemed more interested in the painting than the dinosaur tracks, declared, "I'm not going over there to see them. I know there's nothing to it!"

In November 1969 Lester Galbreath came to Dinosaur Valley State Park as the first park superintendent. Fresh out of college, the young ranger faced an area of still-overgrown countryside. He hired seasonal workers to help clean the park. They cleared out silt from the riverbed to uncover more dinosaur tracks. The crew tore down fences and hauled away a broken-down tractor and rusted-out cars—reminders of the bygone farms. But most of the old structures were gone, with the exception of the Wilson house across the river. They remodeled it to make a ranger residence.[13]

The county lane and some weathered dirt byways served as the only roads in the park at that time. Any evidence of the Hendrix–Ramfield crossing had disappeared, and crews had to backtrack and drive a circuitous route to get to parkland across the river.

With little manpower to assist a growing number of visitors and little control over adjacent property, Lester had to be ever vigilant. The Blue Hole illustrated a major case in point. Though not part of the park, it bordered the park boundary and still reigned as a very popular swimming place. Consequently, the area

The main dinosaur track site as it appeared in 1969. Lanham Mill artist and historian Novella Wilson wished to preserve this scene of the Paluxy and its storied footprints that had made so many memories for local folks. Painting by Novella Wilson

saw its share of skinny dippers, which often posed a problem when picnicking families in the park encountered swimmers in the buff.[14]

During his tenure in the early days of Dinosaur Valley State Park, Lester Galbreath introduced a group of twenty-five Longhorn steers that had been part of the state herd at Fort Griffin. The Longhorns grazed in two pastures of approximately forty to fifty acres each across the river. For some eighteen years the Texas symbols were an added attraction for the park and reflected Galbreath's lifelong interest in the cattle.[15]

As park preparation continued, in March 1969 an important event occurred in the business world that would have a direct impact on Dinosaur Valley State Park. Sinclair Oil Corporation merged with Atlantic Richfield Company. In the ensuing months, as the company made plans to abandon its beloved dinosaur trademark, state officials, park personnel, and Glen Rose citizens sought to acquire the life-size models of "Dinoland."[16]

Governor Preston Smith, in a letter to Atlantic Richfield in February 1970, invited the company to retire the dinosaurs to Texas as a permanent educational display in the park. Dan McCarty and his father Jack were two local officials involved in the talks with an Atlantic Richfield representative. Since their grand tour after the World's Fair, the giant dinosaur replicas sat unused and unseen. Donating these striking creatures would generate great publicity for Atlantic Richfield and be a tremendous asset to the park.[17]

"The way that all worked out," Dan McCarty recalled, "he originally told us we'd get everything." A veritable zoo of the behemoths would indeed recreate a new "Dinoland" on the park grounds, but the arrangement fell through.

"Then he called back and he said that, 'I let my mouth overload my head. Now that the word's out on those, everybody in the free world wants a dinosaur!'" The company promised Sinclair's two most impressive models, however, the thundering brontosaur and towering tyrannosaur.

Atlantic Richfield Company gave their monstrous replicas to the park in July 1970. The *Glen Rose Reporter* proudly delivered the news to interested readers:

Good news received here Thursday of last week from State Senator J.P. Word announced that the Governor's office and the State Parks & Wildlife Department had been notified that the new Dinosaur Valley State Park, located on the Paluxy River just west of town, had been presented components of the Sinclair collection of life-size dinosaur replicas including the 70-foot Brontosaurus, largest of the group; two baby Brontos with simulated eggs; Tyrannosaurus Rex, a 50-foot flesh eater, and Archaeopteryz [*sic*], a winged creature about the size of a pheasant....

Arrival of the Brontosaurus came at noon Tuesday when the huge replica of the ancient vegetable-eating monster pulled into the park aboard a 40-foot trailer truck and word was received that two more truckloads bearing the vicious meateater and miscellaneous parts would arrive later that evening.[18]

As for the two baby Brontos, Bronto eggs, and *Archaeopteryx*—there were no facilities to house them at the park itself. One of the small Brontos, a Sinclair promotional model, was given to Oakdale Park in Glen Rose. The fate of the other baby Bronto, Bronto egg, and Archaeopteryx remained a mystery. Though possible that these models went to TPWD headquarters in Austin, Lester Galbreath could not confirm that TPWD had ever taken possession of them.[19]

The mammoth dismantled figures caused quite a stir when they rolled into the park on July 14, 1970. Frank Sogorka, their "wrangler" who had traveled with them while on exhibit, and several other Atlantic Richfield officials accompanied the models to Glen Rose and were treated to a luncheon at the Chamber of Commerce with then-president Loyan Walker. Lester Galbreath and his workers went about the heavy yet delicate work of erecting the replicas for permanent display.[20]

"The *Tyrannosaurus* was in two parts, bottom half and top half," Lester explained. "I built a foundation to set it on."

With a crane the men carefully positioned the bottom half, then hoisted the top half. A trapdoor underneath the figure enabled Lester and another park employee to crawl inside of the creature, while another worker guided the head with the crane. A series of turnbuckles inside the model clipped the two halves together.

Lester and his helper guided the top into position. As Lester began fastening turnbuckles to secure the halves, the other worker climbed up into the head to unhook the cable of the crane. Suddenly the whole *Tyrannosaurus* began to topple. Lester bailed out the trapdoor and ran for safety, barely avoiding being

Installation of Rex and Bronto, the Sinclair dinosaur models, required care and precision by Park Superintendent Lester Galbreath and his staff. Courtesy Eugene Connally Collection, Somervell County Historical Commission Archives

crushed. His assistant, still trapped in the model's head, had no choice but to ride it all the way to the ground.[21]

Thankfully, no one was hurt—except for the *Tyrannosaurus* that is. His tail cracked. Within a few days, its sculptor Louis Paul Jonas flew out and refiber-glassed the dinosaur. Having learned a valuable lesson about the care and danger involved with erecting the mammoth models, the men took extra precaution with the brontosaur. The all-day job went off without a hitch.

The following day Lester completed the finishing tasks for securing the sauropod. It too had a trapdoor in its belly, and he crawled inside to clip on additional turnbuckles. Bronto, with his "swallowed" stowaway, naturally attracted visitors eager to admire the park's newest reptilian resident.

Through a thin slit in the model's head, Lester could see a woman approach the Thunder Lizard. "Oh you're a pretty thing," she praised.

Hidden from view, the park superintendent could not control his mischievous side. "Why thank you very much!" he answered.

The lady looked shocked. Bronto had spoken! "Did you talk?" she asked.

"Why yes m'am," Bronto replied chipperly, "I said thank you very much!"

Flabbergasted, the woman ran to get her husband, who humored his wife and tromped up to the giant brontosaur. She tried everything she could to coax a reply, much to the chagrin of her husband, but Bronto remained silent. Lester chuckled as they walked away—just another day in the life of a park superintendent![22]

With the dinosaur models in place and a series of new signs to guide visitors to the tracks, officials and residents looked forward to the park dedication. It would be a ceremony filled with dignitaries, oil company executives, state and national park personnel, and many local citizens.[23] One other important guest planned to be there.

After assembling his magnificent trackway at the American Museum and writing of his adventures to the world in *National Geographic*, Roland T. Bird settled into a quiet existence. With his wife Hazel, whom he had married in 1946, he resided in Homestead, Florida. After all these years he still suffered from fragile health. His close friend V.T. Schreiber, an amateur paleontologist, visited Florida each year and also occasionally came to Glen Rose. On one such visit Novella Wilson sent along her own greeting to R.T. Bird through Schreiber.[24]

Bird had followed the saga of his old stomping ground and replied to Novella on September 26, 1970:

I was naturally delighted with the thought that you had remembered me after all these years. Your father-in-law played an important part in the recovery of that brontosaur trailway from the bottom of the Paluxy in allowing me access across the fertile acres of that farm I remember so well—which solved one of the biggest problems of the project.

I have his photograph somewhere among my collection, and I think you will agree it is a good one of him. I will bring it with me to Glen Rose for the opening of the new park skeduled on Oct 2.

For I have decided to get there if possible....

There is just one problem. I am past the age of three-score and ten now, and am victim of a physical disability that makes travel difficult because of diet. I have a form of low blood sugar that involves a high protein intake along with total abstainance from all foods containing refined sugar, a simple matter under controled conditions; but troublesome when one must eat at restaurants. However, I am hoping to get by on the short time involved.

I am most anxious to see what has been done in the "Dinosaur Valley." The model dinosaurs now on exhibition I saw in New York during the World's Fair there....[25]

He also recalled seeing the huge models being carried to their destination. "As I watched from the heights above Riverside Park in the Grant's Tomb area, little did I dream that the big brontosaur would some day end up in Glen Rose!"

Bird arrived by bus from Dallas on September 30, 1970, and Novella was waiting for him. It was his first trip back to Glen Rose since his excavation of the Paluxy in 1940. Novella recognized his deep sense of nostalgia:

He had me take him up there [to the tracksite] and leave him all day. He wanted to reminisce about the tracks, and he stayed up there all day. He told me when to come back in the afternoon.... I don't know how that poor old man got by without any water. He didn't have any water or food or anything with him.[26]

But Bird had his memories, now thirty years past. Perhaps he could hear the sharp clinking of chisels on rock while children played above the bank. The dear old Buick was parked up there again, as the young workers hefted precious

R.T. Bird photographed his old Paluxy quarry on October 1, 1970, the day before the official dedication of the new Dinosaur Valley State Park. Courtesy Novella Wilson, Photo by Roland T. Bird

R.T. Bird returned to his track site thirty years after the excavation to reminisce. Photo by Novella Wilson

blocks of their chiseled quarry up to load on her. Thirty years. He'd fancied himself an old bachelor then, but now at age seventy, in retrospect, they were a sort of salad days, when he had suffered and savored that spring and summer in the Paluxy Valley. Now autumn hovered over him. In the rush of time that so quickly passed, something special was left behind and still here. This valley, the clear Paluxy, old tracks scoured off but new ones revealed—he was home at his quarry one last time. This was a park to be enjoyed by all, but today, he breathed in the scene alone.[27]

After a few hours, Novella returned. "He made a picture of me up there, and I made a picture of him. So it was a really pretty historical day as far as I was concerned, to have the honor of taking him."

Bird made it a point to see another old friend. He stopped in town to meet with Dillard Wilson. "He came back to this country years later when Dad had moved to town and visited Dad," Doyle Wilson recalled. The two shared old stories.

On October 2, 1970, approximately five hundred people witnessed the official dedication of Dinosaur Valley State Park. The sun beamed brilliant on that Friday morning. The Glen Rose High School Band played a rousing "Star Spangled Banner" while members of the local FFA posted the colors. The ceremony was marked by great fanfare. Governor Preston Smith arrived at the grounds by helicopter. He publicly accepted the gift of the dinosaur models from officials of the Atlantic Richfield Company. He also praised the Glen Rose–Somervell County Chamber of Commerce and numerous local business leaders and citizens for their perseverance.[28]

"We are planning for and developing new parks in the state," he said, "but this is the first." Governor Smith also received a bronze plaque from the Department of the Interior recognizing the park as a Natural Landmark.[29]

State Senator J.P. Word served as master of ceremonies and introduced the many VIPs present, including Frank Sogorka, the "Father of the Sinclair Dinosaur Collection;" State Representative J.E. Ward; and of course Roland T. Bird. After the ceremony, guests feasted on barbecue at Oakdale Park in Glen Rose.[30]

The ceremony signified the culmination of years of hard work and was a memorable event for all who attended. Perhaps none quite appreciated the gravity of the occasion as R.T. Bird, who expressed his feelings in a kind note to the people of Glen Rose:

TOP *A large crowd "in the shadow of Bronto" watched the festivities at the dedication of Dinosaur Valley State Park on Friday, October 2, 1970.* **BOTTOM** *State Senator J.P. Word of Meridian was master of ceremonies for the park dedication.* Courtesy Eugene Connally Collection, Somervell County Historical Commission Archives

Rex poses proudly above dignitaries who attended the dedication of Dinosaur Valley State Park. From left to right are Frank Sogorka, "Father of the Sinclair Dinosaur Collection," O.P. Thomas, Chairman of the Executive Committee of Atlantic Richfield Company, Governor Preston Smith, Senator J.P. Word, and Representative J.E. Ward. Courtesy Eugene Connally Collection, Somervell County Historical Commission Archives

Card of Thanks

I want to thank all you wonderful Glen Rose people who made my visit here to attend the new Dinosaur Valley State Park ceremonies the heartwarming, overwhelming experience it proved to be. It was appreciated more, not because I might have expected such a welcome, but because it was so delightfully spontaneous and natural.

I especially want to thank Mrs. Novella Wilson and her mother, and Mrs. Kay White for auto transportation and for the fine courtesies tendered me at Oakdale Park and in every place of business in which I set my foot.

You have furnished me with an unforgetable three days, quite as rewarding as those other days when I came here as a dinosaur hunting representative of the American Museum of Natural History in 1938 and '40.[31]

For Novella he saved a special thank you. He wrote on November 19:

At last I have had some reprints made of the films taken during my Glen Rose visit to attend those ceramonies at the new Dinosaur Valley State Park....

I will feel ever grateful for the part you played in making that visit the resounding success it was for me—and for the extravagant way to which you responded in those matters.

I will never forget the surprise and delight I experienced when the bus I rode from Dallas pulled in, and I found you there on the sidewalk, waiting....

I will never forget those surprisingly lovely paintings of yours at Oakdale Park.... I was especially moved by that masterpiece on the wall depicting my old quarry, with the trailway of one of my old brontosaurs resplendent in the foreground; all of that landscape and riverscape and trailway witness to the many hours of loving care expended upon it. I can see you now as you must have sat there before your canvas and easel, painting; and words fail me, even as they would have failed me had I tried to so express myself on the occasion I made these photos....[32]

He was a man who had come full circle—at least in this aspect of his life. He must have been glad that he took that detour to the Texas village of Glen Rose all those years ago.

CHAPTER NINE
Growing Pains for Dinosaur Valley State Park

Somervell County citizens pinned their hopes on their new state park and believed that Dinosaur Valley symbolized the dawn of a new era of tourism for Glen Rose in 1970. For one of the smallest and poorest counties in the state, securing a portion of the Paluxy Valley for posterity represented an amazing feat.

At the start of the 1970s, many farmers still eked out a living or partial living in agriculture by cultivating peanuts, hay, pecans, and grains as well as raising cattle. The county had also attracted some modest industry with the opening of a garment plant and a cedar oil mill, which utilized one of the region's major resources by extracting oil from cedar trees to produce a base for perfumes.[1] Agriculture and business aside, Dinosaur Valley State Park presented Somervell's public face to the world, and residents eagerly anticipated the park's development.

Park superintendent Lester Galbreath left Dinosaur Valley in the winter of 1971. The Texas Parks and Wildlife Department appointed local man and president of the Glen Rose Chamber of Commerce Loyan H. Walker as new superintendent effective January 4, 1971. Walker, born in Eulogy in nearby Bosque County, had been an active director of the West Texas Chamber of Commerce, and Glen Rose inhabitants respected him as a dynamic civic leader. As superintendent at Dinosaur Valley, Loyan Walker came to a new park still undeveloped. Under his tenure, Parks and Wildlife officials planned and began the first phase of park construction. With a shortage of manpower and funding, the property had demanded most of Lester Galbreath and his staff's time simply to clear part of the land, remove fences, and watch over the tracks. Little else greeted visitors except for the two colossal dinosaur models that rose above the lonely landscape.[2]

Since its dedication, the park was open for day-use only. The lack of facilities precluded any overnight camping. Picnickers gathered around a few benches and fireplaces, all temporary fixtures. The few restrooms were provisional as well. A mobile home served as a park headquarters, and a single faucet in front provided the only drinking water for thirsty tourists. Walker himself lived in the old Wilson house across the river.[3]

During the next two years Walker oversaw major construction in the park at an estimated cost of $475,000, funded equally by state and federal money. The development affected some two hundred acres of the park's total acreage of 1,271 at that time, with the bulk of the work focused on about one hundred acres nestled in the bend of the Paluxy on the former Whitaker land. One of the earliest projects involved building a wooden stairway down the riverbank for easier access to the tracks. "People who haven't visited the dinosaur tracks down in the river in some time," the *Waco News-Tribune* reported, "will be glad to know the parks department has built some wooden stairs down the bank into the streambed. This sure beats shinnying up and down those slippery, sandy banks."[4]

By March 1972 much of the construction was well underway. Visitors did not seem to mind the inconveniences. They still came. Loyan Walker reported that since January 1972, more than 6,800 tourists had enjoyed the park and eyed the dinosaur tracks. "People come here from all over the United States to see them," he declared.[5]

Crews built forty multi-purpose campsites equipped with water, lights, tables, and fire grills. They drilled a well 270 feet deep for water. A sewage treatment plant built across the river would employ a serpentine channel through which sewage would flow continually, and the effluent could irrigate coastal Bermuda grass in the Longhorn pasture rather than flow into a creek. Workers installed playground equipment, cleared trails, and erected a park residence and a maintenance building. "The State Highway Department is constructing the park roads," the *Waco News-Tribune* informed, "including an access road connecting the park with FM 205."[6]

In 1972, with the bustle of work crews, the Paluxy Valley had not seen so much activity since the WPA men swung their hammers in Bird's quarry more than three decades earlier. Glen Rose's recognition and preservation of its scientific and ecological past received an honorable nod in, of all places, Monastir, Tunisia. There, at the meeting of the Society of American Travel Writers (SATW), members agreed to confer upon the people of Glen Rose the prestigious "Connie" Award. The organization gave the annual prize "to individuals and groups who ... made 'outstanding contributions to a quality travel environment through conservation and preservation.'"[7] This "Connie" Award was the first granted to the citizens of an entire town. They praised Glen Rose and its Dinosaur Valley as "a superior example of what can be done to save historic, beautiful or scientifically important parts of our country."[8] Jerry Flemmons, the *Fort Worth Star-Telegram* travel writer and board member of SATW, officially presented the award. Several years earlier he had asked the poignant question, "Where is the fiscal cavalry?" regarding the struggle to purchase Dinosaur Valley.[9] Now residents received one more important validation for their decades-long fight to save the dinosaur tracks.

TPWD and local authorities had desired to acquire additional land for the park, specifically the 258 acres owned by Fort Worth attorney Oliver Fannin, Jr. This property, which accessed the Blue Hole and contained a substantial stretch of the old county road, would be a valuable asset for the overall park. State negotiations with Fannin began in the fall of 1971 and stretched into 1973, because the parties could not agree on the fair market price of the real estate. To complicate matters, in early 1972 Fannin and his wife filed a plan and plat in the Somervell County Clerk's office to subdivide the land into forty-six tracts in a development called Dinosaur Park Country Estates. The presence of a residential subdivision would hamper the future expansion of the park as well as possibly prevent access to a beloved swimming hole and the excellent dinosaur tracks in the riverbed next to it.[10]

TPWD began condemnation proceedings against Fannin, and in April 1972 the Somervell County Commissioners Court voted to join the State in the lawsuit. Finally, after contracting to sell eight of the subdivided tracts, the Fannins reached a settlement and sold all of their land to TPWD in late 1973.[11]

With the purchase of the Fannin land in late 1973, the addition of Blue Hole to the park meant the inclusion of one of the region's favorite and historic swimming holes. That year had seen additional changes at Dinosaur Valley. After the death of Loyan Walker on January 7, 1973, Bob Allen became the third superintendent. Soon the park allowed overnight camping as more amenities became available, including water, electricity, a restroom with showers, a group picnic shelter, and a trailer dump station. Allen continued actively to pursue park development.[12]

Workers put in a primitive camping area, and Allen designed display exhibits. An outdoor amphitheater facilitated educational programs. The dinosaur footprints remained of primary importance for attracting visitors, and the staff performed the daily morning ritual of sweeping silt and debris off the tracks. Large flat stepping stones across the Paluxy afforded a fairly easy way for people to cross the stream while staying dry for a close-up view of the footprints. But periodic floods often washed the rocks out of place, requiring extra cleanup for park personnel.[13]

Even before the land was purchased for a park, state and local officials had voiced ambitious plans for an interpretive center. Bob Slaughter, the curator of the Shuler Museum of Paleontology at Southern Methodist University, had proposed to construct a unique museum. He suggested that crews excavate the earth to expose a new track layer as a permanent exhibit. Then workers would build a museum over the footprints, thus eliminating the threat of erosion and flooding that endangered the tracks in the riverbed.[14]

In the summer of 1974 Allen dug an experimental test pit in the broad field tucked within the bend of the river and to the south of exposed footprints in the streambed. The cavity measured fifteen by twenty feet and twenty-eight feet deep. The excavation at this site of the proposed visitor center revealed excellent dinosaur tracks but crews refilled the hole in the interest of safety.[15]

Under Allen's watch, visitation of the park continued to climb dramatically. In 1974, 112,000 people came to Dinosaur Valley. Summer weekends easily drew three thousand sightseers or more. The park also increased its size. The acquisition, though only one acre, was very significant. In 1975 the State of Texas purchased the Lanham Mill School tract from the Martin family. Historically, this site of the old school building had served as the hub of activity in the valley community. The schoolhouse itself had been purchased a decade earlier by local residents Emmett and Elsie McFall, who moved the structure to their nearby farm.[16]

Park acquisitions and changes in the early 1970s foreshadowed greater developments in the region. In the mid-1970s a series of events and decisions led to a dramatic economic resurgence for little Somervell County. Texas Utilities Company and its subsidiaries applied for building permits for Texas' first nuclear power plant in June 1973. In December 1974 the Atomic Energy Commission granted the permits for the construction of Comanche Peak Steam Electric Generating Station on Squaw Creek, approximately four-and-a-half miles north of Glen Rose. Suddenly Somervell County and sleepy Glen Rose became the focal point of intense media attention. While protest groups from the Dallas/Fort Worth Metroplex and all over the country traveled to the county to voice their

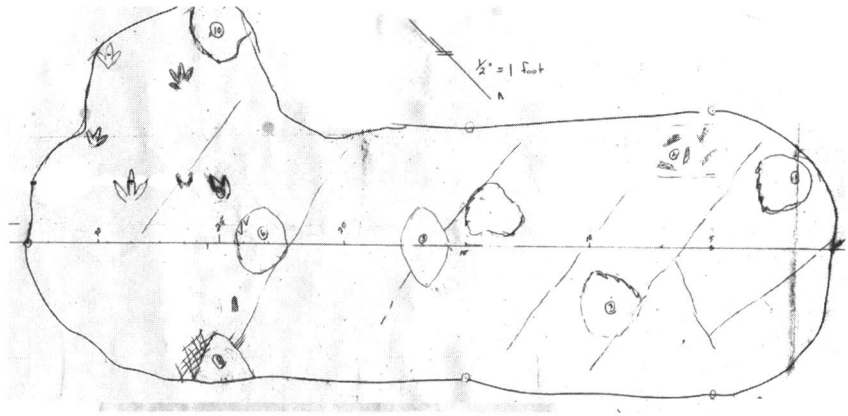

An experimental test pit, dug in the park in 1974, revealed both theropod and sauropod tracks, as shown in this photograph and accompanying sketch. Courtesy Mike O'Brien, Texas Parks and Wildlife Department

objections, most locals favored the nuclear project and hoped for a financial infusion into the area, though some had concerns about safety.[17]

Over the next several years, Somervell County saw the influx of more than four thousand workers needed for building the plant. The county's tax revenue shot up over 400 percent. Housing came at a premium. New businesses arrived, and the county added and enhanced various public programs and services with a bigger budget. The construction of a 3,275-acre lake on Squaw Creek to serve as a cooling reservoir for the plant also provided additional recreational opportunities in the county.[18]

As Somervell County celebrated its centennial in 1975, residents became aware of time's thread from the past to the future in a sensational way. When construction workers blasted through solid rock to excavate a crater for a containment building to house the plant's nuclear reactor, they made a fortunate discovery. Glen Rose resident Curtis Busch recalled the job of gathering the rubble and blowing out debris. "I had a crew down there cleaning the area so the inspectors could come down and check for cracks, and that's when I discovered the dinosaur tracks."[19]

By lucky accident, they had dug down to a rock layer, some fifty feet or more below ground level, imprinted with at least seven theropod tracks. A layer of softer blue shale had covered the fossil footprints. "That's the reason they had to go just a little bit further," Busch explained, "because that shale wasn't suitable for the engineers. We had to keep going til we found harder rock." Digging out those extra couple of feet made all the difference. Busch recognized the tri-toed traces immediately. "There's dinosaur tracks down here!" he hollered to workers above. The ancient had met the modern, and for a week, work at the site stopped as geologists and archeologists, as well as Bob Allen, studied and quarried several tracks. One of the prints went to the Somervell County Museum.[20]

The Glen Rose area coined a new slogan: "From the Dinosaur to the Atom."[21] By the late 1970s newspaper headlines mirrored this great dichotomy of a town whose claim to fame came from the very old dinosaurs and the ultra-modern nuclear plant.

"N-plant radiates new life in town," the *Dallas Morning News* announced. "From Adam to atom, town beginning to make tracks," echoed the *Fort Worth Star-Telegram*. "Here is Glen Rose, city of dinosaurs and nuclear power, one of the few vestiges of the monstrous reptiles that roamed the planet, and one of the few harbingers of a day without fossil fuels."[22]

Two new giants now rose above the rugged landscape. The 265-foot high concrete and steel containment towers were the modern landmarks on the horizon—a stark contrast to their namesake, Comanche Peak, whose silhouette had greeted Native Americans, explorers, and settlers more than a century earlier.

The first decade of Dinosaur Valley State Park's existence had seen dramatic changes both in the park and the county at large. Somervell County experienced fantastic growth with the construction of the Comanche Peak power plant and the resurgence of tourism. This growth was marked by a 49 percent increase in the county's population from 2,793 in 1970 to 4,154 in 1980.[23] The park itself had undergone a transformation from abandoned farms and overgrazed pastures to one of the most popular recreational places in the Texas State Parks System.

In the late 1970s Richard Tafoya became the fourth superintendent at Dinosaur Valley State Park. Under his direction the park continued a reforestation project that had begun in 1975. As of 1979 some nine hundred trees had survived. Part of the overall development plan, especially in the camping areas, the revegetation program added to the privacy and aesthetics of those sections.[24]

By the summer of 1980 Richard Tafoya had relocated to Alaska. During Tafoya's tenure as superintendent, a young park ranger often came to Dinosaur Valley to help. Billy Paul Baker grew up in Buffalo Gap and went to work for the TPWD in the early 1970s, serving first at Possum Kingdom and then Palo Duro Canyon. He recalled:

Then I went to Mineral Wells. Well it was ... under construction and was closed, so during the holidays I would come down and help other law enforcement officers work this park ... since my park was closed. I'd come down here and help Richard Tafoya.[25]

When Richard Tafoya decided to move to Alaska, Billy Paul, fond of the area around Glen Rose, applied for the job and became the fifth superintendent of Dinosaur Valley State Park. He moved to the park in the blistering heat of the summer of 1980 and began his long tenure there. With limited staff and budgets, the park still lacked some features. "When I came here we had two portable buildings sitting down there as headquarters," Billy Paul remembered. The future years would present both challenges and opportunities for further park development and preservation.

That same summer of 1980 a young college graduate ventured to the Paluxy Valley. Glen Kuban had studied biology at the College of Wooster in Ohio. Creationist writings had piqued his interest in the alleged giant human-like tracks in the Paluxy River.[26]

Creationist teams, eager to prove that man and dinosaurs coexisted, had continued to journey to the Paluxy in the attempt to uncover human footprint trails. Creationist filmmaker Stanley Taylor advocated the human track claims and produced and narrated a movie called *Footprints in Stone*, released in 1973, after conducting a series of Paluxy expeditions from 1968 to 1972.[27] Creationist proponents published books on the "man tracks." These included Cecil Dougherty's *Valley of the Giants* (1971) and John Morris' *Tracking Those Incredible Dinosaurs ... and the People Who Knew Them* (1980). Author Erich von Däniken even sent a cameraman to film examples of the "man tracks" in the effort to give credence to his theory of ancient astronauts. Von Däniken asserted that aliens introduced to primitive cultures on Earth the arts, technologies, and social organizations that ancient peoples took as their own myths and building blocks of civilization.[28]

Many of the most prominent examples of trails of human-like footprints were located upstream of Dinosaur Valley State Park on the Emmett McFall property. Creationists, however, had also espoused the existence of a human-like track on the rock shelf layer near the old Bird quarry site. The scientific community had long ignored the "man track" claims. Therefore, the contention of the existence of human footprints in the same rock layer as dinosaur tracks had largely gone unchallenged.[29]

Fascinated by the "man track" scenario, Kuban initially hoped to prove the authenticity of the creationist assertions. In the summer of 1980 he and a colleague, Tim Bartholomew, set out to document and photograph these prints for careful study. With local residents as guides, they combed the riverbed and

Park Superintendent Billy Paul Baker. Photo by Laurie E. Jasinski

examined various named trails and isolated examples of tracks that had vaguely human-like features.[30] Kuban wrote:

> We soon concluded ... that some of the alleged human tracks, such as those on the "State Park Shelf" were merely erosional features and random irregularities of the rock surface. When we selectively applied water to the markings, we found that we could closely replicate the features in creationist photos. However, without such enhancement none of the markings showed clear or convincing human features, and many contained features incompatible with real human prints, especially in regard to bottom contours.[31]

Further study at a number of sites revealed additional information regarding the strange elongated tracks. Bird himself had originally noted the "curious elongated heel" of the "mystery print" pointed out by Jim Ryals many years earlier.[32] After a careful examination of the photos, casts, and measurements taken of the tracks and comparison to sketches and photos of the anatomical structure of the dinosaur leg and foot, Kuban arrived at an interesting and unexpected conclusion:

> Suddenly it occurred to me that the elongate shapes of the tracks probably did not relate to an unusually-shaped foot, but more likely to an unusual locomotor behavior or way of walking. That is, I realized the elongated heel-like posteriors on these prints were best interpreted as just that–impressions of the heels and soles of the dinosaur's foot (technically the metatarsal or metapodial segments), which are normally held above the ground by bipedal dinosaurs.[33]

Kuban asserted that the elongated tracks were produced by dinosaurs that moved in a crouching or flat-footed manner. Perhaps this particular movement involved stalking prey or signified that the mud was especially goopy. He concluded:

> Such metatarsal dinosaur tracks not only appeared to explain the "best" of the creationist "man tracks," but in my view are also the most likely source of the original "giant man track" sightings by local residents decades earlier. After all, metatarsal dinosaur tracks with indistinct digits marks often look more like large human tracks than anything else the townspeople would have been familiar with at the time.[34]

Kuban made subsequent studies and trips to the Paluxy for several years. He also discovered that some of the tracks had interesting color distinctions that he hypothesized were "related to secondary sediment infillings." He wrote:

> The colorations, ranging from bluish gray to rust-brown, more precisely defined the track boundaries than did the topographic relief (indentations) alone, and occurred on some newly discovered tracks with little or no relief, and in

some cases even positive (raised) relief. On many of the tracks both the dinosaurian digit marks and the metatarsal segments were more distinctly defined by these color/texture boundaries, further confirming the metatarsal dinosaur track identification.[35]

Over the years many of the creationist groups that strongly endorsed the "man tracks" tempered their claims or refuted them altogether. One creationist, Carl Baugh, continued to promote the elongated prints as genuine human tracks. Baugh came to Somervell County from Missouri in 1982. In 1984 he purchased land near the old Murphy crossing off Farm Road 205 and established the Creation Evidence Museum. Since its founding, activities have included programs for school, religious, and community groups. The museum continued into the twenty-first century to present exhibits and carry on periodic track excavations, mainly on the McFall property, in the attempt to prove the existence of human fossilized footprints.[36]

Surprisingly, the paleontological scientific community had conducted very little analysis of the Paluxy tracks since R.T. Bird's work in 1940, though vertebrate paleontologist Wann Langston of the University of Texas had done some cursory examinations. But the 1980s saw a resurgence in the study of ichnology. This renewal reflected a renaissance of dinosaur studies in general that took place in the latter part of the twentieth century and continues in the twenty-first. This "Second Golden Age" has resulted in more dinosaur collecting and research leading to a greatly expanded knowledge of dinosaurs.[37]

Paleontologist James Farlow of Indiana University–Purdue University Fort Wayne has been a modern pioneer in the ongoing study of fossil footprints, especially those of the Cretaceous limestone in Texas and specifically the Paluxy River. He admitted that his following in the dinosaur footsteps came about in a surprising way:

I did graduate work at Yale working on dinosaurs, but I was never particularly interested in dinosaur footprints. In fact my advisor ... did everything he could to discourage me from having anything to do with footprints, 'cause he thought it was kind of a dead-end area of study. But when I got my degree and I'm [teaching at] a small college in Michigan ... a college friend of mine had married into a family in Texas. There was a flood on the family ranch in 1980 that uncovered dinosaur tracks

Paleontologist James Farlow has conducted extensive studies of fossil footprints, especially the tracks at Dinosaur Valley State Park. Photo by Laurie E. Jasinski

out there, and he knew I was interested in dinosaurs and he wanted to know if I'd like to come down and...maybe work on the footprints.... I had to take some students on a field trip that spring during spring break, [so I thought] okay we'll come down. We came down. We worked on the site. I wrote up a little article on it, and I figured ... I would write this up because of all the work Bird had done, I figured there had been an extensive study of dinosaur footprints here in Texas. So I would compare the results of what we had found with this literature that I thought had to be there and then write a paper, and then that would be it. But then I discovered there was no literature! Basically it had been ignored, except for a few minor things Wann Langston had done, ever since Bird's time. So I figured, well, okay I need to do something. So I started working on it....[38]

He began his work at Dinosaur Valley State Park in the early 1980s. He later wrote:

I knew that there were dinosaur footprints at sites across much of central Texas, but I also knew that for the number and quality of preservation of dinosaur tracks, the Paluxy River would be hard to beat. Even though I would ultimately visit tracksites all over the state, I would return again and again to Glen Rose and spend a lot of time in the river.[39]

Over the years, Farlow's field trips have also included groups of students, colleagues, and even documentary crews. He has published his studies as scientific articles and as chapters in paleontology volumes. Track investigation has given insight into a wealth of information about the animals that made them. His examinations of the footprints as compared to the skeletal structure of existing fossils have helped identify the most likely track candidates: the three-toed *Acrocanthosaurus* and the sauropod now called *Paluxysaurus*. Farlow and colleagues designated the Texas sauropod tracks as *Brontopodus birdi*—combining *Brontopodus*, a name originally conceived by R.T. Bird, with birdi, a tribute to Bird. Wann Langston designated the theropod prints as *Irenesauripus glenrosensis*, a combination of two previously-used scientific names.[40]

Track studies provide clues to the animals' size, locomotion, gait, and, to a limited degree, speed. "You can certainly tell the gait, and you make some rough estimates of how fast the animal is going, but whether these are completely accurate speed estimates, it's hard to say," Farlow assessed.[41] Measurements of the pace ("the distance from a track made by one foot to the next print made by the opposite foot") and the stride ("the distance between two successive tracks made by the same foot") also offer clues regarding the speed of the dinosaur.[42]

Unfortunately, the Paluxy tracks cannot positively tell the precise sequence of events that happened on that "day" in the ancient past. The menacing theropod trails that shadow the sauropod prints suggested an impending carnivorous attack upon the lumbering sauropod to R.T. Bird. Farlow wrote:

This is a spectacular scenario—a carnosaur pack harassing a sauropod herd—and I would love for it to be true. Unfortunately, there is little to back it up other than the fact that some theropod trails are associated with and head the same direction as the sauropod trackways, and were made after the latter. Bird's grand interpretation is not impossible, but it is equally plausible, given their mirror-image directional pattern ... that the various theropod trails were made independently of each other.[43]

Whether or not an attack did happen does not diminish the significance and impressiveness of the tracks themselves:

An unusually dry summer on the Paluxy exposed this excellent trackway marching through the streambed. The scene, photographed in Dinosaur Valley between Blue Hole and the Main Track Site in August 1978, perfectly illustrates the stony footprints as "moving pictures" in time. Photo by Novella Wilson

The best footprints here I would put up in quality with nearly anywhere in the world—particularly the sauropod footprints here.... Sauropod footprints in most places in the world are just awful, just these oblong big bathtub impressions mostly.... But particularly Glen Rose—the preservation on some of the sauropod tracks there is just exquisite.... Theropod too.[44]

Farlow's studies on the Paluxy have been both rewarding and enlightening. The fieldwork has evoked fascination, curiosity, and questions from onlookers as well. Sometimes comments illustrate that old preconceptions, and perhaps old memories, die hard!

One day Jim Farlow and Billy Paul Baker cleared away gravel that had covered the trackway of a small sauropod after one of the Paluxy's typical rises:

Billy and I hauled out rocks and shoveled gravel for hour after backbreaking hour, putting on an impressive display of manual labor for park visitors while we became soaked with sweat and river water. Finally the tracks were once again uncovered. A gentleman who'd sat and smoked while watching the last half hour of our efforts bestirred himself to take a look at what we'd dug up. "You boys carve those things?" he asked.[45]

Perhaps R.T. Bird himself heard such a question while he slogged away at his Paluxy quarry. He might have delighted in the thought that new fieldwork still ignited spellbound attention and lively debates. Roland T. Bird had passed away on January 24, 1978. Laid to rest in Grahamsville, New York, surrounded by the

A toddler plays in a sauropod track in a scene that is reminiscent of little Tommy Pendley almost forty years earlier. Photo by Novella Wilson

beloved Catskills of his youth, Bird's headstone contained a fitting epitaph bestowing a much deserved title: "Discoverer of Sauropod Dinosaur Footprints."[46]

He could be proud that his pioneering track work on the Paluxy had inspired a new generation of paleontologists in this new golden age, resulting in "unprecedented attention to dinosaur tracks and trackways, with a new appreciation of such fossils as keys to dinosaurian locomotion and other behavior traits."[47] Of the resurgence in the study of vertebrate ichnology of the 1980s, paleontologist Martin Lockley later wrote, "The renaissance in fossil-footprint research during the past ten years has made these 'moving pictures' of dinosaurs a mainstay of paleontology."[48]

Dinosaur track research officially came into its own with the First International Symposium on Dinosaur Tracks and Traces held in Albuquerque, New Mexico, in 1986. James Farlow took part in the two-day event, which brought track enthusiasts from all over the world. A number of presentations detailed studies of the tracks of Dinosaur Valley State Park and other sites on the Paluxy. Glen Kuban presented his work involving the elongated dinosaur footprints and the color distinctions of some of the tracks in the Glen Rose area. University of Texas paleontologist Wann Langston participated in sessions about the Lower Cretaceous Texas dinosaur prints. David Riskind and wife Peggy Maceo of the Texas Parks and Wildlife Department presented a seminar on the latest methods in the moldmaking and casting of dinosaur tracks. The successful symposium surveyed both a historic overview of track work as well as the latest discoveries and research and helped establish guidelines for fieldwork, track preservation, data synthesis, and interpretation with the meeting of the world's track researchers.[49]

The event also resulted in the publication of a compilation of the papers presented. This volume, called *Dinosaur Tracks and Traces,* rightly pronounced:

The science of vertebrate paleoichnology is emerging from the shadows of vertebrate paleontology after over a century of obscurity. It has long been a neglected field outside the mainstream of traditional paleontology and unappreci-

The park headquarters greets visitors with this sauropod image set in stone.
Photo by Gary S. Hickinbotham

ated as a legitimate branch of ichnology and sedimentology. The unprecedented resurgence of research in dinosaur ichnology, as a specialty within the broader discipline of vertebrate ichnology, has been stimulated by numerous new discoveries of dinosaur eggs and tracksites. These in turn have led to provocative interpretations related to dinosaur behavior and dinosaur ecology.[50]

The "Images of Dinosaurs" exhibit features a spectacular mural by Texas Parks and Wildlife Department artist Nola Montgomery that depicts a carnosaur attack of a sauropod on the ancient coastal plains of North Central Texas. Painting by Nola Montgomery, Courtesy Texas Parks and Wildlife Department

In the mid-1980s Dinosaur Valley State Park was also coming into its own with new developments and informative displays. The staff finally moved into a new park headquarters building. During 1986 and 1987 a two-year $30,000 improvement program focused on enhancing the park's educational and interpretive profile for visitors. Installing an exhibit in one wing of the headquarters was a major project. Display planners and writers John Williams and Georg Zappler worked with a team of designers, artists, craftsmen, and others to produce an informative expo titled "Images of Dinosaurs." Paleontologists Wann Langston and James Farlow were special consultants to the project.[51]

Artistic renderings of Texas dinosaurs and their ancient environment graced painted wall panels. A spectacular twenty-foot-by-sixteen-foot mural by Texas Parks and Wildlife artist Nola Montgomery invited viewers to practically walk into the past and witness a scene imagined by R.T. Bird as a possible scenario—a hungry carnosaur, with bared teeth and menacing claws, lunging into a fleeing sauropod. Photographs and geologic and geographic maps offered historic perspectives and site documentation, and an animated film tied the information together.[52]

In the center of the exhibit room sat the showpiece, a seventeen-foot replica of part of the trackway Bird quarried for the American Museum of Natural History. Its magnificent prints strike awe into children and adults alike who want to follow in the footsteps of dinosaurs. Outside the headquarters, another section of replica trackway was installed by exhibit sculptor Peggy Maceo and other technicians for the benefit of visitors.[53]

The park headquarters building itself boldly celebrates the valley's namesake. The exterior stonework has inlaid a thunderous sauropod, visible as drivers approach the building. Another reptilian reminder, a large, colorful, and intricate dinosaur mosaic, greets visitors at the entrance. The mosaic originally hung in the lobby of Sinclair company offices in Dallas. When offered the artwork, *Glen Rose Reporter* editor Dan McCarty accepted the piece and eventually suggested that the mosaic would be appropriate for the headquarters of Dinosaur Valley State Park.[54]

Ironically, at the same time the dinosaur tracks of the Paluxy received extraordinary scientific recognition and study, a proposal placed them in serious jeopardy. In 1982 the cities of Granbury, Stephenville, and Glen Rose and the counties of Hood and Somervell applied to the Texas Water Commission to receive a "permit to construct a dam and reservoir on the Paluxy River."[55] Granbury and Hood County withdrew from the process, but Stephenville, Glen Rose, and Somervell County pressed on and filed for an amended application in 1985. Reservoir proponents cited the area's need for an aboveground water supply. A dam built less than two miles upstream of Dinosaur Valley State Park would impound a 3,800-acre lake.[56]

The Paluxy was a primitive stream, one of the few rivers in the state unfettered by any impoundment. For landowners, family farms in the upper region of the historic Lanham Mill community along with the village of Paluxy would disappear forever under a six-mile-long lake. For Dinosaur Valley State Park, the release of water downstream from the dam would seriously reduce the river flow.[57]

Billy Paul Baker remembered the alarming prospect of a reservoir constructed on the doorstep of Dinosaur Valley:

Hydromorphology. Anytime somebody does something on a stream … it affects the downstream flow, because it will change the hydrology. It'll change the flow. It'll change the stream's ability … up and down flushing action. It'll change a lot of things.[58]

Even worse was the applicants' plans to limit downstream river flow to 2 cubic feet per second (cfs). This is in comparison to a 38-year average discharge of 63.1 cfs.[59] "I didn't know what 2 cfs was, but it didn't sound like much," Billy Paul commented, "and we had an average flow of about 16 to 24 [cfs] at that time it was in a drought situation…. It would be a trickle." Lower water levels would expose more tracks to the elements and accelerate the erosion process, especially in wintertime. Frost was a real killer. Trapped water that froze in the tracks easily caused the fracture of the footprints.[60]

In this case, landowners joined forces with the Texas Parks and Wildlife Department to contest the proposed Paluxy Reservoir before a hearing of the Texas Water Commission. As a TPWD representative, Baker faced the challenging task of presenting testimony on the effects of the proposed dam in an intimidating, high-stakes environment for all parties in 1986.[61]

"You have five or six high-paid water rights lawyers.... By the time you get through, you walk out and know you don't know anything. Kind of staggering!"[62]

But Billy Paul's testimony, along with the information of park planner John Williams, conservation biologist David Riskind, and track expert James Farlow, outlined before the Commission a series of compelling reasons against the dam and reservoir.[63]

The Paluxy River was the lifeblood of Dinosaur Valley State Park. Since opening, the park had received 2,088,327 visitors, and its very existence attested to the determination of many people to preserve and enjoy the dinosaur tracks. And though the periodic rises and falls of the river resulted in the erosion of some of the stony prints, the Paluxy's scouring action was the best method to clean the riverbed and reveal new trackways. Water covering the tracks offered the best natural protection for them.[64]

Baker laid out for the commissioners how restricted streamflow would be a detriment for the fossil footprints:

The construction and operation of the proposed project, in my opinion, would result in direct adverse impact to the paleontological resources downstream of the dam site. Most tracks would become exposed and start to deteriorate rapidly. All data I have seen does not address this to any great extent. I know that at a reduced flow tracks will be exposed. When these tracks become exposed they tend to deteriorate.

In the 5-1/2 years at Dinosaur Valley State Park I have observed what exposure to the elements can do to the tracks. I have observed the effects of people, water, and temperature on the tracks. Park visitors do harm them sometime, river rises expose more tracks and cover others, but the biggest and worst threat I have noticed is when the water drops below the tracks. A track exposed after being inundated for long periods of time will soon be obliterated by the freezing temperatures upon them. This would happen if a reduced flow is allowed in the river. When the spalling begins there is very little that can be done to save the tracks.

Flooding of these trackways is a plus as I see it....[65]

He then made a case for the river itself:

The river is the main attraction in the park. It is one of very few rivers in the State that does not have an impoundment on it. The flow of a natural river compared to an impoundment flow is different in that there is not the scouring effect of periodic flushing from floods in an impoundment stream. The encroachment of plant life and increased organic matter and sedimentation in the water holes reduces the public ability to enjoy the river. Encroachment of terrestrial vegetation creates a problem for the public by limiting the access to the river. Reduced flow will alter the habitat of fish and species that inhabit the numerous pools in the park. With reduced flow, such as has been indicated, there will not be sufficient water to fill even the holes near the dam.... This would in all probability not even reach the park due to evaporation on the rocks during the summer months leaving stagnating pools for the public to deal with.

Reduced flow deteriorates the water quality in the park. Increased algae growth, sedimentation, and potential for water born diseases such as amebic meningoencephalitis creates a public health hazard. The public would not be able to utilize the river by wading, swimming or other activities associated with a free flowing stream.

The park staff's workload would increase due to the build up of debris and plant matter in the river.

The Blue Hole, a favorite swimming area in the park, has been used by the people since this area has been populated. It would be severely impacted by the proposed dam. This water hole is full year round and is approximately 20 feet deep. It requires a periodic rise in the river to flush sedimentation and debris from it. The way the river makes a bend at this point assists in removing sedimentary build up. If there is no flooding this landmark will soon be full of sediments and debris.[66]

Numerous trees along the river bank were also at risk. Hardwoods such as pecan and bur oak could suffer decreased growth and reproduction. Reduction in flow could negatively impact the wildlife in the area, including the endangered Black-capped Vireo and Golden-cheeked Warbler. Also of great concern were the potential significant archeological and paleontological sites that would be lost in the inundation.[67]

TPWD requested at least a minimum flow of 8 cfs during the cold weather months in the event the reservoir project was approved. The Hearing Examiner recommended permit approval, allowing dam applicants the right to divert a maximum of 10,630 acre-feet per year instead of their requested diversion of 17,600 af/year. At this point no parties were happy with the decisions. Lake proponents also asserted that, with the reduced diversion amount, a lake project would not be feasible. Both the applicants and contestants filed exceptions to the Hearing Examiner's proposal. Upon consideration of the filed exceptions, Texas Water Commissioners Ralph Roming and Paul Hopkins adopted most of the examiner's proposal but voted for an amended diversion of 12,950 af/year. Both parties then filed motions for rehearings.[68]

In June 1987 the Texas Water Commission informed both sides that it would consider hearing dam supporters' request for an increase in diverted water, but it would not consider most of the issues associated with the motion of the lake opponents. June 23, 1987, was a dark day for Paluxy Valley landowners and the park. Texas Water Commissioners Roming and Hopkins reversed their earlier decision regarding the amount of diverted water and instructed granting a permit to the Paluxy Reservoir applicants. At this point it looked like the reservoir backers had won.[69]

TPWD and the landowners who saw their life's work threatened would not back down. Thus, the unique circumstances came together whereby one state agency filed suit against the other.[70] The case took a corrupt turn that ultimately worked in the park's favor. The plaintiffs alleged that the Somervell County Judge, one of the lake's most vocal supporters, and Frank Booth, the attorney for the lake proponents, promised political favors to Texas Water Commissioner Roming in exchange for securing a positive vote for the applicants. Roming was seeking reappointment to the Commission.[71]

Parks and Wildlife and the landowners also stated that the Commissioners Hopkins and Roming had violated the Open Meetings Act by making their decision prior to a rehearing. Legal wrangling over the matter stretched into the 1990s. On January 30, 1995, Judge Paul R. Davis in the District Court of Travis County ruled that attorney Booth and his clients had acted unethically, to the point of bribery, and that the Texas Water Commission in deciding the rehearing in private had indeed violated the Open Meetings Act.[72] Davis ordered that the entire reservoir project and application process would have to start over and wrote, "The taint on the decision-making process in this case so permeates the final [Commission] order that the final decision simply cannot stand...."[73]

In this case, dirty politics did not stand. In July 1996 the Third District Court of Appeals upheld this decision and rejected the appeal of the reservoir supporters. Given that the Hearing Examiner's original proposal to divert only 10,630 af/year of water did not make the reservoir project feasible and the Commissioners' initial amendment of his recommendation to allow 12,950 af/year did not make the project feasible, this final decision in effect killed the project.[74]

In retrospect of the long battle Billy Paul Baker said, "They lost. One state agency sued another state agency and won." The Paluxy would remain a free river and subject the valley to the whims of Mother Nature as it had done through history.

CHAPTER TEN

Maintaining the Dinosaur Highway

"Dinosaur hunters" young and old make tracks to the Paluxy riverbed to spy traces of the ancients. They follow in the footsteps of several generations that have traipsed along Somervell County's streambeds to see for themselves a piece of the region's past set in stone. Floods and drouths, farmers, nuclear reactors, treasure seekers and magnetic healers, and scientific studies and debates have all called attention to the story of this place. Dinosaur Valley State Park's layers of history embody the quintessential life of the area from the very old to the modern, and the park has continued to face both rewards and challenges into the twenty-first century.

The Sinclair dinosaur models watch over the park to the delight of visitors. Photo by Gary S. Hickinbotham

In September 2003 the Texas Parks and Wildlife Department purchased property from Helen Lee Kerr Shults, whose father John Kerr had bought the land in 1961. These 62.6 acres, part of the old Daniel place and not far from Tiddle Town, gave the park additional river frontage. Much of the acreage had been used as pasture for grazing, and two small frame houses stood on the property.[1]

As of 2008, Dinosaur Valley State Park contained a total of 1,588 acres. With close to two hundred thousand visitors each year, it ranked among the top ten of the most-visited parks in the Texas State Parks System and employed approximately nine full-time staff (including several park rangers) and five seasonal workers.[2]

Campers and picnickers can partake of the park's amenities—forty-six water and electrical sites and forty picnic sites—as well as experience primitive

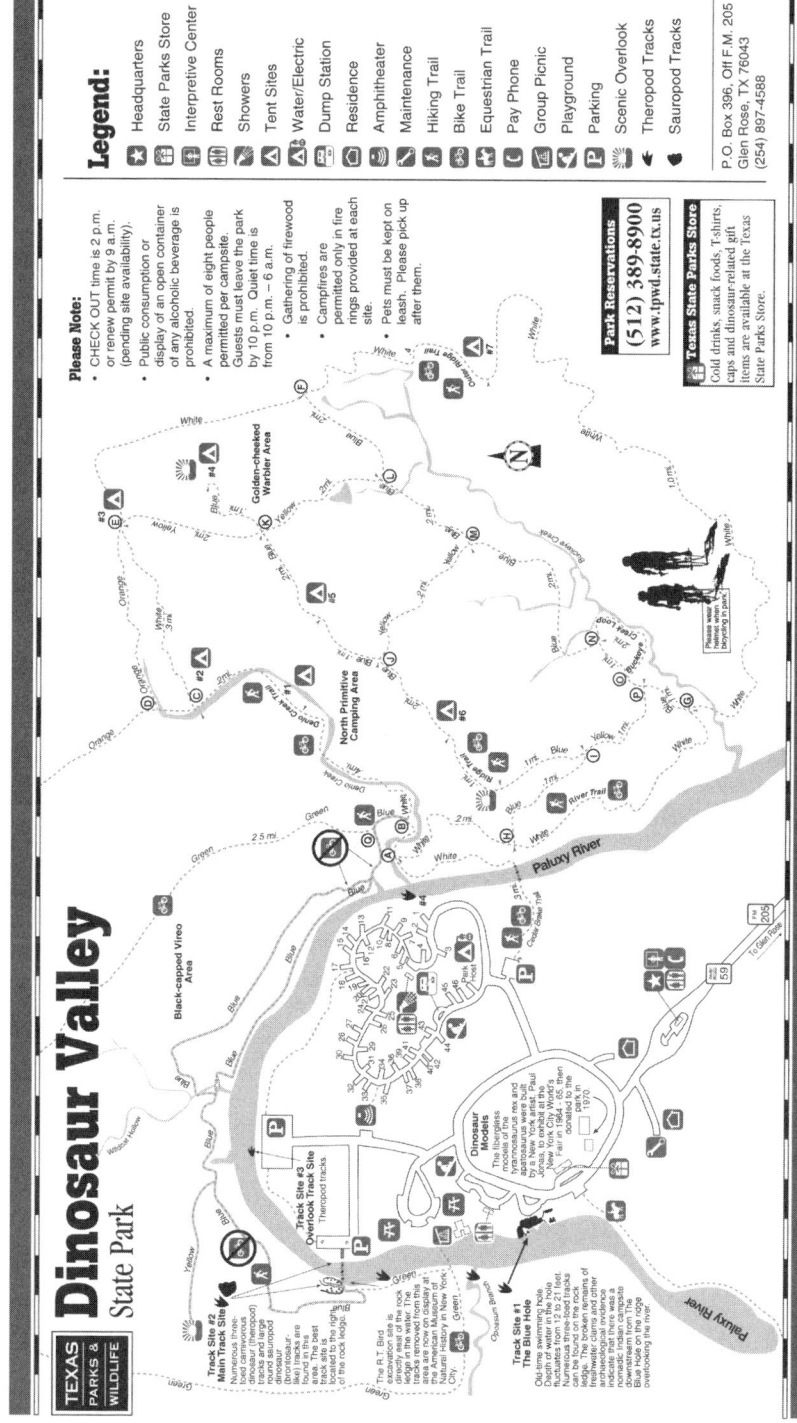

Dinosaur Valley
State Park

TEXAS PARKS & WILDLIFE

Legend:

- Headquarters
- State Parks Store
- Interpretive Center
- Rest Rooms
- Showers
- Tent Sites
- Water/Electric
- Dump Station
- Residence
- Amphitheater
- Maintenance
- Hiking Trail
- Bike Trail
- Equestrian Trail
- Pay Phone
- Group Picnic
- Playground
- Parking
- Scenic Overlook
- Theropod Tracks
- Sauropod Tracks

P.O. Box 396, Off F.M. 205
Glen Rose, TX 76043
(254) 897-4588

Please Note:

- CHECK OUT time is 2 p.m. or renew permit by 9 a.m. (pending site availability).
- Public consumption or display of an open container of any alcoholic beverage is prohibited.
- A maximum of eight people permitted per campsite. Guests must leave the park by 10 p.m. Quiet time is from 10 p.m. – 6 a.m.
- Gathering of firewood is prohibited.
- Campfires are permitted only in fire rings provided at each site.
- Pets must be kept on leash. Please pick up after them.

Park Reservations
(512) 389-8900
www.tpwd.state.tx.us

Texas State Parks Store
Cold drinks, snack foods, T-shirts, caps and dinosaur-related gift items are available at the Texas State Parks Store.

Golden-cheeked Warbler Area

North Primitive Camping Area

Black-capped Vireo Area

Paluxy River

Dinosaur Models
The fiberglass models of the Tyrannosaurus rex and apatosaurus were built by a New York artist, Paul Jonas, for exhibit at the New York City World's Fair in 1964 – 65, then donated to the park in 1970.

Track Site #2 Main Track Site
Numerous three-toed carnivorous dinosaur (theropod) tracks and large round sauropod (brontosaur-like) tracks are found in this area. The best track site is located to the right in the rock ledge.

Track Site #3 Overlook Track Site
Theropod tracks

The R.T. Bird excavation site is directly east of the rock ledge in the water. The tracks removed from this area are now on display at the American Museum of Natural History in New York City.

Track Site #1 The Blue Hole
Old-time swimming hole. Depth of water in the hole fluctuates from 12 to 21 feet. Numerous three-toed tracks can be found on the rock ledge. The broken remains of a threshold/weir dam and other archaeological evidence indicate that there was a nomadic Indian campsite downstream from The Blue Hole on the ridge overlooking the river.

Please wear helmet when bicycling in park.

Paluxy River

To Glen Rose

camping. Horseback riders enjoy some one hundred acres set aside as an equestrian area. Dinosaur enthusiasts can find all manner of souvenirs and educational materials in the park store, located at the site of the original headquarters buildings.[3]

Nearby, fascinated children and delighted adults stand in the shadow of Rex and Bronto, the two Sinclair dinosaur models. These reptilian sentinels have stood watch over the valley since before the park's dedication. Bronto, however, has not talked since Lester Galbreath left! He did undergo a transformation though. In the mid-1980s sculptor John Fishner reworked the head of the sauropod. It seemed that all of those years the precise features of the snake-like head were inaccurate. However, the new head was not built to scale: the mighty Bronto became pinheaded! Conventional taste won out, and visitors in 1995 welcomed back the technically-incorrect but aesthetically-pleasing old brontosaur head. Periodically, personnel spruce up the models with fresh coats of paint and other maintenance.[4]

Beyond the imposing dino figures, the park's thirteen miles of trails beckon sightseers to explore winding paths through the cedar brakes across the Paluxy. These trails meander past several creeks, including Buckeye Creek, Denio Branch, Wildcat Hollow, and Opossum Branch, and cross the historic land of the Martins, Abells, and Rowlands. Scenic overlooks along the way afford hikers expansive views of the rugged valley of this Northern Hill Country. The implementation of a new quarter-mile nature trail with wayside exhibits along the Paluxy in 2007 enhanced ecological educational opportunities for visitors. The park employs a color system of blazes on trees to identify the different loops and trails in the effort to locate or direct lost hikers. A hike and bike trail through the Longhorn pastures makes use of the country byways left over from the past. For years the Longhorn herd was an added attraction and served as a celebration of Texas' cowboy heritage. Due to limited staff and the daily attention required to care for the herd, however, the Longhorns were moved out of Dinosaur Valley State Park and returned to the state herd at Fort Griffin around 1999.[5]

The park is home to abundant wildlife common to North Central Texas. Deer, bobcats, coyotes, and ringtails roam through the wooded country, as do turkey, quail, beaver, and other small animals such as raccoons and opossums. One creature common to some other state parks has not been seen in Dinosaur Valley—the feral pig. "I think I've always said that the people around Glen Rose are too hungry!" Billy Paul grinned. Some campers have reported mountain lion sightings, but rangers have not confirmed this.

Birds both common and endangered make their nests in the hardwoods and scrub cedar in the valley. Watchers can spy a wide variety of sparrows, the Yellow-billed Cuckoo, Summer Tanager, and Painted Bunting along the Paluxy. The cedar woodlands along Denio Branch provide good habitat for the rare Golden-cheeked Warbler, and tourists tromping the trail that skirts the ridge might glimpse the Black-capped Vireo.[6]

Hikers should take care against the Western Diamondback rattlesnake, however. The reptiles sometimes hide under the rocky ledges of the limestone terrain. Years and years ago the farmers of the valley were overwhelmed by the large population of rattlers. Locals knew of a huge rattlesnake den located high on a rock bluff over the Paluxy within the boundaries of the present park. Novella Wilson remembered this site called Rattlesnake Hollow:

There was a county agent here who decided to help the farmers eliminate some of the rattlesnakes, and they would come and get out there and chunk up the holes with concrete or mud. I guess it was mud instead of concrete, to where the gas would stay in there. You'd pump gas in through that and kill the rattlesnakes. And it really did help, because we used to have a lot of rattlesnakes.[7]

From time to time folks have also seen a few cottonmouth moccasins along the creek as well.

Dinosaur Valley's crystal river, cedar hills, and grassy savannas give nature lovers a bounty of scenic beauty. Stately hardwoods, including bur oak, pecan, live oak, post oak, elm, walnut, and cottonwood, provide shade for picnickers and along trails. Open fields contain different prairie grasses such as Little Bluestem, Big Bluestem, Indiangrass, Sideoats grama, and Switchgrass, calling to mind the land's historic past. The large field (the site of the test excavation in 1974), nestled between the roads that lead to Track Sites #2 and #3, contains native grasses. Park personnel now leave it alone. Springtime finds Dinosaur Valley covered by glorious blankets of bluebonnets.[8]

Visitors frolic along the stepping stones to the Main Track Site. Though the dinosaur tracks offer the initial draw to the park, the cool, clear Paluxy River typically entices people to return again and again. Photo by Laurie E. Jasinski

The green river, lifeblood of the valley, is the connecting thread for the park. Its exposed secrets spellbind new generations, while its waters offer themselves for recreation. Visitors wade the shallow Paluxy in search of dinosaur tracks or tiptoe across the rocks near the old Bird quarry site to view the sauropod and theropod prints. An overlook (Track Site #3) allows people to peer down into the riverbed to see the tracks. "A vast majority of people come to see the dinosaur tracks and end up coming back because of the river," Billy Paul commented. The Paluxy provides the opportunity for fishermen to spend a long lazy afternoon on its banks. A good day might result in catches of catfish and perch. Blue Hole still refreshes swimmers on hot summer days.[9]

Educational events are popular at the park. Billy Paul noted:

We get lots of school groups ... busload after busload. We get lots of folks—colleges and universities on their field trips. Teachers' groups, we're on [the] science agenda for ... science teachers that get ... together and go on their field trips.

The park interpreter often presents Friday and Saturday night programs to groups of a hundred or more. The tracks, of course, draw visitors from all over the world. But with a small staff, the duties of maintaining park facilities, watching over visitors and providing law enforcement, offering public outreach programs, and stewarding the tracks present daily challenges in funding, prioritizing, and patience.[10]

Billy Paul Baker explains the significance of the tracks. Often routine inspections and cleaning of the prints lead to impromptu programs to interested onlookers. Photo by Laurie E. Jasinski

"We go give walk-throughs on the tracks as much as we can. You melt down out there after a while. We all work together to do what we can," Billy Paul explained. The Paluxy is no less temperamental than in historic times. Sudden rises still plague the valley and raise concern both for the tracks and for the safety of swimmers and waders who seek them. Even minor flooding often tumbles the rocks carefully positioned for visitors to cross the river. Then the wet and backbreaking work to put the boulders back in place begins.[11]

Sometimes the daily care of the dinosaur tracks presents its own educational opportunities. "Lot of it's when we're cleaning up the tracks. That's the perfect program. People sitting there watching you do it, and you get people to volunteer to help us clean out." Children seem thrilled to sweep out sand, leaves, and silt to uncover where the ancients trod. Different local groups, such as the Boy Scouts, have participated in cleaning and maintaining some of the park attractions like the trails and tracks.[12]

The dinosaur footprints continue to be the hallmark of Dinosaur Valley State Park. Throughout the 1990s and into the twenty-first century, they have inspired ongoing research and attracted worldwide attention. Popular and scientific magazine articles inform new audiences. The trackways have earned mention in paleontological volumes, and noteworthy publications have helped to tell the Paluxy story and its ancient past.[13] In Roland T. Bird's own memoir, *Bones For Barnum Brown: Adventures of a Dinosaur Hunter* (TCU Press, 1985), Bird devoted considerable chapters to his historic work on the Paluxy. James Farlow wrote *The Dinosaurs of Dinosaur Valley State Park* (Texas Parks and Wildlife Department, 1993) and carefully explained the ancient landscape of North Central Texas, the science behind the tracks, and the creatures that made them. Paleontologist Louis Jacobs, then director of SMU's Shuler Museum of Paleontology, wrote *Lone Star Dinosaurs* (Texas A&M University Press, 1995) which presented a detailed overview of the ancient reptiles that roamed the Lone Star State and its dynamic prehistoric environment.

Though the dinosaurs certainly left their calling cards in the form of tracks imprinted in the Cretaceous limestone of Texas, people are often puzzled as to why scientists have discovered so few fossil bones. Several explanations make this point understandable. Since the animal likely had many years and many miles to make tracks, given the right geological conditions, the possibility of finding the dinosaur's trackways is statistically much greater than finding the dinosaur's bones. Also, the ancient landscape itself played a major role. North Central Texas was a vast coastal plain, including shoreline and inland areas. The shoreline was probably not a typical habitat but rather served as a migratory region. In this open environment, fossils would be more widely dispersed.[14]

Limestone areas are less conducive to containing caches of fossil bones of dinosaurs than other regions, such as sandstones and shales. James Diffily, who spent thirty-five years working for the Fort Worth Museum of Science and History and served as Vice President and Curator of Collections from 2003 until his retirement in 2007, explained the "layer cake" geology of North Central Texas:

The Paluxy River is still notorious for its sudden rises, as demonstrated in July 2004. Often park personnel must move stepping stones or replace them after flooding. **TOP** Photo by Laurie E. Jasinski **BOTTOM** Photo by Gary S. Hickinbotham

The geology of the Prairies and Cross Timbers region of Texas consists of layers of sandstone, shale, and limestone. Dinosaurs were land animals, and their remains are found in river valley, delta, and lagoon deposits dominated by sandstones and shales. Only rarely did their carcasses make it out to an open marine environment.[15]

Those bones, of primarily marine animals, that are found in the hard limestone are very difficult to excavate. Fossilized remains of dinosaurs have been discovered and excavated from sandstones and shales in North Central Texas and contribute stronger evidence of the kinds of dinosaurs that roamed present Somervell County. In 1992 Louis Jacobs helped direct the excavation of perhaps the most complete *Acrocanthosaurus* skeleton ever discovered up to that time. The rare find took place on a ranch in Parker County near Fort Worth and north of Somervell County.[16]

Closer to home in Hood County, within ten miles of Dinosaur Valley State Park, a team of scientists unearthed a giant sauropod, remnants of several of the beasts in fact. In 1993 the Fort Worth Museum of Science and History and Southern Methodist University began excavation at the Jones Ranch site. The sauropod bones have fueled the excitement of scientists and dinosaur enthusiasts who have long sought skeletal evidence in the region. In fact, the discovery has provided sufficient fossil materials for the Texas sauropod to earn its own name different from the long-used designation of *Pleurocoelus*.[17]

For years the name *Pleurocoelus*, coined in the late 1800s from fossil materials found in Maryland, had been applied to the scant sauropod fossils found in Texas—until the bone discoveries at the Jones Ranch. In 2007 Peter Rose, formerly a graduate student at Southern Methodist University, proposed the new name of *Paluxysaurus jonesi* for the Texas sauropod in an article published in *Palaeontologia Electronica*, an online journal. The designation honors the Paluxy River and the Hood County town of Paluxy and William R. Jones, owner of the Jones Ranch where the bones were found. Both *Acrocanthosaurus* and *Paluxysaurus* skeletons are housed in the Fort Worth Museum of Science and History.[18]

Given the large stature of the sauropod and its legacy in the Lone Star State, it is only fitting that Texas honored this thundering giant. In 1997, with the signing of Concurrent Resolution #57, the Texas Legislature named *Pleurocoelus* as the official state dinosaur, reflecting the commonly-accepted name at that time. As of 2008, paleontologists expected a future legislature to amend the resolution and bestow the state dinosaur title on *Paluxysaurus*.[19]

Dinosaur Valley State Park has continued to garner international attention. The park has served as a model for a proposed footprint park in Korea. Media and personnel journey to the Paluxy to photograph its excellent dinosaur tracks,

For more than three decades this Sinclair promotional Bronto has greeted visitors at Oakdale Park in Glen Rose. Photo by Gary S. Hickinbotham

and film crews have come from as far away as Japan to see the prints. In 1999 the Discovery Channel produced a program called *Dinosaur Attack!* that featured Dinosaur Valley State Park prominently. "They did an hour-long program on trackways," Billy Paul recalled. Also in the wake of the Hollywood *Jurassic Park* blockbuster movies, the public has once again gone dinosaur crazy. "A lot of series came out about dinosaurs, and we're mentioned in quite a few of those."[20] As recently as August 2004, James Farlow accompanied a British Broadcasting Corporation documentary crew to film the theropod prints for a television special.[21]

Glen Rose celebrates its dinosaur heritage in shops and businesses. Novella Wilson's postcards honor the town's claim to fame–the sauropod tracks and the mild giant that made them. Art by Novella Wilson

Somervell County and the town of Glen Rose still benefit from the forward-thinking citizens and landowners who fought for the tracks. The Texas village celebrates its dinosaur heritage. Everywhere, in offices, motels, restaurants, and gift shops, dinosaur emblems appear. The Somervell County Museum has its own artifacts as well as many souvenirs honoring the ancient creatures. A special holding is the replica of the *Tyrannosaurus* jaw, meticulously built by R.T. Bird himself in 1975. As one of his final projects, it was a thoughtful and fitting tribute to his life and a gift to the little town he grew to love.[22]

Near the bandstand on the courthouse square rests the superb theropod track encased in petrified wood. For all these decades, the track has symbolized

1985   2000   2006

This series of images taken of the Roland Bird quarry site (Main Track Site) in the park shows the startling rate of erosion of some of the dinosaur prints. Several large tracks are clearly visible in 1985 (paleontologist James Farlow stands in the background). By 2000 and 2006 some of those tracks had washed away.
Courtesy Mike O'Brien, Texas Parks and Wildlife Department

the ancient heritage of the area, an area that in the early twenty-first century is growing at unprecedented rates. The 2000 census reported a population of 6,809 for Somervell County. Glen Rose had 2,122 residents. Many worked at the Comanche Peak plant or commuted to Fort Worth. As the old generations passed away, often their children divided or sold the family farms and ranches. Retirees and investors from the Metroplex bought land in and around the Paluxy Valley to build dream homes and weekend getaways.[23]

With the continuous action of the Paluxy River and the heavy visitation of the park, track documentation and preservation have received greater priority. Inevitably over time, some of the tracks will erode away. Comparison of past and current photographs has already proven this point. Mapping the tracks on the Paluxy and its tributaries remains a major ongoing project. Mike O'Brien, an exhibit sculptor and track enthusiast at the TPWD headquarters in Austin, has contributed considerable time, energy, and equipment to this project. Even before he worked for the department full-time, he assisted Peggy Maceo in putting together the replica trackway outside the Dinosaur Valley State Park headquarters. Since coming to work for TPWD as an exhibit sculptor in 1990, he has labored on the dinosaur tracks mapping project.[24]

A digitized resource map depicting all of the trackways, their specific locations, and characteristics would be an invaluable asset to the park, allowing for greater scientific analysis as well as assessment of the rate of track erosion. O'Brien has accumulated a remarkable collection of historical notes, maps, and photographs, including a copy of R.T. Bird's track chart. He has worked with Glen

DINOSAUR VALLEY STATE PARK
MAIN TRACK SITE
(Track Site #2)

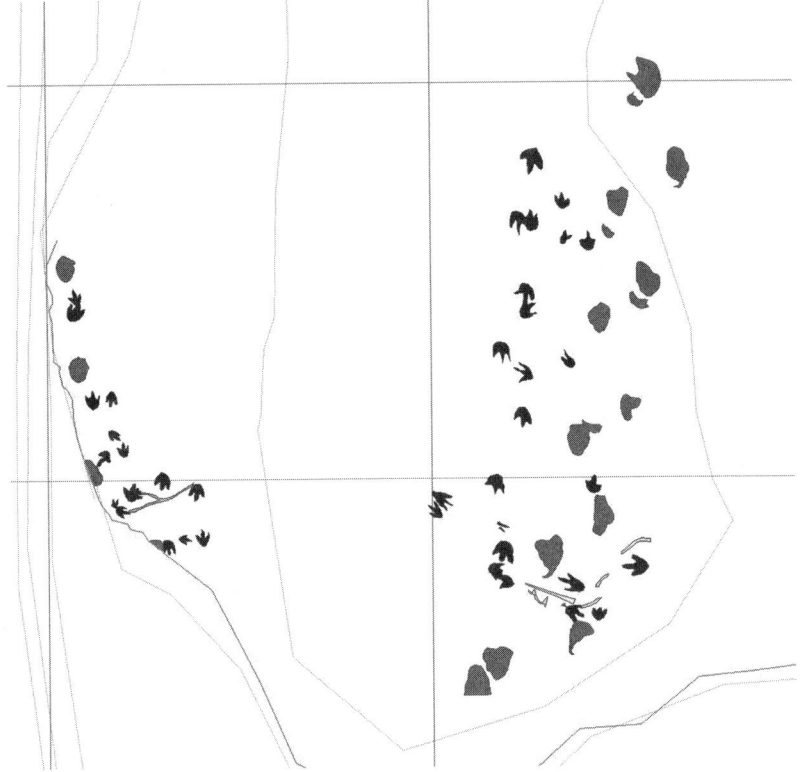

Theropod tracks appear in black and sauropod tracks are shaded gray. (10-meter-cell grid)
Courtesy Mike O'Brien, Texas Parks and Wildlife Department

Kuban through the years in order to document his extensive drawings and notes regarding his study of the elongated tracks. His growing database has also caught the attention of James Farlow.[25]

The systematic and meticulous compilation of track charts, notes, and even photographic documentation of the dinosaur footprints exposed in the excavated test pit in 1974 all contribute to pieces of an emerging big picture of an ancient coastal plain that served as a dinosaur highway of sorts, where potentially dozens of sauropods tromped south through the limy sludge. Theropod trails marched both north and south.[26]

The great historic heritage of the Paluxy dinosaur footprints is not only tied to onsite tracks. In recent years the quarried trackway housed at the Texas Memorial Museum on the campus of the University of Texas at Austin has gained increasing attention and concern from paleoichnologists and Texas Parks and Wildlife personnel. The small WPA-built trackhouse has stood next to the Texas

Memorial Museum building since 1941. In 1988 TPWD exhibits specialist Peggy Maceo noted that the trackway surface was deteriorating and notified William Reeder, Director of the Texas Memorial Museum at that time. Subsequent reports confirmed problems such as roof leakage, improper ventilation, and biological growth, all factors contributing to the slow destruction of the trackway.[27]

Mike O'Brien explained:

As I understand it, the original design for the trackhouse would have been better suited in protecting the tracks than what was actually built. The original design called for a vaulted roof, but a flat one was built. The roof has leaked. The windowsills have leaked. Moisture migrates up through the ground, and the building is poorly ventilated. The limestone of the tracks is slowly turning to mush, and it is so soft in places that the weight of a person is enough to leave human footprints on the trackway. The trackhouse windows provide a very limited

This small WPA-built structure outside the Texas Memorial Museum in Austin houses part of the trackway that R.T. Bird excavated in 1940. Unfortunately, roof leakage and improper ventilation have contributed to the deterioration of the tracks. Photo by Laurie E. Jasinski

view of the tracks. A visitor at the trackhouse can read about the tracks, but there are no photographs, illustrations, or maps that would help the visitor visualize the tracks. Even though the tracks have been in Austin for almost seventy years, very few people really know what they look like.[28]

University of Texas conservation experts produced in-depth reports in 1993 and 1997 detailing the deterioration of the tracks. Suggestions were made ranging from renovating the WPA structure to moving the fossil footprints inside Texas Memorial Museum, moving them to another museum such as the Fort Worth Museum of Science and History, or even giving the tracks to Parks and Wildlife to be displayed at Dinosaur Valley.[29]

In 2004 O'Brien prepared a presentation for Texas Memorial Museum outlining the condition of the trackway. His recommendations included placing the tracks over an impermeable slab in a climate-controlled environment with access for maintenance. The plight of the fossil footprints received media attention in July 2005 and November 2006, when the *Austin American-Statesman* printed stories about the deteriorating trackway. In the fall of 2007, according to Museum Director Ed Theriot, the best solution carried an estimated $250,000 tab and included hiring a stone conservator for assessment of the tracks to ultimately bring the trackway inside the Texas Memorial Museum and establish it as the showpiece of the facility.[30]

"If there is a lesson in this," O'Brien summarized, "it is that dinosaur tracks should be preserved in the ground where they are found. If they are in pristine condition like the Glen Rose tracks, they should be molded and displayed as casts."[31]

The constant issues of track preservation, park stewardship, and public service occupy all the time of the small staff at Dinosaur Valley. But another group of dedicated volunteers has also made valuable contributions to the park. The LDL Friends of Dinosaur Valley State Park, the environmental component of the LDL Foundation, has served Dinosaur Valley for more than a decade.[32]

"I've got a good Friends group," Billy Paul smiled proudly.

The foundation had humble but sincere beginnings in 1993. Three friends, elementary school teachers, Leta Yocham, Dorothy Lewis Gibbs, and Liz Sherrell, saw a need for community service and invested $375 to create a non-profit charitable organization.[33] They wrote:

Back in 1993 we chose the three areas of health, education, and the environment because it was there we felt we could best help the youth and families of the county, as well as possibly making Glen Rose more attractive as a tourist destination. We hoped to complement existing school, county, and state programs.[34]

They took their name from the first three letters of their first names. In addition to their other activities, LDL worked with the Texas Parks and Wildlife Department and opened a park store in the spring of 1994. All sales from the store go to improvements at Dinosaur Valley. Texas Utilities donated a building

TPWD exhibit sculptor Mike O'Brien has contributed considerable time and effort to mapping the fossil footprints at Dinosaur Valley State Park, as well as advocating the preservation of the excavated trackway on display at the Texas Memorial Museum. Photo by Laurie E. Jasinski

that the LDL Friends in turn gave to the park, which paid to have it moved onsite for the store. The LDL Friends group has worked closely with Louis Jacobs at the Shuler Museum of Paleontology as well as the Fort Worth Museum of Science and History, and LDL funded a series of wayside exhibits that helped explain the history of the tracks and dinosaur models to visitors. In 2001 LDL Friends funded the River Ecology Trail. The paved, handicap-accessible path enables easier travel for physically-challenged visitors by connecting one of the parking lots to the Paluxy and down to the main track site (Track Site #2).[35]

The LDL Friends group has bold plans to enhance the educational features at the park. They envision a complex with an interpretive center, park stores, and outdoor amphitheater. The facility would be the ideal setting for interpretive presentations. A special children's area would feature a Dino Dig, where youngsters could excavate their very own "fossils."[36]

Except for the two frame houses on the Kerr property, no structures remain from the old farms that now comprise Dinosaur Valley State Park, but hidden remnants serve as reminders of the Paluxy Valley's past. Abandoned artesian wells recall the region's boom days when water flowed freely. Relics of an old still reflect the important role the abundant water played in that hidden valley industry—bootlegging. Not far from the park headquarters and near a maintenance facility, the old Lanham Mill country road rolls past a hardly-noticeable clearing surrounded by cedar—the site of the Lanham Mill School. This historic center of the valley community lies silent now, except perhaps for the distant laughter of children playing in the park or squealing in front of the dinosaur models. Beneath tangled branches, two rocks, placed between tree trunks, once served as homemade benches and still wait to accommodate schoolchildren playing in the old

The restored Lanham Mill School sits in Heritage Park in Glen Rose. Photo by Gary S. Hickinbotham

yard. The historic building itself, however, was given new life. In 2002 the Robert McFall family donated the structure to be preserved. The crisp white little schoolhouse now sits in Heritage Park in Glen Rose.[37]

Families and descendants of the old Lanham Mill community had worked diligently and lovingly to honor their country home, a little place in the Paluxy Valley that played so big a role in paleoichnological history. On June 22, 1995, they formed the Lanham Mill Cemetery Association to protect and preserve this historic graveyard, located upstream from Dinosaur Valley. The Lanham Mill community was honored with a Texas Historical Marker on October 25, 1997,[38] and writer Novella Wilson recorded the events and families of the valley in her book *Historic Lanham Mill Community and Cemetery* (rev. ed. 1999).

Novella still delights in showing visitors the now-wild countryside of the park and its environs, where as a girl she traipsed through valley lanes to school. "This was all open fields," she says. A driving tour of the Paluxy Valley rekindles memories of the old farms and families who made their lives here. A road off the beaten path follows an old but familiar route to the Hamberlin–Moss crossing downstream from the park.[39]

"Now I hope you're a brave soul! Some people are frightened when they come down here, drive across this. But I'll assure you you're not in any danger." With eyes twinkling she smiles at the driver. With her clear directions, the vehicle fords the Paluxy like a dream. Other motorists make more of an adventure out of crossing with their hot rods. "The kids, they love to get out there and spin you know ... scare the visitors half to death!"

For years the area that is now a state park represented the heart of the valley community. For those who reflect on their old way of life, Dinosaur Valley recalls swimming at Blue Hole, skipping along the old road to school, chopping cedar, and a host of other memories. Before he passed away, John Wilson, Novella's husband, found comfort in driving through the park.[40]

His youngest brother, Doyle, likewise enjoys traipsing the bank of the Paluxy:

I walked ... from Glen Rose to Lanham Mill Cemetery, up the Paluxy. Took three days to do it. I'd just do it and another sometime I'd go back and start where I'd quit. And there are dinosaur tracks in that Paluxy everywhere.[41]

Perhaps the walk harkened back to his boyhood treks among the dinosaur tracks and his daily watch over R.T. Bird and his men hard at work in their quarry.

The memory of those days also burns brightly for Glen Evans, Bird's colleague on the project. "It makes me ... wish I was about twenty years old and had the foreknowledge that I would need and could get in there and work," he exclaims. "God I'd like to do it again."[42]

Doyle and Charlidell Wilson fondly remember their childhood days when the Paluxy riverbed buzzed with the activity of a dinosaur hunter and his crew. Photo by Laurie E. Jasinski

For that matter, perhaps the dinosaur tracks themselves are the ultimate remnants of the past. They tie an ancient landscape to this modern countryside. The park protects a worthy and unique legacy for the enjoyment of the young and the young at heart. Children dream about the reptilian behemoths, and adults become as children again splashing in the footprints of the dinosaurs. The ancient creatures evoke a universal curiosity. For a century now, from a boy's remarkable find on Wheeler Branch to the scientific breakthroughs discovered in the Paluxy streambed, the tracks have inspired wonder and delight.

Dinosaur Valley State Park, tucked in the bend of the Paluxy River, holds a special connection to the Lone Star State's ancient past and preserves a unique legacy for future generations.
Photo by Gary S. Hickinbotham

Art by Novella Wilson

THE DINOSAUR WALTZ

In the Northern Hill Country many miles away
There flows a green river with a story they say.
Tracks in that streambed tell a tale in stone.
They've weathered the ages—the years that have flown.

Time flows that sweet river back to an ancient seashore
And the coastal domain of the great dinosaurs.
The footprints they left there later buried in stone
Show a gentle plant-eater. But she was not alone.

Some say she was followed by a fierce carnosaur
In a life-and-death struggle by that ancient seashore.
I see something different in their footprints by chance
Lined up two-by-two as they started to dance.

The Dinosaur Waltz.
The Dinosaur Waltz.
They swayed to and fro to the Dinosaur Waltz.

From that primitive landscape water carved through the hills
To the pretty Paluxy that's flowing there still.
Through the Hill Country valley with its mystery and charms
Many people would settle on their homesteads and farms.

They planted corn and cotton. Grazed cows in the field.
Hard sweat for the bounty—a good harvest to yield.
And the children would walk to the schoolhouse each day,
And they'd splash in that river where the dinosaurs played.

The Dinosaur Waltz.
The Dinosaur Waltz.
They swayed to and fro to the Dinosaur Waltz.

The valley held treasures in its creeks and its springs
Of good mineral waters and the healing they bring.
Magnetic healers, psychics and such
Drank from the wells with a magical touch.

Deep in the country, moonshine was made.
Good stiff corn whiskey asked a price to be paid.
Bootleggers hid there—white lightning booze,
And the takers might spy while drinking their brews.

The Dinosaur Waltz.
The Dinosaur Waltz.
They swayed to and fro to the Dinosaur Waltz.

Townfolk from Glen Rose came calling to see
Those tracks in the river with wonder and glee.
Tourists would journey from far and from near
For a look and a picnic and a photo held dear.

Dinosaur hunters with science would view
The traces in rock—and they captured some too,
While the folks got together to play old mountain tunes,
And young valley couples would sway and they'd swoon.

The Dinosaur Waltz.
The Dinosaur Waltz.
They swayed to and fro to the Dinosaur Waltz.

That green river valley in those Texas hills
Harbors the secrets of the dinosaurs still.
Tri-toed meat-eaters and "potholes" with claws
Can stop one in his tracks to marvel in awe.

Some say their story was an epic fight
Of the fiercest and fastest and the Bronto in flight.
I say that the footprints that tiptoe the creek—
They trailed into the night.
What a whimsical sight
Cheek to cheek.

The Dinosaur Waltz.
The Dinosaur Waltz.
They swayed to and fro to the Dinosaur Waltz.

The Dinosaur Waltz.
The Dinosaur Waltz.
They swayed to and fro to the Dinosaur Waltz.

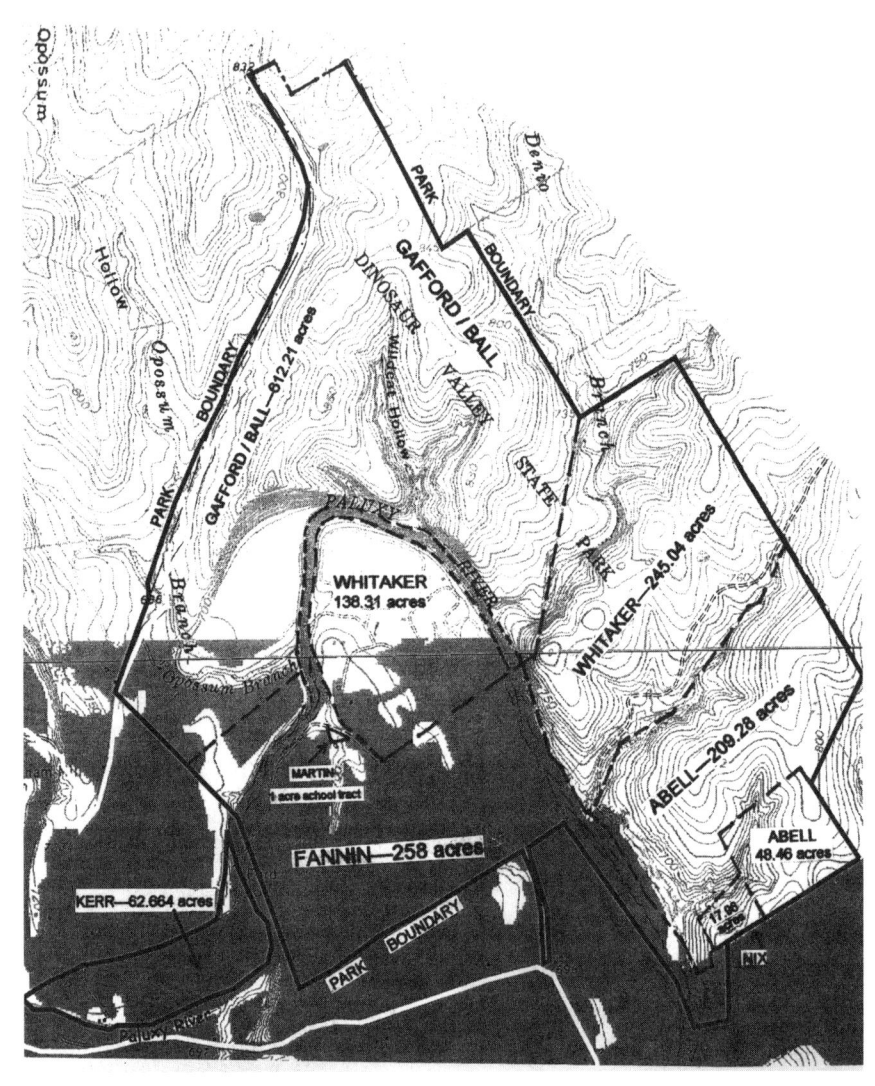

DINOSAUR VALLEY STATE PARK
REAL ESTATE TRACTS

NOTES AND OTHER TRACKWAYS

Chapter 1: The Changing Face of North Central Texas

1. Texas Department of Transportation, *Official Travel Map*, Austin, Texas, 1995; Texas Parks and Wildlife Department, *Dinosaur Tracks State Park*, map prepared by Williams-Stackhouse and Associates, Dinosaur Valley State Park, Archeology Files, Texas Parks and Wildlife Department, Austin; United States Department of the Interior, *Hill City Quadrangle*, Texas, 7.5 minute series, 1961, photorevised 1979; United States Department of the Interior, *Glen Rose West Quadrangle,* Texas, 7.5 minute series, 1966, photorevised 1979; John Clements, *Flying the Colors: Texas* (Dallas: Clements Research, Inc., 1984), p. 402; Ron Tyler, editor-in-chief, *The New Handbook of Texas* (6 vols.; Austin: Texas State Historical Association, 1996), Vol. 5, "Somervell County," pp. 1144-1145; *Texas Almanac,* 1961-1962 (Dallas: A. H. Belo Corporation, 1961), p. 636; *Texas Almanac, 2004-2005* (Dallas: *The Dallas Morning News,* 2004), p. 270; *Texas Almanac and State Industrial Guide,* 1972-1973 (Dallas: A. H. Belo Corporation, 1971), p. 331. *The New Handbook of Texas* will hereafter be cited as *NHOT.* The total park acreage is based on 2008 figures.

2. Albert G. Fiedler, *Artesian Water in Somervell County, Texas,* United States Department of the Interior, Water-Supply Paper 660, Prepared in cooperation with the Texas State Board of Water Engineers and State Department of Health (Washington, DC: Government Printing Office, 1934), pp. 6-7; Diane Dismukes Interview, July 27, 2004; Ken Fry Interview, July 30, 2004; *NHOT,* Vol. 3, "Grand Prairies and the Lampasas Cut Plain," p. 278, Vol. 2, "Cross Timbers," pp. 421-422; J. Stewart Nagle, *Glen Rose Cycles and Facies, Paluxy River Valley, Somervell County, Texas* (Austin: University of Texas, Bureau of Economic Geology, May 1968), p. 2.; John Graves, *Hard Scrabble: Observations on a Patch of Land* (New York: Alfred A. Knopf, 1982), pp. 9-10; Billy Paul Baker, Park Superintendent, Dinosaur Valley State Park, Interview, July 27, 2004; James Farlow Interview, August 6, 2004; Robert T. Hill, *Geography and Geology of the Black and Grand Prairies, Texas,* United States Department of the Interior, Twenty-first Annual Report of the United States Geological Survey, Part VII (Washington DC: Government Printing Office, 1901), pp. 473-475; Darwin Spearing, *Roadside Geology of Texas* (Missoula, Montana: Mountain Press Publishing Company, 1991), pp. 242-244; R. Jay Parker, "The Geomorphic Evolution of the Glen Rose Prairie, North-Central Texas," BS Thesis, Baylor University, Waco, August 1980, pp. i, 1-2. The subtitle of the Robert T. Hill report reads: ... *with detailed descriptions of the Cretaceous formations and special reference to artesian waters.* Geologically, the Glen Rose Formation is part of the Trinity Group, Comanchean Series. The Paluxy valley area of the park lies within a subdivision of the Lampasas Cut Plain called the Glen Rose Prairie.

3. Graves, p. 10.

4. Baker Interview; Farlow Interview; Mike O'Brien, Texas Parks and Wildlife, Interview, July 20, 2004; Louis Jacobs, *Lone Star Dinosaurs* (College Station: Texas A&M University Press, 1995), pp. 3-4; Roland T. Bird, *Bones for Barnum Brown: Adventures of a Dinosaur Hunter* (Fort Worth: Texas Christian University Press, 1985), p. 8.

5. James O. Farlow, *The Dinosaurs of Dinosaur Valley State Park* (Austin: Texas Parks and Wildlife Department, 1993), no page number, section under heading "How the Tracks were Created and Preserved"; Jacobs, pp. 61-65; Spearing, p. 243; Robert T. Hill, "Paleontology of the Cretaceous Formations of Texas—The Invertebrate Paleontology of the Trinity Division," *Proceedings of the Biological Society of Washington,* Vol. VIII, (June 3, 1893): 12-15.

6. Farlow, "Of Tracks and the River," in W. H. Shore, ed., *Mysteries of Life and the Universe: New Essays from America's Finest Writers on Science* (New York: Harcourt Brace Jovanovich, 1992), pp. 68-69; Farlow, *A Guide to Lower Cretaceous Dinosaur Footprints and Tracksites of the Paluxy River Valley, Somervell County, Texas,* South-Central Section, Geological Society of America, Field Trip Guidebook, Baylor University, Waco, Texas, 1987, p. 8; Jacobs, pp. 61-65; Ron Ralph, *An Inventory of Cultural Resources Within the Texas Park System: November 1976 through October 1981,* Texas Antiquities Permit 128 (Austin: Texas Parks and Wildlife Department, August 1996), p. 96; Nagle, p. 1; Baker Interview; Dismukes Interview; O'Brien Interview. Paleontologists, geologists, and ichnologists cannot determine an exact date for the dinosaur tracks. Parks and Wildlife personnel and brochures generally give the age of the tracks at about 113 million years. In his Cultural Resources inventory, archeologist Ron Ralph estimated 110 million years (Ralph, p. 96). Paleontologist James Farlow estimated "just over 110 million years ago" ("Of Tracks and the River", p. 67). Paleontologist and author Louis Jacobs wrote "111 million years" (Jacobs, p. 3), while various other journal articles and reports have listed a generalized estimate

that the tracks are older than one hundred million years. While specific tracks and/or trackways were made on individual days, according to Farlow, the total accumulation of tracks was made probably on many such days, given that the prints occurred in more than one layer. Scientists don't really know exactly how long the surface was recording tracks.

7. Jacobs, p. 3.

8. Glen Evans Interview, July 15, 2004; O'Brien Interview; Baker Interview; Farlow, "Of Tracks..." pp. 67-72; Farlow, *The Dinosaurs of Dinosaur...*; Glen J. Kuban, "An Overview of Dinosaur Tracking," *M.A.P.S. Digest* (April 1994), Mid-America Paleontology Society, Rock Island, Illinois, reprinted on The TalkOrigins Archive Website (http://www.talkorigins.org/faqs/paluxy/ovrdino.html), accessed June 30, 2004; Jacobs, pp. 3-4; Wann Langston, Jr., "Dinosaur Tracks," manuscript copy in Archeology Files, Texas Parks and Wildlife Department, Austin, pp. 1-5; J. Michael Hawthorne, "Stratigraphy and Depositional Environment of the Dinosaur Track-Bearing Glen Rose Limestone in the Paluxy Basin, Texas," BS Thesis, Baylor University, Waco, August 1983, pp. 84-85. The preservation of a track is best obtained when the settling sediment is of a different composition from the track itself. A different, softer layer, composed of shale for example, does not bond with the harder limestone, and therefore the softer layer can more easily break away, exposing the hard limestone layer and the tracks it holds. See also J. Michael Hawthorne, "Dinosaur Track-bearing Strata of the Lampasas Cut Plain and Edwards Plateau, Texas," *Baylor Geological Studies, Bulletin 49* (1990): 47 pp.; Jeffrey G. Pittman, "Stratigraphy, Lithology, Depositional Environment, and Track Type of Dinosaur Track-bearing Beds of the Gulf Coastal Plain," in David D. Gillette and Martin G. Lockley, eds., *Dinosaur Tracks and Traces* (Cambridge: Cambridge University Press, 1989); and James O. Farlow, Wann Langston Jr., E. Everett Deschner, Richard Solis, William Ward, Brenda L. Kirkland, Susan Hovorka, Tamra L. Reece, and James Whitcraft, *Texas Giants: Dinosaurs of the Heritage Museum of the Texas Hill Country* (Canyon Lake, Texas: Heritage Museum of the Texas Hill Country, 2006).

9. Farlow, *The Dinosaurs of Dinosaur...*, no page number, section under heading "Footprint Makers of the Paluxy River Area" and "Meat-Eaters"; Farlow, "*Acrocanthosaurus* and the Maker of Comanchean Large-Theropod Footprints," in Darren H. Tanke and Kenneth Carpenter, eds., *Mesozoic Vertebrate Life* (Bloomington and Indianapolis: Indiana University Press, 2001), pp. 408-409, 421-422, 424; Louis Jacobs, Telephone Interview, January 26, 2005; Jacobs, pp. 22-23, 80-81; Hawthorne thesis, p. 90; Farlow, "Of Tracks...," p. 70. See also J.D. Harris, "A Reanalysis of *Acrocanthosaurus atokensis,* Its Phylogenetic Status, and Paleobiogeographic Implications, Based on a New Specimen From Texas," *New Mexico Museum of Natural History and Science, Bulletin 13* (1998): 1-75; and Philip J. Currie and Kenneth Carpenter, "A New Specimen of *Acrocanthosaurus atokensis* (Theropoda, Dinosauria) from the Lower Cretaceous Antlers Formation (Lower Cretaceous, Aptian) of Oklahoma, USA," *Geodiversitas,* 22, no. 2 (2000): 207-246.

10. Farlow, *The Dinosaurs of Dinosaur...*, no page number, section under heading "Giant Four-Legged Plant-Eaters"; Jacobs, pp. 80-83; Jacobs Telephone Interview; James Diffily Telephone Interviews, July 25, 2005, August 15, 2005; Peter J. Rose, "A New Titanosauriform Sauropod (Dinosauria: Saurischia) from the Early Cretaceous of Central Texas and its Phylogenetic Relationships," *Palaeontologia Electronica,* 10, no. 2 (2007): 65pp. (http://palaeo-electronica.org/2007_2/00063/index.html), accessed October 20, 2007; *Dallas Morning News,* October 3, 2007. A sauropod skeleton was found in Hood County, and a mass accumulation of skeletons has been found at Stephenville in Erath County. For years the name *Pleurocoelus,* a name coined in the late 1800s from fossil materials found in Maryland, has been applied to the scant sauropod fossils found in Texas, but the fossil finds in North Central Texas in the 1990s have led to the reevaluation of the Texas sauropod and the proposal of a new name, *Paluxysaurus jonesi.* The new name (genus) refers to both the Paluxy River and the Hood County town of Paluxy, Texas, and the name (species) honors William R. Jones, owner of the Jones Ranch where the bones were found. According to James Farlow, the sauropods may or may not have been feeding on tidal zone vegetation, if at all, when they made the footprints. They may simply have been moving from one feeding ground to another. Paleontologists cannot ascertain information about feeding from the trackways, and the trackways do not give indication of feeding.

11. Jacobs Telephone Interview; Jacobs, pp. 23, 81-82; Baker Interview; O'Brien Interview; James Farlow, Telephone Interview, February 7, 2005; Farlow, *The Dinosaurs of Dinosaur...*, no page number, section under heading "Large Two-Legged Plant-Eaters"; Kuban, "An Overview of Dinosaur Tracking." One group of early ornithopods, the iguanodonts, lived in North America, including Texas, during the Early Cretaceous, and fossil bones have been found in Texas. See also Farlow et al., *Texas Giants: Dinosaurs of the Heritage Museum of the Texas Hill Country.*

12. Jacobs, pp. 83-84; Bird, pp. 11-12; Spearing, pp. 11-19; Farlow, *The Dinosaurs of Dinosaur...*,

no page number, section under heading "How the Tracks were Created and Preserved."

13. Your Gemologist—Petrified Wood Website (http://www.yourgemologist.com/Kids/petrifiedwood/petrifiedwood.html), accessed February 3, 2005; Somervell County Genealogical and Heritage Society, *History and Families: Somervell County, Texas, 1875-2001* (Paducah, Kentucky: Turner Publishing Company, 2001), p. 168; W.C. Nunn, *Somervell: Story of a Texas County* (Fort Worth: Texas Christian University Press, 1975), p. 3; Hill, *Geography and Geology of the Black and Grand Prairies...*, pp. 149-152; Ralph, p. 96; Fry Interview; Dismukes Interview; Baker Interview.

14. Ken Fry, Telephone Interviews, July 30, 2004, February 3, 2005; Kathy Lenz, Park Interpreter, Dinosaur Valley State Park, Telephone Interview, February 7, 2005; Nunn, pp. 3-5; Baker Interview; Thomas T. Ewell, *History of Hood County* (Granbury, Texas: Frank Gaston, pub., 1895; reprinted by The Junior Woman's Club, Granbury, 1956), pp. 1-2; Dismukes Interview.

15. Ralph, pp. 96-97; Archeology Files, Texas Parks and Wildlife Department, Austin; Stephen M. Carpenter, Dan K. Utley, Steve Carlson, and Solveig A. Turpin, *Cultural Resources Survey of Dinosaur Valley State Park, Somervell County, Texas* (Austin: Texas Parks and Wildlife Department, Cultural Resources Program, 1999), pp. 7-8, 49, 79-80; Joseph G. Gallagher, *A Reconnaissance Survey of the Dinosaur Valley State Park* (Dallas: Archaeology Research Program, Southern Methodist University, 1974), pp. 1-3; Fry Interview; Baker Interview; Dismukes Interview; Nunn, p. 4. Area archeological surveys have included Lake Whitney and environs southeast of Somervell County in 1949 and 1950 and the Lake Granbury and Squaw Creek Reservoir regions in the 1970s.

16. Jacobs Telephone Interview; Fry Interview; Baker Interview; Farlow, "A Guide to the Lower Cretaceous Dinosaur...," p. 1; Farlow, Telephone Interview, February 7, 2005. Some have speculated that the Native American Thunderbird mythology may have a connection to dinosaur tracks and that perhaps large bird-like footprints in stone may have been linked to the Thunderbird by Indian peoples. This is merely speculation and not based on positive evidence. Native American depictions of dinosaur trackways have been confirmed in the Southwest. Folklore scholar and author Adrienne Mayor wrote about dinosaur trackways (regarded as giant bird tracks) that were known to the Navajos of Arizona, for example. She also mentioned rock art found in that state (Adrienne Mayor, *Fossil Legends of the First Americans* [Princeton, New Jersey: Princeton University Press, 2005], p. 139).

17. Fry Interview; Dismukes Interview; Jean F. King Interview, July 25, 2004; Dayton Kelley, "The Tonkawas" in *Indian Tribes of Texas* (Waco: Texian Press, 1971), pp. 151-164; W.W. Newcomb, Jr., *The Indians of Texas* (Austin: University of Texas Press, 1961), pp. 93, 133-135, 138-139; Dayton Kelley, "The Tonkawas" in Dorman H. Winfrey, W.C. Nunn, Rupert N. Richardson, James M. Day, Harold B. Simpson, Sandra L. Myers, Dayton Kelley, and Billy M. Jones, in *Indian Tribes of Texas* (Waco: Texian Press, 1971), pp. 151-164; Charles Shaw, *Indian Life in Texas* (Austin: State House Press, 1987), p. 9.

18. Newcomb, pp. 137-139.

19. Fry Interview; Dismukes Interview; King Interview; Newcomb, pp. 280-282, 135. Historically the Tonkawas and Apaches were enemies and constantly warring with each other. Initially the Tonkawas maintained peace with the Comanches to the west and Wichitas to the north as those groups began to exert their influence in Texas beginning in the eighteenth century, but this condition eventually changed when the Tonkawas established friendly relations with the Apaches and became enemies of the Comanches (Kelley, "The Tonkawas" in *Indian Tribes...*, p. 152).

20. Fry Interview; Nunn, pp. 4-6; Newcomb, pp. 150-153.

21. Billy M. Jones, "The Wichitas" in *Indian Tribes of Texas,* pp. 169-170, 173; Newcomb, pp. 247-249; Fry Interview; Dismukes Interview; Lydia Lowndes Maury Skeels, *An Ethnohistorical Survey of Texas Indians* (Austin: Texas Historical Survey Committee, Report Number 22, October 1972), no page number, Figure 7 titled "Location of Texas Indians, Eighteenth Century." In *The Indians of Texas,* Newcomb wrote that the Wichita were believed to have originated somewhere in the area of the lower Red River and from there migrated north.

22. Jones, "The Wichitas" in *Indian Tribes of Texas,* p. 173; Newcomb, pp. 250-251, 253-257, 270-272.

23. Newcomb, pp. 155-159; Fry Interview; King Interview; Rupert N. Richardson, "The Comanches" in *Indian Tribes of Texas,* pp. 39, 44.

24. Newcomb, pp. 185-188, 159; Fry Interview.

25. Graves, p. 15; Fry Interview; King Interview; Newcomb, pp. 157, 163.

26. Vance J. Maloney, *The Story of Comanche Peak, Landmark of Hood County, Texas* (n.p.: Vance J. Maloney, 1970), p. 2; King Interview; *History and Families: Somervell County, Texas, 1875–2001*, p. 21.

27. Maloney, p. 2.

28. Ibid., pp. 2–4; King Interview; *History and Families: Somervell County, Texas, 1875–2001*, pp. 21, 171-172.

29. Donald W. Olson, et. al., "Piñon Pines and the Route of Cabeza de Vaca," *Southwestern Historical Quarterly, 150,* no. 2 (October 1997): pp. 175-186. *History and Families: Somervell County, Texas, 1875–2001*, p. 17, and W.C. Nunn's Somervell: Story of a Texas County, p. 7, suggest that Cabeza de Vaca may have been the first European to traverse Somervell County.

30. *NHOT,* Vol. 4, "Moscoso Expedition," pp. 851-852. James Bruseth and Nancy Kenmotsu relied on sixteenth-century archeological sites and published their findings in *North American Archeologist* in 1993. Vance J. Maloney in *The Story of Comanche Peak...* (p. 5) indicated that between 1611 to 1634 Catholic missionaries explored the area of what became Fort Belknap (in Young County, northwest of Somervell County) on the Brazos River and visited Indians up and down the river for approximately 150 miles. Some of these men included Juan de Salas, Diego León, and Fray Juan de Ortega. W.C. Nunn in *Somervell: Story of a Texas County* repeated this information and cited Maloney's work as the source. Maloney wrote his information based on Joseph Carroll McConnell's *The West Texas Frontier* (pp. 3-4). McConnell speculated that the Juan de Salas expedition in 1611 "perhaps, reached the Brazos, some-where in the vicinity of Old Fort Belknap." During the seventeenth century Franciscan missionaries did explore West Texas as they traveled east from their colonies in New Mexico in attempts to initiate mis-sionary activity among the Jumanos, Indian groups of the South Plains. Exploration included the Canadian, Pecos, Concho, and upper Colorado River basins (*NHOT,* Vol. 2, "Exploration," p. 919).

31. *NHOT,* Vol. 2, "Exploration," p. 922; Herbert Eugene Bolton, *Texas in the Middle Eighteenth Century* (Berkeley: University of California Press, 1915), p. 120. Spain acquired the French territory of Louisiana with the Treaty of Paris in 1763.

32. Bolton, pp. 120-124, 122 (quote).

33. Ibid., pp. 127-129; *NHOT,* Vol. 6, "Vial, Pedro," pp. 732-733.

34. Bolton, pp. 129-130.

35. *NHOT,* Vol. 4, "Nolan Expeditions," pp. 1028-1029.

36. Maurine T. Wilson and Jack Jackson, *Philip Nolan and Texas: Expeditions to the Unknown Land, 1791-1801* (Waco: Texian Press, 1987), p. 66.

37. Ibid., pp. 65-73, 133-134; "History of Somervell County," in WPA Archives, Somervell County, Center for American History, University of Texas at Austin.

38. *NHOT,* Vol. 4, "Mexican Texas," pp. 689-695.

39. Ibid.; Robert Sidney Martin and James C. Martin, *Contours of Discovery* (Austin: Texas State Historical Association, 1982), pp. 46-48; Stephen Fuller Austin, comp., *Map of Texas With Parts of the Adjoining States* (Philadelphia: H. S. Tanner, 1830).

Chapter 2: Fountains of Youth: Settlement in the Valley of the Paluxy

1. Nunn, p. 10; David H. Burr, *Texas* (New York: J. H. Colton & Co., 1833).

2. *NHOT,* Vol. 4, "Milam County," pp. 719-720; Robert Creuzbaur, *J. De Cordova's Map of the State of Texas* (Houston: Robert Creuzbaur, 1849). Nashville-on-the-Brazos was an early town in present-day

Milam County and served as county seat from 1837 to 1846 until Cameron was made the county seat (*NHOT*, Vol. 4, "Nashville-on-the-Brazos," p. 938).

3. Jacob De Cordova, *Texas: Her Resources and Her Public Men* (Philadelphia: J. B. Lippincott & Co., 1858), p. 203.

4. Ibid., pp. 206-208; *NHOT*, Vol. 6, "Texan Santa Fe Expedition," p. 270; Nunn, p. 13; Horace Bailey Carroll, "The Route of the Texan Santa Fe Expedition," PhD thesis, University of Texas at Austin, June 1935, pp. 94-101; George Bernard Erath, *Memoirs of Major George Bernard Erath* (Austin: Texas State Historical Association, 1923), p. 59. George Erath, early surveyor along the Brazos in Somervell County, led two reconnaissance parties up the Brazos in the area of Comanche Peak in 1840 and early 1841.

5. Erath, p. 59 (quote); *NHOT*, Vol. 6, p. 270; Carroll, pp. 94-101; Maloney, pp. 7-8; George Wilkins Kendall, *Narrative of the Texan Santa Fé Expedition* (2 vols.; New York: Harper & Brothers, Publishers, 1856), Vol. I, pp. 107-108; Ken Fry, Personal Conversation, Somervell County, Texas, May 18, 2007. Erath commented that the party "pushed on parallel with the Brazos to the mouth of the Paluxy, and then passed east of the Comanche Peak." Diarist Gallagher stated that they "Crossed the brassos below Comanche peak..." (Horace Bailey Carroll, p. 96). George Wilkins Kendall in his *Narrative* stated that they crossed the Brazos "a short distance below Comanche Peak..." (Carroll, p. 97). Though the landmark was mentioned prominently, Carroll raised doubts that the expedition actually crossed the Brazos River within sight of the peak, but argued instead that they crossed the Brazos near Bee Mountain in the vicinity of the Kimball's Bend area of the Brazos River in northern Bosque County well below Comanche Peak. If they then headed northwest to the Western Cross Timbers, it is still quite possible that the expedition passed through or very near the area of Somervell County. Carroll (pp. 107-108) does acknowledge the accuracy of eyewitness accounts that describe a high prairie between Nolan's River and the Brazos and the view of Comanche Peak to the west (Kendall, pp. 107-108).

According to Somervell County Historical Commission member Ken Fry, in the late 1990s, grapeshot was discovered by an area resident along the Brazos River bottoms in Somervell County. This was located at the site of an old river ford at Porter's Spring on the Brazos. Buckets of the rusty balls were excavated and later examined by a historical arms consultant who identified the artifacts as grapeshot from early nineteenth-century cannons. This area, the site of a historic ford, would have facilitated crossing the river, not only for pioneer travelers, but for Native American groups long before them. This particular location also offers a clear view of Comanche Peak. While this discovery cannot verify positively that the Texan Santa Fe Expedition crossed that specific spot on the Brazos, it does present a compelling possibility that the chroniclers of the Texan Santa Fe Expedition may indeed have been more accurate in their geographic descriptions than some twentieth-century historians have acknowledged.

6. Kendall, p. 103. The entire title reads: *Narrative of the Texan Santa Fé Expedition, comprising a description of a tour through Texas, and across the great southwestern prairies, the Comanche and Caygüa hunting-grounds, with an account of the sufferings from want of food, losses from hostile Indians, and final capture of the Texans, and their march, as prisoners, to the city of Mexico, with illustrations and a map.*

7. *NHOT*, Vol. 6, p. 270; Nunn, pp. 12-13; Texas Historical Commission, marker files, "Barnard's Trading Post No. 2," Texas Historical Commission Library, Austin.

8. H. P. N. Gammel, comp., *The Laws of Texas*, 1822-1897 (10 vols.; Austin: The Gammel Book Company, 1898), Vol. 2, pp. 842-843.

9. THC marker files; Nunn, pp. 13-14; Ewell, p. 53; *NHOT*, Vol. 1, "Barnard, Charles E.," p. 384. Sam Houston was also an investor in the trading post business. The Torreys and Barnards were childhood friends in Connecticut. In 1848 Charles Barnard married Juana Josefina Cavasos, a Comanche captive whom George Barnard had ransomed at the Tehuacana Trading Post.

10. Ferdinand Roemer, *Texas with Particular Reference to German Immigration and The Physical Appearance of the Country,* Translated from the German by Oswald Mueller (San Antonio: Standard Printing Company, 1935, reprinted Waco: Texian Press, German–Texan Heritage Society, 1983), pp. 192-194; Fry Interview; Ewell, p. 4; Nunn, pp. 15-16.

11. Roemer, *Texas...*, p. 203 (quotes), pp. iv-vi, 150-152; Roemer, "Contributions to the Geology of Texas," *American Journal of Science and Arts,* Vol. 55 (July 1848): 21-23. The author's statement that Roemer traveled as far as just southeast of the Paluxy is based on Roemer's account that he traveled to a Caddo village "about sixty miles up on the Brazos" from the trading house on Tehuacana

Creek near Waco (p. 197). This distance would have brought Roemer very near Somervell County. Also Roemer's accompanying map of Texas shows "Dorf d. Caddoes" on the east side of the Brazos near the mouth of the Nolan River in present-day northern Hill County southeast of Somervell County. Comanche Peak is clearly marked just to the northwest. Unfortunately Roemer took ill and was forced to return to the Tehuacana Trading Post at this point. Because of his pioneering observations, Roemer has some-times been called the "father of Texas geology," a title more often given to geologist Robert T. Hill.

12. Maloney, p. 20.

13. THC marker files; Ewell, p. 53. Sources differ as to the exact year when the Comanche Peak trading post was constructed. Thomas Ewell in his *Hood County History* gives 1847 as the year. *The New Handbook of Texas* lists 1849, while the historical marker files give both dates (but 1849 is actually listed on the marker).

14. Roemer, *Texas...*, pp. 203-204.

15. Nunn, p. 12 (quote); "Categories of Land Grants in Texas," Handout, General Land Office, Archives and Records Division, Austin. Erath County was named for George Erath.

16. School Land Certificate—Galveston County School Land, Galveston County School Land Papers, File No. 632, Original Land Grant Collection, Archives and Records Division, Texas General Land Office, Austin.

17. Ibid., Field Notes—George Green; Texas General Land Office, Somervell Co., Austin, Texas, Compiled and drawn by Geo. J. Thielepape, August 1884. One league of land equals 4,428.4 acres. In addition to the large three-league grant, Galveston County also had a smaller survey fronting the Brazos River near the northeast corner of Somervell County.

18. Creuzbaur, J. *De Cordova's Map of the State of Texas;* Fry Interview; Fry Telephone Interview, February 23, 2005; King Interview; *Somervell County Centennial...*, p. 1; *Tour of Dinosaur Valley & Paluxy Town-Site,* Sunday October 15, 1995, booklet produced for National Trust for Historic Preservation, copy at the Texas State Archives; *History and Families: Somervell County, Texas...*, p. 106. County sources have stated that Paluxy means "beautiful stream" (*Somervell County Centennial*, p. 1). Other sources say it was named by or after the Biloxi Indians. According to the *New Handbook of Texas* (Vol. 1, "Biloxi Indians," p. 545), European chroniclers have used the spelling of Paluxy to refer to the Biloxi Indians of southern Mississippi. By the late 1820s some Biloxis had migrated west into eastern Texas and had allied themselves with the Cherokees in the 1830s. By the early 1840s some Biloxis had migrated far-ther westward to the Trinity River, and still others continued a westward movement after that (as far west and south as Brackettville and even south into Mexico).

Tour of Dinosaur Valley & Paluxy Town-Site, p. 5, presents an interesting but probably unprovable origin for the name of the Paluxy River:

The name, Paluxy, is probably a Spanish/Anglo corruption of a word taken from Caddoian beginnings. Found in a newspaper article from the *"Glen Rose Reporter Newspaper,"* housed with the former Glen Rose Mayor [Eugene] Connally's Collection, dated July 6, 1967, it states the Paluxy River was named by the Biloxi Indians, which is an Anglo-Saxon spelling of the French rendition of the tribal name, which meant "Turkey"....

The Biloxi Indians are said to have been part of a group of Indians who endured a forced march through the Paluxy River Valley en route to the Indian Reservations farther west then located in Young County, Texas. Whether or not the Biloxi Indians, who originated in Mississippi are responsible for naming the river is unproved....

The name Paluxy appeared on surveys long before the creation of the Brazos Indian Reservation in Young County in the 1850s. The reference to the meaning of "turkey" does present a curious, however remote possibility. Could this name have possibly been applied to the river as a reference to giant turkey-like tracks in the limestone bed? This question represents pure speculation by the author.

19. THC marker files; *NHOT*, Vol. 1, "Brazos Indian Reservation," pp. 714-715, Vol. 2; "Comanche Indian Reservation," p. 242; Ewell, pp. 53-54; Kelley, "The Tonkawas" *in Indian Tribes...*, pp. 162-163. The two reservations never functioned as agents had idealized. Though the Comanches learned to culti-vate crops, they were plagued by drought and division. Elements within the Penateka wished to leave the reservation and eventually did. Others joined hunting expeditions or raids. Comanche and Kickapoo

bands from the west often raided settlements, but the reservation Indians received the blame and hostility of the settlers. Unscrupulous traders illegally sold whiskey. The Brazos Reservation fared better for a time, with some of the more agricultural Indians, but they too eventually faced the ire of settlers. The reservation Indians wrongly received the blame for raids perpetrated by western Comanche bands. Military officers and Texas Rangers even enlisted the help of some reservation Indians as scouts in actions against the warring bands, but it did little good in the long run. White settlers committed depredations on some of the Brazos Reservation Indians and demanded their removal. The removal and relocation of the Tonkawas led to a tragic episode in their history. They settled in Indian Territory (near present Anadarko, Oklahoma). In 1862 Caddo, Delaware, and Shawnee warriors attacked the Tonkawas, killing almost half of the three hundred members. Though the perpetrators claimed that they had attacked because of the Tonkawas' Confederate sympathies, it is also quite likely that these Indians saw an opportunity to retaliate against the Tonkawas for old grievances, including their assistance as military scouts and their historic practice of ritual cannibalism. Gradually the shattered remnants of the Tonkawas straggled back into Texas. Some served as army scouts.

In 1895 in his *History of Hood County* (p. 54) author Thomas Ewell relayed Charles Barnard's view of the Indians:

He believes the Indians, so long his friends, associates and allies, have been [maligned in] many respects; that they are not, without cause, the blood thirsty wretches and thieves, that many writers have credited them with being.

20. THC marker files, "Barnard's Trading Post No. 2," "Barnard's Mill"; Nunn, p. 16. George Barnard returned to Waco.

21. Ewell, p. 61.

22. Ibid., p. 12.

23. Graves, p. 20.

24. Johnson County History Book Committee, *History of Johnson County, Texas* (Dallas: Curtis Media Corp., 1985), pp. 25-26; THC marker files, "Barnard's Trading Post No. 2"; *NHOT*, Vol. 5, "Somervell County," p. 1144. In 1880 Somervell County had a total population of 2,649. This number included an African-American population of only twenty-four.

25. Dorman H. Winfrey and James M. Day, eds., T*he Indian Papers of Texas and the Southwest, 1825-1916* (5 vols.; Austin: Texas State Historical Association, 1995), Vol. 4, pp. 8-11, 183-184; Joseph Carroll McConnell, *The West Texas Frontier* (Vol. 2; Palo Pinto, Texas: Texas Legal Bank & Book Co., 1939), p. 117; Fry Interview; Dismukes Interview; THC marker files, "Squaw Creek Indian Fight"; Ewell, pp. 67-68; Nunn, p. 28.

26. THC marker files, "Squaw Creek Indian Fight"; Ewell, pp. 57-58; Nunn, pp. 35-37; Fry Interview. The last Indian raid into Somervell County occurred in 1868. Settlers pursued the Native American group who sought refuge in the overhang of a ravine, which proved to be an effective defensive position. One settler was shot and another severely wounded when they approached the hiding place of the Indian band. This defensive location, however, ultimately proved to be the Indians' entrapment when heavy rains flooded the ravine and forced them out. As the Indians became exposed in the water, they were shot.

27. Betty Gosdin, Personal Conversation, July 15, 2005; THC marker files, "Barnard's Trading Post No. 2"; Ewell, pp. 125, 147; King Interview; *History and Families: Somervell County, Texas...*, pp. 106-107; *Somervell County Centennial,* p. 9. Somervell County histories have stated that Mrs. Jordan suggested the name of Rose Glen after the scenery of her native Scotland. Newspaper articles, encyclopedia entries, and popular literature have subsequently reported this story. In recent years, Betty Gosdin and Rhonda Duffie of the Somervell County Heritage Center have researched this story and the Jordan family history. In fact, they discovered, based on genealogy and census records, that Annie R. Lewis Jordan was born in Alabama, and her father and mother were born in Georgia and Alabama, respectively. As of 2007 there was no evidence that the family had a connection to Scotland. This raises suspicion that the "Scottish" connection may have been a marketing ploy invented by citizens in the mid-twentieth century. Some alternate theories exist regarding the naming of Glen Rose. Perhaps T.C. Jordan, who hailed from Bedford County, Virginia, renamed the town. Another story suggests that a local resident suggested naming the town after his/her two daughters, Rosa and Glenna.

Jordan had a dam built across the Paluxy, but a spring flood in 1873 destroyed it. He then commissioned Charles Barnard to construct a new sturdier structure.

28. *The Texas Almanac for 1867 with Statistics, Descriptive and Biographical Sketches, Etc, Relating to Texas* (Galveston: W. Richardson & Co., 1867), p. 234; Gammel, Vol. VIII, pp. 471-473; THC marker files, "Somervell County," "Somervell County Courthouse," "Barnard's Trading Post No. 2"; *Somervell County Centennial,* pp. 5-6; Nunn, pp. 44-45. The Somervell Expedition was a planned invasion of Mexico in 1842, but the force was soon disbanded. For a brief time, another Somervell County village, Sulphur Springs, contested for the county seat, but voters, spurred on by the fact that T.C. Jordan specifically proposed to construct a courthouse there, overwhelmingly approved Glen Rose. Sulphur Springs soon vanished.

29. Novella Wilson, *Historic Lanham Mill Community and Cemetery* (Glen Rose: Novella Wilson, 1999), pp. 1, 4-5; THC marker files, "Lanham Mill Community."

30. Wilson, *Historic Lanham Mill...*, pp. iv, 1, 3-5.

31. Ibid., pp. iv, 4-5; THC marker files, "Lanham Mill Community"; Novella Wilson Interview, July 28, 2004; Novella Wilson Historical Driving Tour, July 28, 2004; Doyle Wilson Interview, July 28, 2004; Dorthy Ketter, Mary Ann Millian, and Angela Sanders, comps., *The Cemeteries of Somervell County Texas* (Duncanville, Texas: Green Dog Press, 1991), pp. 145-149.

32. Dinosaur Valley State Park, Legal Acquisitions Files, Land Conservation Program, Texas Parks and Wildlife Department, Austin; Somervell County Deed of Records, Vol. C, pp. 179-182, Vol. D, pp. 544-547, Vol. H, pp. 343-346; Wilson, p. 5.

33. Somervell County Deed of Records, Vol. C, pp. 179-182; Dinosaur Valley State Park, real estate maps, Legal Acquisitions Files, Land Conservation Program, Texas Parks and Wildlife Department, Austin; Wilson, *Historic Lanham Mill...*, pp. 264-265; Somervell County Marriage Records, Vol. 2, pp. 47, 175; Somervell County Probate Minutes, Vol. 1, pp. 327-333; Somervell County Deed of Records, Vol. Q, p. 55; Wilson Telephone Interview, March 2, 2005. A tributary called Opossum Branch runs through the property originally purchased by Adams. This parcel overlooks the Main Track Site (Track Site #2). Samuel Adams and his wife Ester are both buried in Lanham Mill Cemetery. Samuel Adams died on March 15, 1884. After the death of his wife on January 17, 1888, Delila, then only about sixteen, inherited the family farm, where she resided until her death. She had married Marion C.A. Stephens on August 25, 1887, and they had a son, Charlie Henry. She died on September 25, 1896, and willed the property to her son. Charlie Henry Stephens died in Walnut Springs, Texas, on June 2, 1911. Upon the death of Charlie Henry Stephens before the age of twenty-one in 1911, the land was given to Charley Pair as conditional beneficiary.

34. Somervell County Deed of Records, Vol. H, pp. 343-348; Wilson, pp. iv, 8, 14-15, 54; *History and Families: Somervell County, Texas...,* p. 16; Wilson Historical Driving Tour; Wilson Interview. The author has also seen the spelling of Wylie.

35. Wilson, pp. 36-38, 65. Novella Wilson's *Historic Lanham Mill Community and Cemetery* contains a very thorough listing of the teachers at the Lanham Mill schools, including the years they taught.

36. Novella Wilson Interview; Wilson Historical Driving Tour; Doyle Wilson Interview; Baker Interview.

37. Wilson, *Historic Lanham Mill...*, pp. 21, 23, 41-45; Wilson Historical Driving Tour; Somervell County Deed of Records, Vol. 44, p. 643, Vol. F, p. 163, Vol. 2, pp. 550-553; Dinosaur Valley State Park, real estate maps—Legal Acquisitions Files. George Abell was born in Indiana on December 8, 1837. He married Polly Cox, and they had a son Matt, born on February 15, 1860. Matt Abell married Emma Josephine Roach on February 1, 1891, in Hood County. Matt and his wife Emma purchased the sixty acres from landowner Felix Walton.

38. Wilson, *Historic Lanham Mill...*, p. 41. About 1902 the Abells added side rooms to their house (p. 42).

39. Ibid., pp. 41-42, 220; Somervell County Deed of Records, Vol. J, pp. 169-171, Vol. 55, pp. 592-593; Affidavit of Mrs. Dillard Wilson and Charlie Moss, Somervell County Deed of Records, Vol. 55, pp. 86, 628; Affidavit copies in Dinosaur Valley State Park, Legal Acquisitions Files, Land Conservation Program, Texas Parks and Wildlife Department, Austin. Cassie Florence Beck, born on June 12, 1875, in Bosque County, was one of eight children of James and Cassie Beck. James and Cassie's grandson, Walter Erostus Beck, born on July 24, 1898, owned the forty-eight acres throughout much of the twenti-

eth century but eventually sold it to J.B. Abell (the son of Matt Abell) in 1969 (Vol. 55, pp. 592-592).

40. Graves, p. 20; Nunn, p. 60. The Chisholm Trail led to Fort Worth and eventually to railheads in Kansas (map of cattle trails in T. U. Taylor, *The Chisholm Trail and Other Routes* [San Antonio: The Naylor Company, 1936]); A.W. Spaight, *The Resources, Soil, and Climate of Texas* (Galveston: A.H. Belo & Co., 1882), pp. 288-289; Frank W. Johnson, *A History of Texas and Texans* (5 vols.; Chicago and New York: The American Historical Society, 1914), Vol. II, p. 777.

41. Wilson, *Historic Lanham Mill...*, pp. 4-5.

42. *Texas State Gazetteer and Business Directory, 1884-5* (St. Louis: R. L. Polk & Co., 1884), pp. 398-399.

43. *Glen Rose Citizen*, January 22, 1885.

44. *Texas State Gazetteer...1890-91*, pp. 564-565; Nunn, pp. 69-70; Wilson, p. 41.

45. *Glen Rose Citizen*, April 2, 1885.

46. Fiedler, *Artesian Water in Somervell County Texas...*, p. 1.

47. Spaight, pp. 288-289.

48. James U. Vincent, *A Pen Picture of General Robert Toombs with a Glimpse of the Mental Characteristics of Hons. A.H. Stephens and Benj. H. Hill* (Louisville, Kentucky: Courier-Journal Job Printing Company, 1886), pp. 26-27; Doyle Wilson Interview. In 1886, of the total of 130 artesian wells county-wide, 86 of those wells were in Glen Rose.

49. Jacobs, pp. 9-13; *NHOT*, Vol. 3, "Hill, Robert Thomas," p. 616. The U. S. Geological Survey was established in 1879.

50. Fiedler, p. 18; Robert T. Hill, "Paleontology of the Cretaceous Formations of Texas—The Invertebrate Paleontology of the Trinity Division," *Proceedings of the Biological Society of Washington*, Vol. VIII (June 3, 1893): p. 11. In this report, Hill commented that the Trinity Division, which included the "Glen Rose, or alternating, beds" and the "Trinity, or basal, sands," "constitutes a paleontologic and stratigraphic division of the utmost importance in the interpretation of the North American Cretaceous." He also referenced his dinosaur bone find near Millsap, Texas, in Parker County, which occurred in 1886 (p. 13).

51. Hill, *Geography and Geology...*, p. 472.

52. Ibid., pp. 474, 478 (quote).

53. Ibid., pp. 475 (quote), 476.

54. Ibid., p. 476 (quote); Baker Interview; Wilson Historical Driving Tour; Wilson, p. 21.

Chapter 3: Making Tracks: Moonshiners, Model Ts, and the Lime Mud Strider

1. Elna Martin, *Glen Rose and Geo. P. Snyder: A Texas Town, The American Coue* (Dallas: Bradford Printing Co., Inc., 1927), p. 5. All future references to Martin in the endnotes refer to author Elna Martin and her book.

2. *Texas Almanac and State Industrial Guide, 1904* (Galveston: A.H. Belo & Co., 1904), p. 365. Glen Rose had 890 citizens.

3. Somervell County Deed of Records, Vol. J, pp. 4-5; Wilson, pp. 5, 16-17, 314, 350; Wilson Historical Driving Tour. H.O. Tidwell, born in 1843, brought his wife Elizabeth and ten children from Georgia to Texas in the 1880s.

4. Wilson, *Historic Lanham Mill...*, pp. 16, 56; Nunn, pp. 75-79.

5. Nunn, pp. 75-79; Gene Fowler and the Somervell County Historical Commission, *Images of*

America: Glen Rose, Texas (Chicago: Arcadia Publishing, 2002), pp. 125-128.

6. Wilson, *Historic Lanham Mill...*, pp. 16, 313-314; Somervell County Deed of Records, Vol. K, p. 126.

7. Somervell County Deed of Records, Vol. G, pp. 30-31, Vol. K, p. 465, Vol. V, pp. 12-13, Vol. I, p. 354; Wilson, *Historic Lanham Mill...*, pp. 58-60; Novella Wilson Interview; Doyle Wilson Interview; Baker Interview; Nunn, p. 136. J. T. Martin had already moved to Texas by the time the Civil War broke out, but not wanting to fight against his brother, he consequently returned to Illinois to join the Union army. He married Janette Turner. After her death he married Susan Bates. He eventually owned interest with son-in-law Henry A. Tidwell, son of H.O. Tidwell, in another 16 1/2 acres sandwiched between the Abell and Beck land and located near the present park entrance. Isaac Edgar "Ed" Martin was the son of Jacob and Janette Martin. The Martins later owned Martin and Sons, a longtime grocery and hardware business in Glen Rose.

8. Somervell County Deed of Records, Vol. K, p. 207.

9. Doyle Wilson Interview; Novella Wilson Interview; Baker Interview; Wilson, *Historic Lanham Mill...*, pp. 61-62; *Glen Rose Herald*, June 15, 1905. The Lanham Mill School may have been built as early as 1901 and served children during the 1901-1902 year.

10. Somervell County Deed of Records, Vol. M, pp. 101-103, Vol. K, p. 186; Wilson, pp. 54, 56, 74-75, 109, 183.

11. Wilson, *Historic Lanham Mill...*, pp. 8-15; Doyle Wilson Interview; Charlidell Davis Wilson Interview, July 28, 2004; Novella Wilson Historical Driving Tour; *History and Families...*, pp. 51-52; Novella Wilson Telephone Conversation, March 10, 2005.

12. Wilson, *Historic Lanham Mill...*, p. 9.

13. *Glen Rose Herald*, May 11, 1905 (quotes), February 15, 1906, August 30, 1906; Fowler, p. 56.

14. *The Weekly Enterprise* (Cleburne), April 23, 1908.

15. Ibid.

16. Ibid.; Wilson, *Historic Lanham Mill...*, p. 128.

17. *The Weekly Enterprise* (Cleburne), April 23, 1908.

18. Dorothy Leach Interview, July 29, 2004; B.J. Morris, Personal Conversation, July 30, 2004; *The Weekly Enterprise* (Cleburne), April 8, 1909.

19. Robert E. McDonald, Leander, Texas, letter to Mrs. Wayland G. Adams, Glen Rose, Texas, April 11, 1965, copy in THC marker files, "Dinosaur Tracks," Texas Historical Commission Library, Austin.

20. *The Weekly Enterprise* (Cleburne), April 8, 1909. The article to which Ravenel referred was: Dr. Richard S. Lull, "Nature's Heiroglyphics," *The Popular Science Monthly*, Vol. 66 (December, 1904): 139-149. Lull wrote primarily about the dinosaur tracks in the valley of the Connecticut River.

21. Edwin H. Colbert, "North American Dinosaur Hunters," in James O. Farlow and M. K. Brett-Surman, eds., *The Complete Dinosaur* (Bloomington: Indiana University Press, 1997), pp. 26-28.

22. Bird, *Bones for Barnum Brown*, pp. 1-2.

23. Ellis W. Shuler, "Dinosaur Tracks in the Glen Rose Limestone near Glen Rose, Texas," *The American Journal of Science*, Vol. XLIV (October 1917): 294. The author cannot explain the discrepancy of Shuler's accounting of a total of eight tracks versus the total of twelve originally reported in *The Weekly Enterprise* on April 8, 1909.

24. Ibid., pp. 296-298.

25. John D. Morris, *Tracking Those Incredible Dinosaurs ... and the People Who Knew Them* (San Diego: CLP Publishers, 1980), pp. 10 (quote), 11; Glen J. Kuban, "On the Heels of Dinosaurs: An Informal History of the Texas 'Man Track' Controversy," 1995-2006, (http://paleo.cc/paluxy/onheel.htm),

accessed on December 18, 2006; Ilo Hiller, "Where the Dinosaurs Roamed," *Texas Parks & Wildlife*, Vol. 41, No. 7 (July 1983): 7-8; Mrs. Luba (Ora Lee) LeBoeuf and William B. Cowan, Jr., "History of Dinosaur Valley State Park," unpublished manuscript, Park Files, Dinosaur Valley State Park, Glen Rose, Texas. Some sources also claim that the Moss brothers first found sauropod tracks at this time. The dates vary from 1910 to 1912. Charlie Moss provided a written statement on December 19, 1950, stating that he found tracks from the time of "about 1908 to 1918." This statement was published in the John D. Morris book. His statement includes the following description of the human-like prints:

... about 15 tracks or footprints of apparent giant human beings. The tracks measured about 18 inches from heel to toe, the five toes being plainly marked. The first few tracks were about 6 feet apart; then from 8 to 10 feet apart as the person started to run. In these prints only the toes and balls of the feet were in evidence. They were in an 8-inch layer of limestone along the river bank.

26. Somervell County Deed of Records, Vol. R, p. 446, Vol. X, pp. 42-43; Wilson, *Historic Lanham Mill...*, p. 127. Muse's fences consisted of painted white posts that lined the road.

27. Martin, pp. 25-27.

28. Somervell County Deed of Records, Vol. W, pp. 74-75; Wilson, *Historic Lanham Mill...*, pp. 34, 107, 361, 365; Novella Wilson Telephone Interview, March 2, 2005. Two of the twelve Wilson children died in infancy. Dillard's brother George Eugene Wilson was already living on the Rowland farm when he died of pneumonia in April 1920.

29. Novella Wilson Telephone Interview, March 2, 2005. According to Novella Wilson, the old Adams dogtrot cabin was not a typical residence in the Lanham Mill area by the 1920s. Most homes were of frame construction.

30. Doyle Wilson Interview; Nunn, p. 136.

31. Nunn, pp. 121-124; Fowler, pp. 99-101.

32. THC marker files, "Snyder Sanitarium"; Novella Wilson, Personal Conversation, May 18, 2007.

33. Martin, pp. 49, 66. The name Coue refers to the popular French psychotherapist Emile Coue (1857-1926). His well-known catchphrase reflects his teachings of healing by positive autosuggestion: "Day by day, in every way, I am getting better and better." In this context, writer Elna Martin is comparing the practices and philosophies of George P. Snyder, who claimed to be a magnetic healer in Glen Rose, to Emile Coue. Hence, Snyder is "The American Coue."

34. Ibid., p. 6.

35. Ibid., p. 11.

36. *Glen Rose Herald*, August 30, 1906; Glen Rose Reporter, May 29, 1975; Rhonda Mears Duffie, "Bootlegging," *Somervell Settlers*, Vol. 6, No. 2 (Summer 2001): 41-45; Nunn, pp. 130-134; Fowler, pp. 50-52; Doyle Wilson Interview; Novella Wilson Interview; Wilson, pp. 137-142; King Interview; Kenneth Hopson, Personal Conversation, July 15, 2005; Murray Dehtan, Personal Conversation, July 15, 2005. I.E. "Ed" Martin led the petition with over two hundred others to hold an election to prohibit the sale of liquor in Somervell County in 1906.

37. Novella Wilson Interview, March 2, 2005.

38. Wilson, *Historic Lanham Mill...*, pp. 25-28, 139-142. John A. Hamberlin, the grandfather of Charlie Moss, built a shingle mill above Murphy crossing and owned a farm. After Charlie's father William Boone Moss died, his mother Lallah Hamberlin Moss, moved the family onto her parents' farm.

39. Ibid., pp. 139-142; King Interview; Doyle Wilson Interview; Hopson Conversation; Dehtan Conversation. Charlie Moss claimed that he and a partner netted $25,000 in one year from the production of moonshine.

40. Fowler, p. 50; Nunn, pp. 125, 131; Hopson Conversation; Dehtan Conversation. Some sources have also quoted the phrase, "Moonshine Capital of Central Texas" for Somervell County. Old-timers of Somervell County have surmised that the term "hoe beer" may have been slang for homebrew beer.

41. Doyle Wilson Interview; Hopson Conversation; Dehtan Conversation; King Interview. Some families carried on a tradition of making their own moonshine, even into the twenty-first century.

42. Fowler, p. 40.

43. Ibid.

44. Doyle Wilson Interview; Charlidell Davis.

45. "History of Somervell County" in WPA Records, Somervell County, Center for American History, University of Texas at Austin; *NHOT*, Vol. 3, "Highway Development," pp. 607-608.

46. "History of Somervell County" in WPA Records.

47. Martin, p. 36.

48. *The WPA Guide to Texas* (Austin: Texas Monthly Press, 1986, orig. published New York: Hastings House, 1940), p. 593; *Dallas Morning News*, July 25, 1937; Fowler, pp. 111-119; *History and Families...*, p. 168. Petrified wood was not prevalent in the Lanham Mill community, but upstream in the town of Paluxy just inside Hood County, farmers often found petrified wood.

49. Leach Interview; Maxie Parker Leach, Telephone Interview, July 6, 2005.

50. Martin, p. 1. According to paleontologist James Farlow, during the early twentieth century, before radiometric dating came into its own, most geologists estimated dinosaur tracks to be significantly younger than they actually were.

51. Ibid., pp. 2-3. The author contacted Texas A&M University regarding the possible whereabouts of a theropod track quarried in the 1920s as mentioned by Elna Martin, but no one was aware of a dinosaur print, and no track was found.

52. Ibid., pp. 44-45.

53. Fowler, p. 7; *Somervell County Centennial*, p. 73.

54. Laurie P. Sanders Interview, New Braunfels, Texas, August 25, 1988; Laurie E. Jasinski, *Hill Country Backroads: Showing the Way in Comal County* (Fort Worth: Texas Christian University Press, 2001), p. 55. Before 2004 the author had mistakenly assumed that her grandmother saw dinosaur tracks in the Paluxy River in 1929, though, in the interview, Mrs. Sanders never actually stated that the stream was the Paluxy. In light of research conducted during 2004 and 2005 in Glen Rose, it is very probable that Joe and Laurie Sanders saw the tracks on Wheeler Branch.

55. Laurie Jo Sanders Jasinski Interview, November 13, 2004; Laurie P. Sanders, various conversations; *Somervell County Centennial*, p. 56.

56. Sanders Interview. Mrs. Sanders never described a trough-shaped wooden cover over the tracks as described by author Elna Martin in her book (p. 45) from 1927. This would indicate that in 1929 the dinosaur tracks were left out in the open.

Chapter 4: Work and Play on Paluxy "Creek"

1. Nunn, pp. 135-136; Johnson, p. 777; *The Texas Almanac and State Industrial Guide* (Dallas: A.H. Belo Corporation, 1936), p. 444. In 1930 almost one-third of the county population lived in Glen Rose, which had 983 residents.

2. Novella Wilson, *Kids and Kinfolk of George Wilson* (Glen Rose, Texas: Novella Wilson, July 1983), p. 54.

3. Ibid.; Novella Wilson Telephone Interview, March 2, 2005.

4. Wilson Historical Driving Tour. The family lived with Vivian's father, Newt May, a widower. The May farm was located just outside the boundaries of the present park.

5. Wilson, *Historic Lanham Mill...*, p. 62; Doyle Wilson Interview.

6. Doyle Wilson Interview.

7. Novella Wilson Interview, July 28, 2004.

8. Fowler, p. 25; Ellis W. Shuler, "Dinosaur Track Mounted in the Band Stand at Glen Rose, Texas," *Field & Laboratory*, Vol. 4, No. 1 (November, 1935): 9. According to Dorothy Leach of the Somervell County Historical Commission, locals called the bandstand theropod track the "verdict" track, used for comparison against other theropod prints. The bandstand with dinosaur track was officially dedicated on April 6, 1933.

9. Shuler, "Dinosaur Track Mounted...," p. 9. Shuler mentions "at least nine localities in Hood County, Texas." (He mistakenly writes Hood County instead of Somervell County.) In "Dinosaur Tracks at the Fourth Crossing of the Paluxy River Near Glen Rose, Texas," *Field & Laboratory*, Vol. 5, No. 2 (April 1937), p. 33, Shuler writes "at least eight localities," perhaps taking into account that one site had been washed away.

10. Shuler, "Dinosaur Track Mounted," p. 13. Shuler's use of the question mark in the name *Eubrontes (?) glenrosensis* reflected his uncertainty (as in 1917 during his initial studies) as to whether his species was correctly attributed to *Eubrontes*.

11. *Dallas Morning News*, August 12, 1934. In his later years, Robert T. Hill wrote occasional columns for the *Dallas Morning News*. This particular column was divided into several subject sections, and the write-up under the heading "Open Season for Dinosaur Hunting" contained the interesting references to the recent discoveries in the field of paleontology.

12. Ibid. Hill was referring to the Howe Quarry site in Wyoming. Among those working there for Barnum Brown was Roland Bird (*Bones for Barnum Brown*, pp. 47-65).

13. Shuler, "Dinosaur Tracks at the Fourth Crossing of the Paluxy River Near Glen Rose, Texas," *Field & Laboratory*, Vol. 5, No. 2 (April 1937): pp. 33-34, 36.

14. Hiller, p. 7; LeBoeuf and Cowan, unpublished manuscript; Fowler, p. 23; Wilson, *Historic Lanham Mill...*, p. 147; THC marker file, "Dinosaur Tracks"; *Somervell County Centennial*, p. 82; *Glen Rose Reporter*, May 29, 1975. Specific years of the sauropod track discovery vary among sources. LeBoeuf and Cowan state that Charlie and Grandy Moss found sauropod tracks as early as 1912 on a ledge near Murphy crossing (about the same time they found the "human-like" tracks). Hiller repeats this date. Most sources agree that the Moss brothers found the first sauropod tracks in the streambed in the present-day park in 1934, and a photograph was taken in August 1934.

15. Fiedler, p. 1.

16. Ibid., pp. 2 (quote), 3. The 360,000 gallons of wasted water was part of a total estimate of 1,000,000 gallons used each day in Somervell County during the summer. The total figure included 150,000 gallons for domestic use, 180,000 gallons for irrigation, 60,000 for watering stock, and 250,000 for recreational pools.

17. Doyle Wilson Interview; *Dallas Morning News*, July 25, 1937.

18. Novella Wilson Historical Driving Tour.

19. Novella Wilson Interview, July 28. 2004; Novella Wilson Telephone Interview, April 2, 2005.

20. Novella Wilson Interview, July 28. 2004; Novella Wilson Telephone Interview, April 2, 2005; Daisy Ryals May Telephone Interview, April 2, 2005; Doyle Wilson Interview; Charlidell Davis Wilson Interview, July 28, 2004; Leach Interview; Roland T. Bird, "We Captured a 'Live' Brontosaur," *National Geographic*, Vol. 105, No. Five (May, 1954): pp. 709, 712; Kuban, "On the Heels of Dinosaurs: An Informal History of the Texas 'Man Track' Controversy"; Morris, pp. 109-110. To carve a track, the sculptor started with an existing block of stone that already had a depression in it.

21. Novella Wilson Interview, July 28, 2004. John and Novella Wilson lived in their home near the Dillard Wilson farm until John was drafted during World War II.

22. Doyle Wilson Interview.

Chapter 5: The Dinosaur Hunter and the Texas Village

1. Doyle Wilson Interview; Doyle Wilson Telephone Interview, April 4, 2005.

2. Doyle Wilson Interview.

3. Bird, *Bones for Barnum Brown*, Introduction (pp. 1-16) by James Farlow, pp. 1, 17. Bird also had a bout with rheumatic fever as a child.

4. Ibid., pp. 1, 17, 19-22.

5. Ibid., pp. 1, 5-6. Barnum Brown was born on February 12, 1873, in Carbondale, Kansas.

6. Colbert, "North American Dinosaur Hunters" in *The Complete Dinosaur*, p. 30. Economic and world events helped discourage dinosaur exploration and scientific funding with the Great Depression and especially World War II. Also, though some exploration and research continued during this time, the paleontological community shifted its focus from dinosaurs to the mammal-like reptiles (the therapsids), that scientists judged were "in the mainstream of evolution" (Colbert, pp. 30-31; Farlow Telephone Interview, February 7, 2005).

7. Jacobs, p. 5.

8. R.T. Bird to Barnum Brown, Thanksgiving Day, 1938, page 3 [and/or] page 4, Field Correspondence 1933-1939, Box 7, Folder 9, Vertebrate Paleontology Archives, Division of Paleontology, American Museum of Natural History, New York. Thanksgiving Day 1938 was November 24, 1938. The quoted passages from Bird's correspondence are faithful to the original typescript and handwritten letters, including misspellings.

9. Bird, *Bones for Barnum Brown*, pp. 146-147.

10. Bird to Brown, Thanksgiving Day, 1938.

11. R.T. Bird to Mr. Adamson, November 30, 1938, Field Correspondence 1933-1939, Box 7, Folder 9, Vertebrate Paleontology Archives, Division of Paleontology, American Museum of Natural History, New York. Hans Christian Adamson, a writer and reporter, was Chairman of Public and Press Information at the American Museum of Natural History from 1938 to 1941. Additionally, he served as Assistant to the President of the American Museum. During the mid-1930s he was also the founding editor of *The Sky* magazine, the forerunner to *Sky & Telescope*.

12. Roland T. Bird, "Thunder in His Footsteps," *Natural History*, Vol. XLIII, No. 5 (May, 1939): p. 256.

13. Bird to Adamson, November 30, 1938.

14. *Dallas Morning News*, July 25, 1937.

15. Bird to Brown, Thanksgiving Day, 1938.

16. Bird, "Thunder in His Footsteps," p. 257.

17. Ibid., p. 260.

18. Fowler, p. 26.

19. Bird to Brown, Thanksgiving Day, 1938.

20. Bird, p. 149.

21. Doyle Wilson Interview; *Texas Almanac and State Industrial Guide*, 1941-42 (Dallas: A. H. Belo

Corporation, 1941), p. 505.

22. Doyle Wilson Telephone Interview, April 4, 2005.

23. Bird, "Thunder in His Footsteps," p. 260; James Farlow Interview, August 6, 2004. Earlier in November 1938, Bird had examined possible sauropod tracks in Colorado, but they were poorly defined, and he was not convinced that the site truly contained sauropod footprints. In later years the site was confirmed as a sauropod tracksite (Farlow, *A Guide to Lower Cretaceous Dinosaur Footprints...*, p. 2).

24. Farlow Interview.

25. Bird, "Thunder in His Footsteps," p. 260; Bird, *Bones for Barnum Brown*, p. 149.

26. Bird, *Bones for Barnum Brown*, p. 149.

27. Bird to Adamson, November 30, 1938.

28. Roland T. Bird, "To Capture a Dinosaur Isn't Easy," Natural History, Vol. 62, No. 3 (March, 1953): p. 106.

29. Ibid.; Roland T. Bird to Mr. Monaco, November 30, 1938, Field Correspondence 1933-1939, Box 7, Folder 9, Vertebrate Paleontology Archives, Division of Paleontology, American Museum of Natural History, New York.

30. Doyle Wilson Telephone Interview, April 4, 2005.

Chapter 6: In the Footsteps of the Dinosaurs

1. Bird to Brown, Thanksgiving Day, 1938.

2. *Dallas Morning News*, November 30, 1938.

3. Farlow, *A Guide to Lower Cretaceous Dinosaur Footprints...*, p. 2.

4. Bird, "Thunder in His Footsteps," p. 302.

5. "Evolution of the Company Symbol," Sinclair Oil Corporation Website, (http://www.sinclairoil.com/history/historys_p1.htm), accessed January 26, 2007; Farlow, *A Guide to Lower Cretaceous Dinosaur Footprints...*, p. 2.

6. Farlow, *A Guide to Lower Cretaceous Dinosaur Footprints...*, pp. 2-3; Nunn, p. 116; Bird, *Bones for Barnum Brown*, p. 156.

7. Glen Evans Interview, July 15, 2004; Bird, *Bones for Barnum Brown*, p. 156.

8. Evans Interview; *NHOT*, Vol. 6, "Texas Memorial Museum," pp. 359-360. Evans earned thirty cents an hour in Austin working at the State Legislature at night, while he studied and attended classes during the day. Sellards was director of the Texas Memorial Museum by the time of its official opening on January 15, 1939.

9. Evans Interview; Bird, *Bones for Barnum Brown*, pp. 156-163; Roland Bird, Bandera, Texas, to Henry Bird, March 26, 1940, copy from Roland T. Bird Dinosaur Tracks Collection, Somervell County Heritage Center, Glen Rose, Texas.

10. Roland Bird to Henry Bird, March 26, 1940, March 29, 1940.

11. Bird to Brown, April 9, 1940, Field Correspondence 1940-1951, Box 8, Folder 2, Vertebrate Paleontology Archives, Division of Paleontology, American Museum of Natural History, New York; Bird, *Bones for Barnum Brown*, p. 164; Doyle Wilson Interview. There is some discrepancy in Bird's writings regarding the exact number of men in his work crew. In his letter to Brown dated March 12, 1940, he specifically states, "So far I have had seven men," but in his memoir *Bones for Barnum Brown* (p. 164) he lists eight men. In his article "To Capture a Dinosaur Isn't Easy," published in *Natural History* in March 1953, he lists a "ten-man crew at the initial job of damming the river" (p. 106). A further compli-

cation—his letter dated March 12, 1940, gives all of the early details of the excavation that took place within a few days of April 9, 1940, as detailed in *Bones for Barnum Brown*. The author suspects that the March 12th letter is misdated and should really be April 12, 1940. Perhaps while recounting the story years later, Bird included all of his major workers at the beginning of the project, while one may have actually signed on a few days or weeks later. In the same letter dated March 12, 1940, in which he describes all of the setup and initial work of the crew, he writes, "I regreted the fact I hadn't a motion picture camera to record this first phase of the work...." In *Bones for Barnum Brown* (p. 165) he writes, "I turned to go for the movie camera to shoot the first pictures [on the first day of work]."

12. Bird, *Bones for Barnum Brown*, p. 164.

13. Bird to Brown, March 12, 1940. See footnote 11 regarding March date.

14. Ibid.; Bird, *Bones for Barnum Brown*, p. 165.

15. Bird to Brown, March 12, 1940.

16. Novella Wilson Telephone Interview, April 2, 2005; letterhead on much of Bird's correspondence.

17. Bird, *Bones for Barnum Brown*, pp. 1, 165-166.

18. Doyle Wilson Interview.

19. Bird to Brown, March 12, 1940. Bird also conducted limited exploration for fossil bones in the area. He reported his observation of three sacral vertebrae of a sauropod at the home of a fossil collector in Stephenville. He also saw the remnants of a skeleton that he theorized was possibly part of a duckbill dinosaur. He was hopeful regarding a major fossil bone discovery, and while he observed some limited specimens, he did not make any major discoveries nor did he have sufficient time for a thorough survey of the region.

20. Ibid., April 17, 1940, copy in Roland T. Bird Correspondence in Park Files, Dinosaur Valley State Park, Glen Rose, Texas.

21. Ibid., April 29, 1940, Field Correspondence 1940-1951, Box 8, Folder 2, Vertebrate Paleontology Archives, Division of Paleontology, American Museum of Natural History, New York.

22. Ibid., May 19, 1940, copy in Roland T. Bird Correspondence in Park Files, Dinosaur Valley State Park, Glen Rose, Texas; Evans Interview.

23. Evans Interview.

24. Doyle Wilson Interview; *Bones for Barnum Brown*, pp. 172-174.

25. Bird to Brown, May 23, 1940, Field Correspondence 1940-1951, Box 8, Folder 2, Vertebrate Paleontology Archives, Division of Paleontology, American Museum of Natural History, New York.

26. Doyle Wilson Interview.

27. Doyle Wilson Telephone Interview, March 30, 2005; *Bones for Barnum Brown*, p. 171; Brown to Bird, May 31, 1940; Bird to Brown, May 27, 1940 (quote), Field Correspondence 1940-1951, Box 8, Folder 2, Vertebrate Paleontology Archives, Division of Paleontology, American Museum of Natural History, New York.

28. Charlidell Davis Wilson Interview (quotes); Charlidell Davis Wilson Telephone Interview, April 9, 2005; Doyle Wilson Telephone Interview, March 30, 2005; Somervell County Deed of Records, Vol. 33, pp. 77-78, 40-41, Vol. 54, p. 605. W.D. Jones purchased 110 acres (the old Martin place) from G.E. and Anna Segelhurst. They had bought the land from C.W. Gravitt in 1931. Johnny Beck, son of landowner Charlie Beck, lived in the old Martin house during the excavation of the dinosaur tracks by R.T. Bird.

29. Novella Wilson Interview; Daisy Ryals May Telephone Interview, April 2, 2005.

30. Bird, *Bones for Barnum Brown*, p. 181.

31. Bird to Brown, May 27, 1940; Doyle Wilson Telephone Interview, March 30, 2005.

32. Doyle Wilson Telephone Interview, March 30, 2005.

33. Bird to Brown, May 27, 1940; Brown to Bird, May 31, 1940; Bird to Brown, June 1, 1940, copy in Roland T. Bird Correspondence in Park Files, Dinosaur Valley State Park, Glen Rose, Texas. In his reply to Bird on May 31, 1940, Barnum Brown wrote:

Sellards released the publicity and he is in the position to counteract any adverse repercussions. I have kept your work out of print here so as to avoid any such possibilities of interference.

For your guidance, I believe a river course is defined by the evidence of the maximum amount of water carried, which would be determined by the drift wood along the banks. Ask your lawyer friend, Adams, about this in case it should come up.

34. Bird, *Bones for Barnum Brown*, p. 179; Bird to Brown, June 12, 1940, Field Correspondence 1940-1951, Box 8, Folder 2, Vertebrate Paleontology Archives, Division of Paleontology, American Museum of Natural History, New York. In his June 12 letter, Bird also mentioned that E.H. Sellards had been in contact with "Gilmore"—Charles Gilmore at the Smithsonian Institute. Bird expressed his belief that, once the excavation was over, area farmers would raid the streambed for more tracks. He wrote, "The farmers nearby, who have taken up many a carnivore print in the past, are already eyeing and considering the sauropod tracks with envy—almost with a hammer and chisel in the hands."

According to paleontologist James Farlow, after long years in storage, the fossil footprint specimen that Bird quarried for Brooklyn College was rediscovered at that institution in June 2005. In 2007 Southern Methodist University was in possession of two prints that appeared to be quarried by someone other than Bird, perhaps by Jim Ryals. Those prints are bound by metal rings that Ryals used to secure his quarry to prevent breakage.

35. Bird, *Bones for Barnum Brown*, p. 171; Jacobs, pp. 8-9; Roland T. Bird, "We Captured a 'Live' Brontosaur," *The National Geographic Magazine*, Vol. 105, No. 5 (May, 1954): p. 720.

36. Roland T. Bird, Homestead, Florida, to Novella Wilson, Glen Rose, Texas, February 8, 1973, copy courtesy Novella Wilson Collection.

37. Ibid.; "Roland T. Bird Dinosaur Tracks Collection" in Research Files, Somervell County Heritage Center, Glen Rose, Texas; Bird, "We Captured a 'Live' Brontosaur," p. 711. In correspondence with the author, paleontologist James Farlow wrote:

In 1986, as part of a symposium on dinosaur tracks, I led a field trip of paleontologists to Dinosaur Valley State Park. When I showed them a sauropod print that was partly underwater, some of them insisted that their picture be taken as they sat in it—paleontologists from around the world deliberately imitating little Tommy Pendley.

38. Doyle Wilson Interview.

39. Ibid.; Novella Wilson Interview; Novella Wilson, *Historic Lanham Mill...*, p. 147; Bird to Brown, May 19, 1940. The Missouri, Kansas and Texas Railway Company (Katy) ran trains through Walnut Springs. Originally the railway through Walnut Springs had been constructed and operated in the early 1900s by the Texas Central Railroad.

40. Bird to Brown, June 12, 1940.

41. Ibid., (quote); Riskind, David. "A Celebration of Glen Evans," Address given April 1, 2001, Texas Memorial Museum of Science and History, in Research Files, Natural Resources Program, Texas Parks and Wildlife Department, Austin; Glen Evans, Personal Conversation, August 4, 2005; Bird, *Bones for Barnum Brown*, p. 186.

42. Bird to Brown, June 12, 1940.

43. Ibid., June 28, 1940, Field Correspondence 1940-1951, Box 8, Folder 2, Vertebrate Paleontology Archives, Division of Paleontology, American Museum of Natural History, New York. A copy of the film is on file at the Somervell County Historical Commission as well as the Texas Parks and Wildlife Department.

44. Ibid., July 7, 1940.

45. Ibid.

46. Ibid., June 28, 1940.

47. Bird to Brown, July 27, 1940; Brown to Bird, July 30, 1940, both letters in Field Correspondence 1940-1951, Box 8, Folder 2, Vertebrate Paleontology Archives, Division of Paleontology, American Museum of Natural History, New York.

48. Bird, *Bones for Barnum Brown*, pp. 6, 17, 204; Bird, "We Captured a 'Live' Brontosaur," p. 722; S.Y. Shelton, R.C. Barnett, and M.D. Magruder, "Conservation of a Dinosaur Trackway Exhibit," Abstract in Vertical Files, "Dinosaur Valley State Park," Texas Parks and Wildlife Department, Cultural Resources Program / Natural Resources Program, Austin; *New York Times*, May 22, 1953.

49. J. R. Hildebrand, Assistant Editor, *National Geographic Magazine*, Washington, DC, to Roland T. Bird, American Museum of Natural History, New York, April 18, 1941, July 1, 1941, July 9, 1941, July 22, 1941, correspondence in "Roland T. Bird Dinosaur Tracks Collection," Somervell County Heritage Center, Glen Rose, Texas.

50. In the 1980s James Farlow and colleagues designated the sauropod tracks as *Brontopodus birdi*.

Chapter 7: The Fight for Dinosaur Valley

1. William Edward Syers, *Off the Beaten Trail* (Fort Worth: F.L. Motheral Company, 1964), Volume 2, p. 133.

2. Wilson, *Historic Lanham Mill...*, pp. 103, 143.

3. Ibid., p. 62; Somervell County Deed of Records, Vol. K, p. 207.

4. Laurie E. Jasinski, *Hill Country Backroads: Showing the Way in Comal County* (Fort Worth: Texas Christian University Press, 2001), p. 146; "Highway Highlights," Bulletins, Austin: Texas Good Roads Association, 1-30-46, 8-27-46, 3-29-47, Center for American History, University of Texas at Austin; General Highway Map, Hood County, Somervell County, Texas, Austin: Texas State Highway Department, 1936, completely revised to July 1947; Wilson, *Historic Lanham Mill...*, p. 14. Upstream from present Dinosaur Valley State Park, another ford, the Kimmel crossing, had been long abandoned.

5. *Texas Almanac and State Industrial Guide*, 1951-1952 (Dallas: A.H. Belo Corporation, 1951), p. 602; *Texas Almanac and State Industrial Guide*, 1941-42 (Dallas: A.H. Belo Corporation, 1941), p. 506; King Interview; Graves, p. 24.

6. Ibid.; Doyle Wilson Interview; Leach Interview; Novella Wilson Historical Driving Tour; Graves, pp. 56-57. Fiedler had warned about the wasted water of many uncapped wells and the decline of the water table in 1934.

7. Graves, p. 56.

8. Ibid., p. 58.

9. Somervell County Deed of Records, Vol. 43, pp. 386-388, Vol. 49, p. 307, Vol. 50, pp. 35-36, Vol. 40, p. 212. The sales to Earnest Winston Whitaker included two tracts (237 acres and 110 acres). Both of these parcels were later resurveyed to show that the properties actually included 245.04 acres and 138.31 acres.

10. Ibid., Vol. 44, pp. 644-645, Vol. 55, pp. 592-593, (Affidavits), pp. 86, 628; Wilson, *Historic Lanham Mill...*, p. 222. Evidently J.B. Abell's uncle, Charlie Walton Beck, and later Abell's cousin, Walter Erostus Beck, had interest in the adjoining forty-eight acres.

11. Somervell County Deed of Records, Vol. 43, pp. 629-633, Vol. 45, p. 73, Vol. 48, pp. 535-536, Vol. 49, pp. 405-407.

12. Ibid., Vol. 38, pp. 184-185, 214-216, 331-333, 584, Vol. 39, pp. 370-371, Vol. 42, p. 404, Vol. 44, pp. 124-125, Vol. 49, pp. 575-576, Vol. 33, pp. 571-575; Wilson, *Historic Lanham Mill...*, pp. 313-314.

13. Somervell County Deed of Records, Vol. 43, p. 423, Vol. 44, pp. 52-53, 56-57, Vol. 43, pp. 528-529, Vol. 48, pp. 181-183. In March 1951 Moody Booker resurveyed the 190 acres to show that the property was actually 183 acres (Vol. 43, p. 285). In 1946 Clay Huffman originally purchased remnants of the Galveston County School Land Grant and sold 451.82 acres to Dwight McDonald. By the end of the 1950s, McDonald, of Midland County, sold his two tracts to Roland and Neva Ball (Vol. 48, pp. 181-183).

14. Doyle Wilson Interview; Novella Wilson Interview; Wilson, *Historic Lanham Mill...*, pp. 143-144, 361-362 (quote).

15. Graves, pp. 44, 58.

16. Bird, "Thunder in His Footsteps," p. 256. Recall that Bird judged that the man-like tracks in Jack Hill's trading post were carved fabrications.

17. Ibid., p. 257.

18. James Farlow, author of the endnotes in Bird, *Bones for Barnum Brown*, p. 215.

19. Glen J. Kuban, "On the Heels of Dinosaurs: An Informal History of the Texas 'Man Track' Controversy," 1995-2006, (http://paleo.cc/paluxy/onheel.htm), accessed December 18, 2006; Glen J. Kuban Telephone Interview, April 23, 2005; Morris, p. 21; Farlow endnotes in Bird, *Bones for Barnum Brown*, p. 215. According to John Morris in his book *Tracking Those Incredible Dinosaurs...and the People Who Knew Them*, Burdick was part of a committee of five appointed to examine claims that the tracks Bird saw in Jack Hill's post were giant man tracks. Scientists judge that these giant man-like tracks are most likely carved fabrications. Burdick, of Los Angeles, found the tracks and used them as examples in subsequent articles and photos he published. Creationists believe that proof of the coexistence of humans and dinosaurs would cast serious doubt about the evolutionary time scale. According to creationists, the earth is approximately six thousand years old, and the dinosaurs were killed in Noah's flood. Creationists also assert that early man was much larger than modern man and that some humans may have been well over twelve feet tall. Author C. N. Dougherty in his *Valley of the Giants* (Cleburne, Texas: Bennett Printing Company, orig. pub. 1971, 4th ed. 1976) suggested that the first man, Adam, was as tall as sixteen feet (p. 51).

20. Farlow endnotes quoting Bird in *Bones for Barnum Brown*, p. 215. Bird regretted his inclusion of the man-like tracks in his May 1939 Natural History article, and his comments in the feature were often taken out of context. Some writers even credited him as the discoverer of the first petrified human footprints. A book by the famous "psychic" Jeanne Dixon made this claim, resulting in an immediate reply by Bird requesting that she retract the statement and delete it from future printings (*Bones for Barnum Brown*, p. 216).

21. *Dallas Morning News*, May 18, 1958. Tolbert also referred to Glen Rose's "courthouse senate" as the "hackberry senate."

22. Ibid., December 31, 1963.

23. *Waco Tribune-Herald*, July 24, 1966.

24. Syers, pp. 130, 132-133.

25. Leach Interview; Dan McCarty Interview, July 29, 2004; Miscellaneous clippings, Eugene Connally Collection, Somervell County Historical Commission Archives, Glen Rose, Texas; *Fort Worth Star-Telegram*, June 8, 9, 1965; *Glen Rose Reporter*, July 15, 1965. The proposed scenic parkway would have run south from Fort Worth roughly along U.S. Highway 377 to Granbury, State Highway 144 through Glen Rose to Meridian, State Highway 6 to Valley Mills, along a route to Mother Neff State Park and then to Belton, U.S. Highway 190 to Lampasas, and down U.S. Highway 281 to San Antonio (identification of route made by comparing drawing of proposed scenic parkway against current Texas highway maps). The Somervell County Historical Society was the forerunner to the Somervell County Historical Commission. Poage's inspiration for proposing a scenic route came from derogatory comments by *New York Daily News* columnist Ted Lewis who wrote: "the Lone Star State is big but its landscape is drab and without

one scenic beauty worth touting" (quote from clipping in Connally Collection, *Fort Worth Star-Telegram*, June 8, 1965).

26. Somervell County Deed of Records, Vol. 51, pp. 602-603; *Glen Rose Reporter*, July 15, 1965; Leach Interview; Baker Interview; Doyle Wilson Interview.

27. Somervell County Deed of Records, Vol. 51, pp. 602-603; *Glen Rose Reporter*, July 15, 1965; Leach Interview; Baker Interview; Doyle Wilson Interview.

28. *Glen Rose Reporter*, July 29, 1965.

29. Ibid., September 16, 1965.

30. Leach Interview; McCarty Interview; Miscellaneous clippings, Connally Collection.

31. *Glen Rose Reporter*, May 5, 1966.

32. Ibid.

33. McCarty Interview; *Fort Worth Press*, June 5, 1966.

34. National Monument Files, Dinosaur Trail National Monument, National Park Service Southwest Regional Office, copies in Historic Sites Program Director Files, Texas Parks and Wildlife, Austin, Texas; *Glen Rose Reporter*, June 2, 1966; *Fort Worth Star-Telegram*, June 1, 1966.

35. *Glen Rose Reporter*, June 2, 1966.

36. *Fort Worth Press*, June 5, 1966.

37. Ibid.

38. Leach Interview; McCarty Interview; *Cleburne Times-Review*, June 9, 1966.

39. Leach Interview; Texas Good Roads Association Newsletter, No. 68-9 (September 1968): p. 3; *Waco Tribune-Herald*, July 24, 1966.

40. Leach Interview; *Waco Tribune-Herald*, July 24, 1966.

41. Sinclair and the Exciting World of Dinosaurs, booklet published in 1967, in Park Files, Dinosaur Valley State Park, Glen Rose, Texas; *Glen Rose Reporter*, September 29, 1966. In addition to Barnum Brown, Dr. John H. Ostrom of the Peabody Museum of Natural History at Yale University also served as a technical consultant. The nine dinosaurs at Dinoland were *Brontosaurus, Struthiomimus, Trachodon, Tyrannosaurus, Triceratops, Ankylosaurus, Corythosaurus, Ornitholestes,* and *Stegosaurus*.

42. Roland T. Bird, Homestead, Florida, to Novella Wilson, Glen Rose, Texas, September 26, 1970, letter in private collection of Novella Wilson.

43. McCarty Interview; *Fort Worth Star-Telegram*, September 22, 1966.

44. Linda Mask Newland Interview, November 30, 2004; *Dallas Morning News*, September 27, 29, 1966. Technically, the Big Town shopping mall was located within the city limits of Mesquite, Texas, just east of Dallas. The Sinclair dinosaur exhibit was in Dallas from September 27 through October 2, 1966. The *Dallas Morning News* commented on the dinosaurs at Big Town: "They'll be there through Sunday, disturbing the sleep of kids and the waking hours of drunks." Dinomania struck "Big D," with local restaurants serving up "dino dogs," "Cretaceous coffee," and "brontosaurus burgers" among other eating delights, and three hundred inflated dinosaurs dangled from the ceiling in the Big Town mall. Big Town was torn down in the summer of 2006.

45. *Fort Worth Star-Telegram*, September 22, 1966; Geneva "Pete" May (Mrs. Alton May), Telephone Interview, June 18, 2005. The dinosaur caravan came from Tulsa and Oklahoma City to Fort Worth. Mrs. May recalled talking with the Sinclair Oil representative who accompanied the dinosaurs (probably Jim Tucker), and she suggested that the dinosaur models should eventually go to what would become Dinosaur Valley State Park at Glen Rose. According to Mrs. May, a place in Florida had already offered $70,000 for the dinosaur models. Alton and Geneva "Pete" May own and operate the Oakdale Park resort in Glen Rose.

46. *Glen Rose Reporter*, September 29, 1966.

47. Legal Acquisitions Files, Dinosaur Valley State Park, Land Conservation Division, Texas Parks and Wildlife Department, Austin; National Monument Files. The National Monument proposal was referred to the Committee on Interior and Insular Affairs.

48. Legal Acquisitions Files, "Preliminary Investigation Report: Proposed Glen Rose Dinosaur Tracks State Park," Research Planning Division, Park Services, Parks and Wildlife Department, March 12, 1967, pp. 3-5, Texas Parks and Wildlife Department, Austin.

49. Ibid., pp. 5 (quote), 6-7.

50. *Fort Worth Star-Telegram*, July 6, 1967; McCarty Interview.

51. *Fort Worth Star-Telegram*, July 6, 1967.

52. *Dallas Morning News*, August 14, 1967. In the summer of 1967 the Paluxy Valley saw considerable weekend visitation. Charlie Moss reported that in one weekend, thirty-nine cars paid to take a tour of the tracks on Saturday, and eighty-two carloads paid on Sunday. Most visitors were from the Dallas area (misc. clippings, Connally Collection).

Chapter 8: To Capture a Park—Landscape and Riverscape and Trailway

1. Misc. clippings, Connally Collection.

2. *Fort Worth Star-Telegram*, August 11, 1968.

3. Ibid.

4. *Glen Rose Reporter*, October 3, 1968. At that time the Whitakers lived in Alvarado, Texas, located about fifteen miles east of Cleburne. According to the *Glen Rose Reporter*:

Making the announcement possible last Friday [September 27, 1968] was sale of $5.75 million in park bonds to Lehmann Bros. & Associates of New York, who submitted the low interest rate bid of 3.5846 per cent last week.

5. McCarty Interview; Leach Interview.

6. Somervell County Deed of Records, Vol. 54, pp. 610-611; *Cleburne Times-Review*, January 1, 1969; *Fort Worth Star-Telegram*, January 1, 1969; Legal Acquisitions Files, "Preliminary Investigation Report," p. 4; McCarty Interview. During the resurvey of the two tracts, the 110-acre tract was shown to actually include 138.31 acres, and the 237-acre tract actually included 245.04 acres.

7. Clipping dated February 13, 1969, in private collection, Novella Wilson, Glen Rose; Lester Galbreath Telephone Interview, April 21, 2005; Baker Interview.

8. National Monument Files; Misc. clippings, Connally Collection; THC marker files.

9. Somervell County Deed of Records, Vol. 55, pp. 328-332; Doyle Wilson Interview; Novella Wilson Interview. Roland Ball and his wife Neva lived in the home almost up to the time of the sale. On May 23, 1969, they sold the property, including 8.1 acres right-of-way of a county road, to William D. Gafford and his wife Ethelene of Bosque County, and the Gaffords in turn sold the land to the state that same day.

10. Somervell County Deed of Records, Vol. 55, pp. 424-426, 435-436, 592-593, Vol. 56, pp. 165-166; Wilson, *Historic Lanham Mill...*, p. 42; Novella Wilson Telephone Interview, April 28, 2005. According to first park superintendent Lester Galbreath, many of the old structures on parkland had deteriorated beyond the point of saving. Also, park personnel at that time were not as aware of the historical aspects of structures.

11. Novella Wilson Interview; Wilson Historical Driving Tour. Novella Wilson has had an art studio in Glen Rose for many years and still taught painting classes in 2008. As of that time, she had pro-

duced more than one thousand paintings in her lifetime.

12. Novella Wilson Interview.

13. Galbreath Telephone Interviews, April 21, 2005, May 28, 2005. Lester Galbreath stated that he received instructions from TPWD Regional Director Billy Smith to get rid of the old tractor and hulls of cars. A local resident took the vehicles for scrap metal. Galbreath did not recall that the old Martin home was still standing by the time he arrived at the park. During his tenure as park superintendent, Galbreath spoke with many old-timers about the history of the area. After its initial use as a ranger residence, the old Wilson house was eventually torn down.

14. Ibid. Lester Galbreath also remembered an old barn in the area of Blue Hole. For years, swimmers used a long rope as a swing out over the Blue Hole. After a tragic accident resulting in a boy's death, the rope was removed.

15. Ibid.; Baker Interview. The Longhorn herd was located at Dinosaur Valley State Park from approximately 1971 to 1999.

16. *Glen Rose Reporter*, July 16, 1970; McCarty Interview. Newspaper articles of the time reported that Sinclair (as acquired by Atlantic Richfield) intended to abandon its dinosaur as a trademark. However, in 1976 Atlantic Richfield Company divested many assets, including retail operations in the Midwest and the rights to Sinclair's logo and brand, which were purchased by Earl Holding. This effectively reestablished Sinclair as a private company. In fact, Sinclair service stations, with the dinosaur symbol and small replica models, continued to operate in the western and midwestern United States in 2008. Sinclair's dinosaur trademark remained an important and highly-recognizable corporate emblem. Texas, however, had no Sinclair stations. ("Sinclair," Sinclair Oil Corporation Website [http://www.sinclairoil.com/about_sinclair.htm], accessed December 1, 2007.)

17. THC marker files, "Dinosaur Tracks"; *Dallas Morning News*, February 13, 1970; McCarty Interview.

18. *Glen Rose Reporter*, July 16, 1970.

19. McCarty Interview; Galbreath Telephone Interviews, April 21, 2005, May 28, 2005; Geneva "Pete" May Telephone Interview. Some discrepancy exists regarding the Bronto egg. Geneva "Pete" May recalled that an egg was located at Dinosaur Valley State Park, but the egg was vandalized. Park Superintendent Lester Galbreath stated that no egg came to the state park.

20. *Glen Rose Reporter*, July 23, 1970; Galbreath Telephone Interviews, April 21, 2005, May 28, 2005.

21. Galbreath Telephone Interviews, April 21, 2005, May 28, 2005.

22. Ibid.

23. Misc. clippings, Connally Collection.

24. Bird, *Bones for Barnum Brown*, p. 219; Roland T. Bird, Homestead, Florida, to Mrs. Novella Wilson, Glen Rose, Texas, September 26, 1970, copy in private collection of Novella Wilson, Glen Rose, Texas. R. T. Bird and Hazel Russell married on June 4, 1946. She had two small adopted daughters from a previous marriage. V.T. Schreiber edited Bird's memoirs into the book *Bones for Barnum Brown*. For a short time, Schreiber had also worked at Dinosaur Valley State Park as an interpreter.

25. Bird to Wilson, September 26, 1970.

26. Novella Wilson Interview.

27. In his letter to Novella Wilson on February 8, 1973, Bird had referred to himself at the time of the track excavation as "still unmarried at the ancient age of 40."

28. *Glen Rose Reporter*, October 8, 1970; *Johnson County News*, October 8, 1970; *Waco Tribune-Herald*, October 3, 1970; Misc. clippings, Connally Collection.

29. *Glen Rose Reporter*, October 1, 1970 (quote), October 8, 1970.

30. Ibid., October 8, 1970.

31. Clipping dated October 8, 1970 in private collection of Novella Wilson, Glen Rose, Texas.

32. Roland T. Bird, Homestead, Florida, to Mrs. Novella Wilson, Glen Rose, Texas, November 19, 1970, letter in private collection of Novella Wilson, Glen Rose, Texas.

Chapter 9: Growing Pains for Dinosaur Valley State Park

1. *Texas Almanac and State Industrial Guide*, 1972-1973, p. 331; *Fort Worth Star-Telegram*, July 24, 1970; Leach Interview. Somervell County's population remained fairly constant from 1960 to 1970, with a small increase from 2,577 to 2,793. The two companies that came to town were the Wall Manufacturing Company of Cleburne and the Texas Cedar Oil Company, Inc.

2. Galbreath Telephone Interviews, April 21, 2005, May 28, 2005; *Glen Rose Reporter*, January 7, 1971. Lester Galbreath's tenure at Dinosaur Valley State Park actually overlapped with Walker for a couple of months. Galbreath then relocated to Lake Whitney and eventually to Fort Griffin State Park where he retired in August 2004.

3. Galbreath Telephone Interviews, April 21, 2005, May 28, 2005; *Fort Worth Star-Telegram*, October 10, 1971; Waco News-Tribune, March 17, 1972; Baker Interview.

4. *Glen Rose Reporter*, January 7, 1971; *Fort Worth Star-Telegram*, October 10, 1971; Waco News-Tribune, March 17, 1972 (quote).

5. Waco News-Tribune, March 17, 1972.

6. Ibid.; Mrs. Luba (Ora Lee) LeBoeuf and William B. Cowan, Jr., "History of Dinosaur Valley State Park," (May 1979) unpublished manuscript, Park Files, Dinosaur Valley State Park, Glen Rose.

7. Misc. clippings, unnamed, dated September 28, 29, 1972, Connally Collection. In 2007 the conservation and preservation award of the Society of American Travel Writers was called the Phoenix Award.

8. *Fort Worth Star-Telegram*, October 1, 1972.

9. Ibid.; Misc. clippings, Connally Collection.

10. Legal Acquisitions Files, Dinosaur Valley State Park, Land Conservation Program, Texas Parks and Wildlife, Austin. Superintendent Walker indicated in a memo to Parks and Wildlife officials that Fannin ultimately aimed to achieve a higher appraisal price. The State appraised the land at $350 per acre. Fannin countered with a suggested price of $700 per acre. In the final sale, the Fannins sold their land for about $950 per acre. The 258 acres included 4.54 acres right-of-way for Park Road No. 59, which had already been previously deeded to the State of Texas (Somervell County Deed of Records, Vol. 53, p. 602).

11. Legal Acquisitions Files, Dinosaur Valley State Park, Land Conservation Program, Texas Parks and Wildlife, Austin; *Glen Rose Reporter*, April 6, 1972; Somervell County Deed of Records, Vol. 61, pp. 162-164. The Fannins removed two small houses from the property.

12. Texas State Library and Archives, Genealogy Department, Texas Death Index Records; Misc. clipping, unnamed, dated May 16, 1973, Connally Collection.

13. LeBoeuf and Cowan, unpublished manuscript; Archeology Files, "Development Plan and Program for Primitive Camping Area and Revegetation in Dinosaur Valley State Park, Somervell County, Texas," June, 1975, Parks Division, Master Planning Branch, Texas Parks and Wildlife Department, Austin, p. 1; Baker Interview; Archeology Files, "National Registry of Natural Landmarks Biennial Inspection Report," Texas Parks and Wildlife Department, Austin.

14. *Dallas Morning News*, August 14, 1967.

15. "National Registry of Natural Landmarks Biennial Inspection Report," p. 4; Baker Interview;

Dismukes Interview. Interestingly, this biennial report also made mention of the two Sinclair dinosaur models at the park and the display panel that Allen erected for them. The report then stated: "A smaller Brontosaurus and 2 eggs will be added to this display." Evidently in 1974 the whereabouts of these extra Sinclair models was still known.

16. "National Registry...," p. 3; Somervell County Deed of Records, Vol. 64, pp. 614-616; Wilson, *Historic Lanham Mill...*, p. 62; plaque on Lanham Mill Schoolhouse, Heritage Park, Glen Rose. The McFalls purchased the Lanham Mill Schoolhouse for $350.

17. Nunn, p. 203; *Dallas Morning News*, January 20, 1980; Vertical Files, "Glen Rose, Texas," Center for American History, University of Texas at Austin; King Interview; Vertical Files, "Cities and Towns—Glen Rose," Texas State Library and Archives, Austin.

18. Vertical Files, "Cities and Towns—Glen Rose," Texas State Library and Archives, Austin; History and Families: *Somervell County, Texas...*, p. 167; *Wichita Falls Times*, July 2, 1978; *Glen Rose Reporter*, May 29, 1975.

19. Curtis Busch Interview, June 3, 2007.

20. Ibid.; Vertical Files, "Paleontology," Texas State Library and Archives, Austin; Vertical Files, "Dinosaurs," Center for American History, University of Texas at Austin; S. Alan Skinner and Charles Blome, "Dinosaur Track Discovery at Comanche Peak Steam Electric Station, Somervell County, Texas," article in Dinosaur Tracks Collection, Somervell County Heritage Center, Glen Rose, Texas, pp. 1-2, 5-6. The track discovery occurred on May 14, 1975. Crews had used explosives for excavating, making this rare find all the more improbable. A difference of six inches above or below the track layer would have resulted in no discovery. According to Jason Sanchez, Park Ranger at Dinosaur Valley State Park, one of the excavated tracks from Comanche Peak went to Dinosaur Valley State Park. The track, however, sat out in the elements and eventually crumbled by the late 1980s. The *Houston Chronicle* (April 25, 1976) reported that Texas Utilities retained some of the tracks. Sources differ as to the exact number of theropod tracks found, varying from eight to as many as thirteen prints. Curtis Busch remembered seven tracks. All were quarried. Sources also conflict regarding the depth of the crater, and the numbers reported vary from fifty to eighty feet. The author is inclined to think that a depth of fifty feet, based on Curtis Busch's explanation and on photographic views of the crater, is more accurate.

21. *Stephenville Empire-Tribune*, July 1, 1976.

22. *Dallas Morning News*, July 2, 1979; *Fort Worth Star-Telegram*, July 10, 1978.

23. John Clements, Flying the Colors: Texas, Dallas: Clements Research, Inc., 1984, p. 402; *Texas Almanac...1982-1983*, p. 333.

24. LeBoeuf and Cowan; Baker Interview; Cultural Resource Files, Dinosaur Valley State Park, Texas Parks and Wildlife Department, Austin; Archeology Files, "Development Plan and Program...," June, 1975, p. 11, Texas Parks and Wildlife Department, Austin.

25. Baker Interview.

26. Glen Kuban Telephone Interview, April 23, 2005; Kuban, "On the Heels of Dinosaurs...."

27. Glen Kuban Telephone Interview, April 23, 2005; Kuban, "On the Heels of Dinosaurs..."; Morris, p. 25-28. Taylor owned a small company called Films for Christ. His film was released in January 1973.

28. Dougherty, pp. 49, 52; Kuban, "On the Heels of Dinosaurs..."; J.R. Cole, L.R. Godfrey, R.J. Hastings, and S.D. Schafersman, "Introduction" in "The Paluxy River Footprint Mystery—Solved," Special Issue, edited by John R. Cole and Laurie R. Godfrey, Creation/Evolution, Vol. 5, No. 1 (Issue XV, Winter 1985): p. 1; Both Dougherty's *Valley of the Giants* and Morris' *Tracking Those Incredible Dinosaurs...* give thorough accounts of the various creationist expeditions to the Paluxy River and outline alleged human trackways that groups believe have been uncovered. Von Däniken's claims were made internationally-famous in his book *Chariots of the Gods? Unsolved Mysteries of the Past*, published in 1968.

29. Morris, pp. 132-140, 156-157; Kuban, "On the Heels of Dinosaurs..."; Kuban Telephone Interview; Baker Interview.

30. Kuban Telephone Interview.

31. Kuban, "On the Heels of Dinosaurs...." In his writings Kuban acknowledged the work of earlier track studies by a team that came to the conclusion that the man-like tracks were actually dinosaurian. This group was a creationist team from Loma Linda University who performed field work on the Paluxy in 1970. They attributed the human-like appearance of some tracks to erosion and documented tridactyl traces on the footprints, indicating dinosaurian features.

32. Bird, "Thunder in His Footsteps," p. 257.

33. Kuban, "On the Heels of Dinosaurs...."

34. Ibid.

35. Ibid.

36. Ibid.; Kuban Telephone Interview; Creation Evidence Museum website (http://www.creationevidence.org), accessed July 12, 2007; R.J. Hastings, "Tracking Those Incredible Creationists," Creation/Evolution, Vol. 5, No. 1 (Issue 15, Winter 1985): pp. 14-15; Baker Interview. Track excavations upstream have been problematic for Dinosaur Valley State Park through the years. The work sometimes involves heavy machinery resulting in the disturbance of gravel and sediments that flow downstream through the park.

37. Farlow Interview; Farlow, "Of Tracks and the River," p. 66; Colbert in Farlow and Brett-Surman, eds., *The Complete Dinosaur*, pp. 31-32.

38. Farlow Interview. Interestingly, Farlow's advisor was John Ostrom, the consultant for the Sinclair Dinosaurs. Ostrom was a pioneering paleontologist who established the evolutionary link between birds and dinosaurs. Farlow taught at Hope College in Holland, Michigan, when he began his dinosaur track studies.

39. Farlow, "Of Tracks and the River," p. 67.

40. Farlow Interview; Farlow, The Dinosaurs of Dinosaur Valley State Park; Farlow, "Of Tracks and the River," pp. 70-71, 73; Jacobs, p. 81; Jeffrey A. Wilson and Matthew T. Carrano, "Titanosaurs and the Origin of 'Wide-gauge' Trackways: A Biomechanical and Systematic Perspective on Sauropod Locomotion," Paleobiology, Vol. 25, No. 2 (April 1999): pp. 252-267; Rose, "A New Titanosauriform Sauropod...," *Palaeontologia Electronica*. Farlow has also done studies of the theropod tracks in Comal County, for example, at the Heritage Museum of the Texas Hill Country in Sattler. Though Bird originally created the name *Brontopodus*, he never published it.

41. Farlow Interview.

42. Farlow, "Of Tracks and the River," p. 71. Farlow wrote that British zoologist R. McNeill Alexander came up with a formula "relating the speed of a track maker to its stride and the length of its footprints, based on observations of living animals." Using this calculation, he suggested that bipedal dinosaurs walked at a speed of 3 to 6 miles per hour. Trackways that have apparent long strides indicate that the animals may have run as fast as about 25 miles per hour. Applying these rules to the Paluxy River tracks, Farlow estimated that the dinosaurs that made the Paluxy River tracks traveled at slow speeds.

43. Ibid., *A Guide to Lower Cretaceous Dinosaur Footprints...*, p. 23-24.

44. Farlow Interview.

45. Farlow, "Of Tracks and the River," p. 73.

46. Unnamed clipping, dated December 15, 1985, titled "Tracking long-dead quarry" by Walter D. Scott, in Park Files, Dinosaur Valley State Park, Glen Rose, Texas; Bird, *Bones for Barnum Brown*, p. 219.

47. Colbert in *The Complete Dinosaur*, p. 33.

48. Martin Lockley, "Track Records," *Natural History*, Vol. 104, No. 6 (June 1995): p. 51.

49. David D. Gillette and Martin G. Lockley, Dinosaur Tracks and Traces (Cambridge: Cambridge University Press, 1989), pp. vii-ix, xv-xvi; David D. Gillette, ed., *First International Symposium on Dinosaur Tracks and Traces, Abstracts With Program*, New Mexico Museum of Natural History, Albuquerque, New Mexico, 1986, p. 5.

50. Gillette and Lockley, p. xv.

51. *Dallas Times Herald*, November 10, 1987; Vertical Files, "Dinosaur Valley State Park," Texas State Library and Archives, Austin; John E. Williams, "Images of Dinosaurs," *Texas Parks & Wildlife*, Vol. 45, No. 8 (August 1987): p. 12.

52. *Dallas Times Herald*, November 10, 1987; Vertical Files, "Dinosaur Valley State Park," Texas State Library and Archives, Austin; John E. Williams, "Images of Dinosaurs," *Texas Parks & Wildlife*, Vol. 45, No. 8 (August 1987): p. 12; Williams, p. 16.

53. *Dallas Times Herald*, November 10, 1987; Vertical Files, "Dinosaur Valley State Park," Texas State Library and Archives, Austin; John E. Williams, "Images of Dinosaurs," *Texas Parks & Wildlife*, Vol. 45, No. 8 (August 1987): p. 12; O'Brien Interview.

54. McCarty Interview. For a time prior to construction of the headquarters the mosaic was located at the high school football stadium in Glen Rose.

55. Cultural Resource Files, *City of Stephenville, City of Glen Rose and Somervell County, Appellants v. Texas Parks and Wildlife Department; Julian S. Crowell; Lometa Wann; Jean Wan Edwards; Cynthia McIntire; Lois H. Crowell; Clinton McIntire; Rosamond C. Berry; Michael Clifton Allen; Dorothy Allen Tiwater; Terry McIntire; Sharon Haley; John H. Crowell; and Pauline Crowell, Appellees*, No. 03-95-00292-CV, Court of Appeals of Texas, Third District, Austin, filed July 3, 1996, Dinosaur Valley State Park, Texas Parks and Wildlife Department, Austin.

56. *City of Stephenville ... v. Texas Parks and Wildlife...*; Cultural Resources Files, "Testimony of Billy P. Baker on the Effects of the Proposed Dam Above Dinosaur Valley State Park," Dinosaur Valley State Park, Texas Parks and Wildlife Department, Austin; Vertical Files, "Paluxy River," Center for American History, University of Texas at Austin; Robert W. Spain, "Instream Flow Technique Used to Protect Dinosaur Tracks in Central Texas," *Instream Flow Chronicle*, Vol. 4, No. 3 (October 1987): pp. 1-2; Baker Interview.

57. *City of Stephenville ... v. Texas Parks and Wildlife....*; "Testimony of Billy P. Baker..."; Vertical Files, "Paluxy River," Center for American History, University of Texas at Austin; Spain, pp. 1-2; Baker Interview.

58. Baker Interview.

59. Ibid.; Cultural Resources Files, Office Memorandum from Tom Hayes and John Williams to Mike Herring, Re: Proposed Paluxy River Reservoir, November 22, 1985, Texas Parks and Wildlife Department, Austin.

60. Baker Interview; Office Memorandum...; "Testimony of Billy P. Baker..."; O'Brien Interview.

61. Baker Interview; "Testimony of Billy P. Baker..."; Spain, p. 2; *City of Stephenville ... v. Texas Parks and Wildlife....*

62. Baker Interview.

63. Ibid.; "Testimony of Billy P. Baker..."; *City of Stephenville ... v. Texas Parks and Wildlife....*

64. "Testimony of Billy P. Baker...."

65. Ibid.

66. Ibid.

67. Ibid.

68. Spain, p. 2; *City of Stephenville ... v. Texas Parks and Wildlife....*

69. Spain, p. 2; *City of Stephenville ... v. Texas Parks and Wildlife*.... The only issue that the Commission would consider out of the Contestants' motion was the "mitigation of adverse impact on wildlife habitation."

70. Spain, p. 2; *City of Stephenville ... v. Texas Parks and Wildlife*...; Baker Interview.

71. *City of Stephenville ... v. Texas Parks and Wildlife*.... George Crump was the Somervell County Judge at the time of the dam controversy. According to the text of the prior history of this case as published in the above cited case:

Shortly before the events at issue, a new Republican Governor had been elected to office. Roming, a Democratic appointee, was concerned that he would not be reappointed as Water Commissioner. At the time of the Paluxy hearings, Roming was soliciting aid in his efforts to persuade the new Governor to reappoint him to the Commission. Thinking that Booth could help him be reappointed, Roming asked Booth to assist in his political efforts.

72. Ibid.; Robert Elder Jr., "Water Case Brings Back Bad Old Days," *Texas Lawyer*, July 29, 1996, p. 5.

73. Elder, p. 5.

74. *City of Stephenville ... v. Texas Parks and Wildlife*...; Elder, p. 5. In this case the Court of Appeals rejected a series of points of error filed by the reservoir applicants. The allowance of 12,950 af/year diversion stems from the "First Order" of the Commissioners in May 1987.

Chapter 10: Maintaining the Dinosaour Highway

1. Somervell County Deed of Records, Vol. 116, pp. 492-495; Legal Acquisitions Files, Dinosaur Valley State Park, Land Conservation Program, Texas Parks and Wildlife, Austin; Baker Interview. According to Helen Kerr Shultz, one of the houses was built in 1910. The other was moved to the property from town (Glen Rose) about 1920. The frame houses were on pier and beam foundations and had metal roofs. The houses had been used as weekend retreats. There was also an old barn and storage facility on the property. Between 2003 and 2008 no additional land purchases had been made for the park.

2. Baker Interview; Lenz Telephone Interview, May 16, 2005; Baker Telephone Interviews, May 27, 2005, April 15, 2007. According to Billy Paul Baker, visitation figures have varied depending on the method of counting cars and visitors entering the park. In the past, the figure of 300,000 has been applied to the number of park visitors. A new counting system, which he indicated seemed to be undercounting visitors, indicated annual visitation of approximately 160,000. The number of park employees varies depending on funding.

3. Baker Interview.

4. Ibid.; O'Brien Interview; Cultural Resources Files. According to park wayside exhibits, the Sinclair brontosaur, actually an *Apatosaurus*, had a head modeled after a type of sauropod called *Camarasaurus*. Over the years, paleontological studies confirmed that "the *Apatosaurus* had a head more like a *Diplodocus*, another type of sauropod." TPWD wished to update the head of the Sinclair sauropod to reflect this new information. In the 1990s, however, in addition to restoring the aesthetics of the original head, TPWD also recognized the historical significance and integrity of the original Sinclair models in their own right.

5. Baker Interview; Baker Telephone Interview, April 15, 2007; Lenz Telephone Interviews, February 7, 2005, May 16, 2005; park maps and real estate maps, Legal Acquisitions Files; Galbreath Telephone Interviews, April 21, 2005, May 28, 2005.

6. Baker Interview; "Birds of Dinosaur Valley State Park: A Preliminary Field Checklist," pamphlet, Austin: Texas Parks and Wildlife Department.

7. Novella Wilson Historical Driving Tour.

8. Baker Interview; Lenz Telephone Interview, February 7, 2005. According to Park Interpreter

Kathy Lenz, the large field has always been left alone.

9. Baker Interview.

10. Ibid.; Lenz Telephone Interviews.

11. In fact, the author witnessed one of the Paluxy's sudden rises during July 2004.

12. Baker Interview; Lenz Telephone Interviews.

13. The bibliography of this work tells the story of just some of the publications that have contained information about the Paluxy tracks.

14. Farlow, "Of Tracks and the River," p. 75; Baker Interview; Dismukes Interview; James Diffily Telephone Interview, August 15, 2005.

15. Diffily Telephone Interview, August 15, 2005.

16. Vertical Files, "Dinosaurs," Center for American History, University of Texas at Austin; Farlow Telephone Interview, May 25, 2005; Jacobs Telephone Interview; Jacobs, pp. 79-80. Since the discovery of the *Acrocanthosaurus* skeleton in Parker County, an even more complete *Acrocanthosaurus* skeleton, including the only known complete skull, was discovered in Oklahoma. See J.D. Harris, "A Reanalysis of *Acrocanthosaurus atokensis*, Its Phylogenetic Status, and Paleobiogeographic Implications, Based on a New Specimen From Texas," *New Mexico Museum of Natural History and Science*, Bulletin 13 (1998): pp. 1-75; and Philip J. Currie and Kenneth Carpenter, "A New Specimen of *Acrocanthosaurus atokensis* (Theropoda, Dinosauria) from the Lower Cretaceous Antlers Formation (Lower Cretaceous, Aptian) of Oklahoma, USA," *Geodiversitas*, Vol. 22, Issue 2 (2000): pp. 207-246.

17. Vertical Files, "Paleontology," Texas State Library and Archives, Austin; *Fort Worth Star-Telegram*, November 20, 1993; Jacobs Telephone Interview; Jacobs, p. 83; Diffily Telephone Interview, July 25, 2005. According to Park Superintendent Billy Paul Baker and track researcher Glen Kuban, what looked like possibly a complete *Acrocanthosaurus* skeleton was discovered in the hard limestone of the Paluxy banks near Dinosaur Valley State Park. Unfortunately, the excavation was conducted by amateur fossil hunters and resulted in damage to the skeleton and the incomplete documentation and preservation of many of the smaller bones.

18. Jacobs Telephone Interview; Diffily Telephone Interview; Peter J. Rose, "A New Titanosauriform Sauropod (Dinosauria: Saurischia) from the Early Cretaceous of Central Texas and its Phylogenetic Relationships," *Palaeontologia Electronica*, Vol. 10, Issue 2 (2007): 65pp. (http://palaeo-electronica.org/2007_2/00063/index.html), accessed October 20, 2007; *Dallas Morning News*, October 3, 2007. The Society of Vertebrate Paleontology holds the copyright for *Palaeontologia Electronica*.

19. "Texas: Pleurocoelus (state dinosaur)," Website, (http://www.statefossils.com/tx/txdino.html), accessed July 13, 2007; *Dallas Morning News*, October 3, 2007.

20. Baker Interview; Jacobs Telephone Interview; Louis L. Jacobs, "The Making of Dinosaur Valley State Park, Glen Rose, Texas, USA," published in *International Dinosaur Symposium for The Uhangri Dinosaur Center and Theme Park in Korea*, Chonnam National University, Kwangju, Korea, and Uhangri Dinosaur Site, Haenam, Korea, September 3-5, 1997. The program *Dinosaur Attack!* was based on R.T. Bird's attack scenario that he hypothesized based on his analysis of the Paluxy trackways.

21. Farlow Interview.

22. Epilogue in Bird, *Bones for Barnum Brown*, p. 204; R.T. Bird, Homestead, Florida, to Ruth Parker, Glen Rose, Texas, March 8, 1975, copy of letter in Roland T. Bird Dinosaur Tracks Collection, Research Files, Somervell County Heritage Center, Glen Rose, Texas. Bird wrote: "Accordingly I will have to ship that *tyrannosaur* jaw by some sort of freight; which is really no problem from this end. At the moment I have been making a latex copy, but I shall be through soon."
The Epilogue in *Bones for Barnum Brown* commented on Bird's final work to construct the Tyrannosaurus jaw replica:

In his last years, I [V.T. Schreiber] worked with him on experiments at making a copy of the lower jaw of the tyrannosaur found by Barnum. R.T.'s working day consisted of two or three stretches of work, each twenty minutes long. The rest of the day was spent in rest. Yet he achieved his goal. The copy of the jaw now rests in the little museum in Glen Rose, Texas, five or six miles from the spot where R.T. uncovered the sauropod tracks in the Paluxy bed.

23. *Texas Almanac*, 2002-2003, Dallas: The *Dallas Morning News*, 2001, p. 260; King Interview; Leach Interview. In the mid-to-late 1980s the Somervell County courthouse was renovated. Unfortunately, since that time the steel silhouette of the *Trachodon* (duckbilled dinosaur) erected in front of the courthouse has disappeared. In the early 2000s there was talk of possibly constructing more reactors at the Comanche Peak plant.

24. O'Brien Interview. Doyle Wilson commented that he has witnessed serious erosion of many of the tracks that he first saw more than sixty-five years ago when he was a child.

25. Ibid.; O'Brien Telephone Interview, April 1, 2007.

26. O'Brien Telephone Interview, April 1, 2007.

27. Ibid.; O'Brien Interview; S.Y. Shelton, R.C. Barnett, and M.D. Magruder, "Conservation of a Dinosaur Trackway Exhibit," *Collection Forum*, Vol. 9 (1993): 18; Vertical Files, "Dinosaur Valley State Park," Texas Parks and Wildlife Department, Cultural Resources Program / Natural Resources Program, Austin.

28. O'Brien Telephone Interview, July 14, 2007.

29. Ibid.; O'Brien Interview; Shelton et al.; Cultural Resources Files, Natural Resources Files, Dinosaur Valley State Park, Texas Parks and Wildlife Department, Austin.

30. O'Brien Interview; *Austin American-Statesman*, July 24, 2005, November 8, 2006; Ed Theriot Telephone Interview, June 29, 2007; O'Brien Telephone Interview, December 15, 2007. The *Austin Chronicle* also published a story on the plight of the tracks in early 2008 (*Austin Chronicle*, January 25, 2008).

31. O'Brien Telephone Interview, July 14, 2007.

32. Liz Sherrell Telephone Interview, May 18, 2005; "A Decade of Service, 1993-2003, LDL Education Resources Foundation," booklet, LDL Educational Resources Foundation, Glen Rose, Texas.

33. "A Decade of Service, 1993-2003...," p. 1.

34. Ibid., inside cover.

35. Ibid., pp. 4-5; Sherrell Telephone Interview.

36. "A Decade of Service, 1993-2003...," pp. 4-5; Sherrel Telephone Interview; Baker Interview.

37. Baker Interview; Dismukes Interview; Archeology Files, Texas Parks and Wildlife Department, Cultural Resources Program, Austin; Novella Wilson Interview; Novella Wilson Historical Driving Tour; Novella Wilson Telephone Interview, March 2, 2005; Doyle Wilson Interview; author observation.

38. Wilson, *Historic Lanham Mill...*, pp. 153-154; THC marker files, "Lanham Mill Community."

39. Novella Wilson Historical Driving Tour.

40. Ibid. John Wilson suffered from Alzheimer's Disease in his later years, but on country drives, he always suggested going through Dinosaur Valley State Park.

41. Doyle Wilson Interview.

42. Evans Interview.

BIBLIOGRAPHY

Newspapers

Austin American-Statesman. July 24, 2005; November 8, 2006.

Austin Chronicle. January 25, 2008.

Cleburne Times-Review. June 9, 1966; January 1, 1969; October 21, 1984.

Dallas Morning News. August 12, 1934; July 25, 1937; November 30, 1938;
    May 18, 1958; December 31, 1963; May 29, 1966; September 27, 1966;
    September 29, 1966; August 14, 1967; February 13, 1970; July 2, 1979;
    January 20, 1980; October 3, 2007.

Dallas Times Herald. November 10, 1987.

Fort Worth Press. June 5, 1966.

Fort Worth Star-Telegram. June 8, 1965; June 9, 1965; May 29, 1966; June 1, 1966;
    September 22, 1966; July 6, 1967; August 11, 1968; January 1, 1969;
    July 24, 1970; October 3, 1970; October 10, 1971; October 1, 1972; July 10, 1978;
    March 20, 1988; November 20, 1993.

Glen Rose Citizen. January 22, 1885; April 2, 1885.

Glen Rose Herald. May 11, 1905; June 15, 1905; February 15, 1906; August 30, 1906.

Glen Rose Reporter. July 15, 1965; July 29, 1965; September 16, 1965; May 5, 1966;
    June 2, 1966; September 29, 1966; October 3, 1968; July 16, 1970; July 23, 1970;
    October 1, 1970; October 8, 1970; January 7, 1971; April 6, 1972; May 29, 1975.

Johnson County News (Cleburne, Texas). October 8, 1970.

Lubbock Avalanche-Journal. April 6, 1969.

New York Times. May 22, 1953.

Stephenville Empire-Tribune. July 1, 1976.

Waco News-Tribune. March 17, 1972.

Waco Tribune-Herald. July 24, 1966; October 3, 1970.

The Weekly Enterprise (Cleburne, Texas). April 23, 1908; April 8, 1909.

Wichita Falls Times. July 2, 1978.

Personal Interviews

Baker, Billy Paul. Park Superintendent. Interview, July 27, 2004, Dinosaur Valley State
    Park, Glen Rose, Texas.

Busch, Curtis. Interview, June 3, 2007, New Braunfels, Texas.

Dismukes, Diane. Cultural Resource Specialist. Interview, July 27, 2004, Dinosaur Valley
    State Park, Glen Rose, Texas.

Evans, Glen. Interview, July 15, 2004, Austin, Texas.

Farlow, James O. Interview, August 6, 2004, Sattler, Texas.

Fry, Ken. Interview, July 30, 2004, Glen Rose, Texas.

Jasinski, Laurie Jo Sanders. Interview, November 13, 2004, New Braunfels, Texas.

King, Jean F. Interview, July 25, 2004, Glen Rose, Texas.

Leach, Dorothy. Interview, July 29, 2004, Glen Rose, Texas.

McCarty, Dan. Interview, July 29, 2004, Glen Rose, Texas.

Newland, Linda Mask. Interview, November 30, 2004, Austin, Texas.

O'Brien, Mike. Exhibits Sculptor. Interview, July 20, 2004, Texas Parks and Wildlife Department, Austin, Texas.

Sanders, Laurie P. Interview, August 25, 1988, New Braunfels, Texas.

Wilson, Charlidell Davis. Interview, July 28, 2004, Glen Rose, Texas.

Wilson, Doyle. Interview, July 28, 2004, Glen Rose, Texas.

Wilson, Novella. Historical Driving Tour—Interview, July 28, 2004, Glen Rose, Texas.

Wilson, Novella. Interview, July 28, 2004, Glen Rose, Texas.

Telephone Interviews

Baker, Billy Paul. Interview, May 27, 2005; April 15, 2007.

Diffily, James. Interview, July 25, 2005; August 15, 2005.

Farlow, James O. Interview, February 7, 2005; May 25, 2005; November 18, 2007.

Fry, Ken. Interview, February 3, 2005; February 23, 2005.

Galbreath, Lester. Interview, April 21, 2005; May 28, 2005.

Jacobs, Louis. Interview, January 26, 2005.

Kuban, Glen. Interview, April 23, 2005.

Leach, Maxie Parker. Interview, July 6, 2005.

Lenz, Kathy. Interview, February 7, 2005; May 16, 2005.

May, Daisy Ryals. Interview, April 2, 2005.

May, Geneva "Pete." Interview, June 18, 2005.

O'Brien, Mike. Interview, April 1, 2007; July 14, 2007; December 15, 2007.

Sherrell, Liz. Interview, May 18, 2005.

Theriot, Ed. Interview, June 29, 2007.

Wilson, Charlidell Davis. Interview, April 9, 2005.

Wilson, Doyle. Interview, March 30, 2005; April 4, 2005.

Wilson, Novella. Interview, March 2, 2005; March 10, 2005; April 2, 2005; April 28, 2005.

Personal Conversation with the Author

Dehtan, Murray, July 15, 2005, Glen Rose, Texas.

Evans, Glen, August 5, 2005, Austin, Texas.

Fry, Ken, May 18, 2007, Somervell County, Texas.

Gosdin, Betty, July 15, 2005, Glen Rose, Texas.

Hopson, Kenneth, July 15, 2005, Glen Rose, Texas.

Morris, B.J., July 30, 2004, Glen Rose, Texas.

Wilson, Novella, May 18, 2007, Glen Rose, Texas.

Publications

Bird, R.T. *Bones for Barnum Brown: Adventures of a Dinosaur Hunter*. Fort Worth: Texas Christian University Press, 1985.

Bolton, Herbert Eugene. *Athanase de Mézières and the Louisiana–Texas Frontier*, 1768–1780. 2 vols., Cleveland, OH: The Arthur H. Clark Company, 1914.

_____. *Texas in the Middle Eighteenth Century*. Berkeley: University of California Press, 1915.

Carpenter, Stephen M., Dan K. Utley, Steve Carlson, and Solveig A. Turpin. *Cultural Resources Survey of Dinosaur Valley State Park, Somervell County, Texas*. Austin: Texas Parks and Wildlife Department, Cultural Resources Program, 1999.

Clements, John. *Flying the Colors: Texas*. Dallas: Clements Research, Inc., 1984.

Colbert, Edwin H. "North American Dinosaur Hunters." In James O. Farlow and M.K. Brett-Surman, eds., *The Complete Dinosaur*. Bloomington: Indiana University Press, 1997.

De Cordova, Jacob. *Texas: Her Resources and her Public Men*. Philadelphia: J.B. Lippincott & Co., 1858.

Dougherty, Dr. Cecil N, D.C. *Valley of the Giants*. Cleburne, Texas: Bennett Printing Company, orig. pub. 1971, 4th ed. 1976.

Erath, George Bernard. *Memoirs of Major George Bernard Erath*. Austin: Texas State Historical Association, 1923.

Ewell, Thos. T. *History of Hood County*. Granbury, Texas: Frank Gaston, pub., 1895, reprinted by the Junior Woman's Club, Granbury, 1956.

Farlow, James O. "Acrocanthosaurus and the Maker of Comanchean Large-Theropod Footprints." In Darren H. Tanke and Kenneth Carpenter, eds., *Mesozoic Vertebrate Life*. Bloomington and Indianapolis: Indiana University Press, 2001.

Farlow, James O., Jeffrey G. Pittman, and J. Michael Hawthorne. "*Brontopodus birdi* Lower Cretaceous Sauropod Footprints from the U.S. Gulf Coastal Plain." In David D. Gillette and Martin G. Lockley, eds., *Dinosaur Tracks and Traces*. Cambridge: Cambridge University Press, 1989.

Farlow, James O. *The Dinosaurs of Dinosaur Valley State Park*. Austin: Texas Parks and Wildlife Department, 1993.

_____. *A Guide to Lower Cretaceous Dinosaur Footprints and Tracksites of the Paluxy River Valley, Somervell County, Texas*. South-Central Section, Geological Society of America, Field Trip Guidebook, Baylor University, Waco, Texas, 1987.

_____. "Of Tracks and the River." In W.H. Shore, ed., *Mysteries of Life and the Universe: New Essays from America's Finest Writers on Science*. New York: Harcourt Brace Jovanovich, 1992.

Farlow, James O. and M.K. Brett-Surman, eds. *The Complete Dinosaur*. Bloomington: Indiana University Press, 1997.

Farlow, James O., Wann Langston Jr., E. Everett Deschner, Richard Solis, William Ward, Brenda L. Kirkland, Susan Hovorka, Tamra L. Reece, and James Whitcraft. *Texas Giants: Dinosaurs of the Heritage Museum of the Texas Hill Country*. Canyon Lake: Heritage Museum of the Texas Hill Country, 2006.

Fiedler, Albert G. *Artesian Water in Somervell County Texas*. United States Department of the Interior, Water-Supply Paper 660, Prepared in cooperation with the Texas State Board of Water Engineers and State Department of Health. Washington, DC: Government Printing Office, 1934.

Fowler, Gene, and the Somervell County Historical Commission. *Images of America: Glen Rose, Texas*. Chicago: Arcadia Publishing, 2002.

Gallagher, Joseph G. *A Reconnaissance Survey of the Dinosaur Valley State Park*. Dallas: Archaeology Research Program, Southern Methodist University, 1974.

Gammel, H.P.N. *The Laws of Texas, 1822–1897*. 10 vols., Austin: The Gammel Book Company, 1898.

Gillette, David D., ed. *First International Symposium on Dinosaur Tracks and Traces*. Albuquerque: New Mexico Museum of Natural History, 1986.

_____ and Martin G. Lockley, eds. *Dinosaur Tracks and Traces*. Cambridge: Cambridge University Press, 1989.

Graves, John. *Hard Scrabble: Observations on a Patch of Land*. New York: Alfred A. Knopf, 1982.

Hill, Robert T. *Geography and Geology of the Black and Grand Prairies, Texas*. United States Department of the Interior, Twenty-First Annual Report of the United States Geological Survey, Part VII. Washington, DC.: Government Printing Office, 1901.

Jasinski, Laurie E. *Hill Country Backroads: Showing the Way in Comal County*. Fort Worth: Texas Christian University Press, 2001.

Jacobs, Louis. *Lone Star Dinosaurs*. College Station: Texas A&M University Press, 1995.

Johnson, Frank W. *A History of Texas and Texans*. 5 vols., Chicago and New York: The American Historical Society, 1914.

Johnson County History Book Committee. *History of Johnson County, Texas*. Dallas: Curtis Media Corp., 1985.

Kendall, George Wilkins. *Narrative of the Texan Santa Fé Expedition*. 2 vols. New York: Harper & Brothers, Publishers, 1856.

Ketter, Dorothy, Mary Ann Millian, and Angela Sanders. *The Cemeteries of Somervell County Texas 1836–1991*. Duncanville, Texas: Green Dog Press, 1991.

Maloney, Vance J. *The Story of Comanche Peak, Landmark of Hood County, Texas*. Granbury, Texas: Vance J. Maloney, 1970.

Martin, Elna, A.B. *Glen Rose and Geo. P. Snyder*. Dallas: Bradford Printing Co., Inc., 1927.

Martin, Robert Sidney and James C. Martin. *Contours of Discovery: Printed Maps Delineating the Texas and Southwestern Chapters in the Cartographic History of North America, 1513–1930, A User's Guide*. Austin: Texas State Historical Association, 1982.

Mayor, Adrienne. *Fossil Legends of the First Americans*. Princeton, New Jersey: Princeton University Press, 2005.

McConnell, Joseph Carroll. *The West Texas Frontier or a Descriptive History of Early Times in Western Texas*. Vol. 1, Jacksboro, Texas: Gazette Print, 1933.

_____. Vol. 2, Palo Pinto, Texas: Texas Legal Bank & Book Co., 1939.

Morris, John D. *Tracking Those Incredible Dinosaurs ... and the People Who Knew Them*. San Diego: CLP Publishers, 1980.

Nagle, J. Stewart. *Glen Rose Cycles and Facies, Paluxy River Valley, Somervell County, Texas*. Austin: University of Texas, Bureau of Economic Geology, May 1968.

Newcomb, W.W., Jr. *The Indians of Texas*. Austin: University of Texas Press, 1961.

NHOT. See Tyler, Ron.

Nunn, W.C. *Somervell: Story of a Texas County*. Fort Worth: Texas Christian University Press, 1975.

Pittman, Jeffrey G. "Stratigraphy, Lithology, Depositional Environment, and Track Type of Dinosaur Track-bearing Beds of the Gulf Coastal Plain." In David D. Gillette and Martin G. Lockley, eds., *Dinosaur Tracks and Traces*. Cambridge: Cambridge University Press, 1989.

Ralph, Ron. *An Inventory of Cultural Resources Within the Texas Park System: November 1976 through October 1981*. Texas Antiquities Permit 128, Austin: Texas Parks and Wildlife Department, August 1996.

Roemer, Ferdinand. *Texas with Particular Reference to German Immigration and The Physical Appearance of the Country*. Translated from the German by Oswald Mueller. San Antonio: Standard Printing Company, 1935, reprinted Waco: Texian Press, German–Texan Heritage Society, 1983.

Shaw, Charles. *Indian Life in Texas*. Austin: State House Press, 1987.

Skeels, Lydia Lowndes Maury. *An Ethnohistorical Survey of Texas Indians*. Austin: Texas Historical Survey Committee, Office of the State Archeologist, Report Number 22, October 1972.

Somervell County Centennial, 1875–1975. Glen Rose, Texas: Somervell County Centennial Association, 1975.

Somervell County Genealogical and Heritage Society. *History and Families: Somervell County, Texas, 1875–2001*. Paducah, Kentucky: Turner Publishing Company, 2001.

Spaight, A.W. *The Resources, Soil, and Climate of Texas*. Galveston, Texas: A. H. Belo & Co., Printers, 1882.

Spearing, Darwin. *Roadside Geology of Texas*. Missoula, Montana: Mountain Press Publishing Company, 1991.

Syers, William Edward. *Off the Beaten Trail*. Vol. 2, Fort Worth, Texas: F.L. Motheral Company, 1964.

Taylor, T.U. *The Chisholm Trail and Other Routes*. San Antonio: The Naylor Company, 01936.

Texas Almanac, 2002–2003. Dallas: The *Dallas Morning News*, 2001.

_____, *1961–1962*. Dallas: A.H. Belo Corporation, 1961.

Texas Almanac and State Industrial Guide, 1982–1983. Dallas: A. H. Belo Corporation, 1981.

_____, *1972–1973*. Dallas: A.H. Belo Corporation, 1971.

_____, *1951–1952*. Dallas: A.H. Belo Corporation, 1951.

_____, *1941–1942*. Dallas: A.H. Belo Corporation, 1941.

_____, *1936*. Dallas: A.H. Belo Corporation, 1936.

_____, *1904*. Dallas: A.H. Belo & Co., 1904.

Texas Almanac for 1867, with Statistics, Descriptive and Biographical Sketches, Etc, Relating to Texas. Galveston, Texas: W. Richardson & Co., 1866.

Texas State Gazetteer and Business Directory, 1884–5. St. Louis: R.L. Polk & Co., 1884.

_____, *1890-91*. St. Louis: R.L. Polk & Co., 1890.

Tyler, Ron, editor-in-chief. *The New Handbook of Texas*. 6 vols., Austin: Texas State Historical Association, 1996.

Vincent, James U. *A Pen Picture of General Robert Toombs, with a Glimpse of the Mental Characteristics of Hons. A.H. Stephens and Benj. H. Hill*. Louisville, Kentucky: Courier-Journal Job Printing Company, Publishers, 1886.

Wilson, Maurine T. and Jack Johnson. *Philip Nolan and Texas: Expeditions to the Unknown Land, 1791–1801*. Waco: Texian Press, 1987.

Wilson, Novella. *Historic Lanham Mill Community and Cemetery*. Glen Rose, Texas: Novella Wilson, 1999.

_____. *Kids and Kinfolk of George Wilson*. Glen Rose, Texas: Novella Wilson, July 1983.

Winfrey, Dorman H. and James M. Day, eds. *The Indian Papers of Texas and the Southwest, 1825–1916*. 5 vols., Austin: Texas State Historical Association, reprinted 1995.

Winfrey, Dorman H., W.C. Nunn, Rupert N. Richardson, James M. Day, Harold B. Simpson, Sandra L. Myers, Dayton Kelley, and Billy M. Jones. *Indian Tribes of Texas,* Waco: Texian Press, 1971.

The WPA Guide to Texas. Austin: Texas Monthly Press, 1986, orig. published New York: Hastings House, 1940.

Magazines and Journals

Bird, Roland T. "A Dinosaur Walks into the Museum." *Natural History*, 47, no. 2 (February 1941): 74-81.

_____. "Thunder in His Footsteps." *Natural History*, 43, no. 5 (May 1939): 254–261, 302.

_____. "To Capture a Dinosaur Isn't Easy." *Natural History*, 62, no. 3 (March 1953): 104-110.

_____. "We Captured a 'Live' Brontosaur." *National Geographic*, 105, no. 5 (May 1954): 707–722.

Cole, John R. and Laurie R. Godfrey, eds. "The Paluxy River Footprint Mystery—Solved," Special Issue, *Creation/Evolution*, 5, no. 1 (no. 15, Winter 1985).

Currie, Philip J. and Kenneth Carpenter. "A New Specimen of Acrocanthosaurus atokensis (Theropoda, Dinosauria) from the Lower Cretaceous Antlers Formation (Lower Cretaceous, Aptian) of Oklahoma, USA." *Geodiversitas*, 22, no. 2 (2000): 207-246.

Duffie, Rhonda Mears. "Bootlegging." *Somervell Settlers*, 6, no. 2 (Summer 2001): 41–45.

Elder, Robert, Jr. "Water Case Brings Back Bad Old Days." *Texas Lawyer*, July 29, 1996.

Godfrey, Laurie R. and John R. Cole. "Blunder in Their Footsteps." *Natural History*, (August 1986): 4, 6, 8–12.

Harris, J. D. "A Reanalysis of *Acrocanthosaurus atokensis*, Its Phylogenetic Status, and Paleobiogeographic Implications, Based on a New Specimen From Texas." *New Mexico Museum of Natural History and Science, Bulletin 13* (1998): 1–75.

Hastings, Morris. "Footprints From the Prehistoric Past." *Texas Parade*, 6, no. 4 (September 1941): 14–15, 26.

Hastings, R.J. "Tracking Those Incredible Creationists." *Creation/Evolution*, 5, no. 1 (Issue 15, Winter 1985): 5–15.

Hawthorne, J. Michael. "Dinosaur Track-bearing Strata of the Lampasas Cut Plain and Edwards Plateau, Texas." *Baylor Geological Studies, Bulletin 49* (1990): 47 pp.

Hill., Robert T. "Paleontology of the Cretaceous Formations of Texas—The Invertebrate Paleontology of the Trinity Division." *Proceedings of the Biological Society of Washington*, 8 (June 3, 1893): 9–40.

Hiller, Ilo. "Where the Dinosaurs Roamed." *Texas Parks & Wildlife*, 41, no. 7 (July 1983): 7–8.

Jacobs, Louis L. "The Making of Dinosaur Valley State Park, Glen Rose, Texas, USA." published in *International Dinosaur Symposium for The Uhangri Dinosaur Center and Theme Park in Korea*, Chonnam National University, Kwangju, Korea, and Uhangri Dinosaur Site, Haenam, Korea, September 3–5, 1997.

Kuban, Glen J. "An Overview of Dinosaur Tracking." *M.A.P.S. Digest* (April 1994), Mid-America Paleontology Society, Rock Island, Illinois, reprinted on The TalkOrigins Archive Website (http://www.talkorigins.org/faqs/paluxy/ovrdino.html), accessed June 30, 2004.

_____. "On the Heels of Dinosaurs: An Informal History of the Texas 'Man Track' Controversy," 1995-2006 (http://paleo.cc/paluxy/onheel.htm), accessed December 18, 2006.

_____. "On the Heels of Dinosaurs: An Informal History of the Texas 'Man Track' Controversy," 1995, 1996,The TalkOrigins Archive Website (http://www.talkorigins.org/faqs/paluxy/onheel.html), accessed July 7, 2007.

Lockley, Martin. "Track Records." *Natural History*, 104, no. 6 (June 1995): 46–51.

Lull, Richard S. "Nature's Heiroglyphics." *The Popular Science Monthly*, 66 (December, 1904): 139–149.

Olson, Donald, et. al. "Piñon Pines and the Route of Cabeza de Vaca." *Southwestern Historical Quarterly*, Vol. CI, No. 2 (October 1997): pp. 175–186.

Roemer, Ferdinand. "Contributions to the Geology of Texas." *American Journal of Science and Arts*, Second Series, 150 (November 1848): no. 16, 21–28.

Rose, Peter J. "A New Titanosauriform Sauropod (Dinosauria: Saurischia) from the Early Cretaceous of Central Texas and its Phylogenetic Relationships." *Palaeontologia Electronica*, 10, no. 2 (2007): 65 pp. (http://palaeo-electronica.org/2007_2/00063/), accessed October 20, 2007.

Shelton, S.Y., R.C. Barnett, and M.D. Magruder. "Conservation of a Dinosaur Trackway Exhibit." *Collection Forum*, 9 (1993): 17–26.

Shuler, Ellis W. "Dinosaur Track Mounted in the Band Stand at Glen Rose, Texas." *Field & Laboratory*, 4, no. 1 (November 1935): 9–13.

_____. "Dinosaur Tracks at the Fourth Crossing of the Paluxy River Near Glen Rose, Texas." *Field & Laboratory*, 5, no. 2 (April 1937): 33–36.

_____. "Dinosaur Tracks in the Glen Rose Limestone Near Glen Rose, Texas." *The American Journal of Science*, 44 (October 1917): 294–298.

Skinner, S. Alan and Charles Blome. "Dinosaur Track Discovery at Comanche Peak Steam Electric Station, Somervell County, Texas." Located in Dinosaur Tracks Collection, Somervell County Heritage Center, Glen Rose, Texas.

Spain, Robert W. "Instream Flow Technique Used to Protect Dinosaur Tracks in Central Texas." *Instream Flow Chronicle*, 4, no. 3 (October 1987): 1–2.

Williams, John E. "Images of Dinosaurs." *Texas Parks & Wildlife*, 45, no. 8 (August 1987): 2–17.

Wilson, Jeffrey A. and Matthew T. Carrano, "Titanosaurs and the Origin of 'Wide-gauge' Trackways: A Biomechanical and Systematic Perspective on Sauropod Locomotion." *Paleobiology*, 25, no. 2 (April 1999): 252–267.

Maps

Austin, Stephen F., comp. *Map of Texas With Parts of the Adjoining States*. Philadelphia: H.S. Tanner, 1830.

Burr, David H. *Texas*. New York: J. H. Colton & Co., 1833.

Creuzbaur, Robert. *J. De Cordova's Map of the State of Texas*. Houston: Robert Creuzbaur, 1849.

Texas Department of Transportation. *Official Travel Map*. Austin, Texas, 1995.

Texas General Land Office. *Somervell County*. Austin, Texas. Compiled and drawn by Geo. J. Thielepape, August 1884.

Texas Parks and Wildlife Department. *Dinosaur Tracks State Park*. Map prepared by Williams-Stackhouse and Associates from Archeology Files, Texas Parks and Wildlife Department, Austin.

Texas Parks and Wildlife Department. *Kerr Acquisition, Dinosaur Valley State Park* from Legal Acquisitions Files, Texas Parks and Wildlife Department, Austin.

Texas State Highway Department. *General Highway Map, Hood County, Somervell County, Texas, Austin, Texas*, 1936, completely revised to July 1947.

United States Department of the Interior Geological Survey. *Glen Rose West Quadrangle*. Texas, 7.5 minute series, 1966, photorevised 1979.

United States Department of the Interior Geological Survey. *Hill City Quadrangle*. Texas, 7.5 minute series, 1961, photorevised 1979.

Scrapbooks, Brochures, Compilations, Research Files, Correspondence, and Personal Collections

Archeology Files. Texas Parks and Wildlife Department, Cultural Resources Program, Austin.

Bird, R.T. Correspondence with Barnum Brown, 1938, 1940, in Park Files, Dinosaur Valley State Park, Glen Rose, Texas.

Bird, R.T. Correspondence with Novella Wilson, 1970, 1973, private collection of Novella Wilson, Glen Rose, Texas.

"Birds of Dinosaur Valley State Park: A Preliminary Field Checklist." Pamphlet. Texas Parks and Wildlife Department, Austin.

"Categories of Land Grants in Texas." Handout. Texas General Land Office, Archives and Records Division, Austin.

Connally Collection. See Research Files.

Cultural Resources Files. Dinosaur Valley State Park. Texas Parks and Wildlife Department, Cultural Resources Program, Austin.

"A Decade of Service, 1993–2003, LDL Education Resources Foundation." Booklet. LDL Educational Resources Foundation, Glen Rose, Texas.

Field Correspondence 1933–1939, Box 7, Folder 9, Vertebrate Paleontology Archives, Division of Paleontology, American Museum of Natural History, New York.

Field Correspondence 1940–1951, Box 8, Folder 2, Vertebrate Paleontology Archives, Division of Paleontology, American Museum of Natural History, New York.

"Highway Highlights." Bulletins. Austin: Texas Good Roads Association, 1-30-46, 8-27-46, 3-29-47, Center for American History, University of Texas at Austin.

Langston, Wann, Jr. "Dinosaur Tracks." Manuscript copy in Archeology Files, Texas Parks and Wildlife Department, Austin.

LeBoeuf, Mrs. Luba (Ora Lee) and William B. Cowan, Jr. "History of Dinosaur Valley State Park." (May 1979), Unpublished manuscript, in Park Files, Dinosaur Valley State Park, Glen Rose, Texas.

Legal Acquisitions Files. Texas Parks and Wildlife Department, Land Conservation Division, Austin.

Maceo, Peggy J. and David H. Riskind. "Field and Laboratory Moldmaking and Casting of Dinosaur Tracks." Abstract in Research Files, Natural Resources Program, Texas Parks and Wildlife Department, Austin.

National Monument Files. Dinosaur Trail National Monument, National Park Service Southwest Regional Office, copies in Historic Sites Program Director Files, Texas Parks and Wildlife, Austin, Texas.

Park Files. Dinosaur Valley State Park, Glen Rose, Texas.

Research Files. "Dinosaur Tracks Collection," Somervell County Heritage Center, Glen Rose, Texas.

_____. Eugene Connally Collection, Somervell County Historical Commission, Glen Rose, Texas.

_____. "The Famed Tommy Pendley Track." Manuscript. Somervell County Historical Commission, Glen Rose, Texas.

_____. "Roland T. Bird Dinosaur Tracks Collection," Somervell County Heritage Center, Glen Rose, Texas.

_____. "T.C. Jordan File," Somervell County Heritage Center, Glen Rose, Texas.

Riskind, David. "A Celebration of Glen Evans." Address given April 1, 2001, Texas Memorial Museum of Science and History, in Research Files, Natural Resources Program, Texas Parks and Wildlife Department, Austin.

Sinclair and the Exciting World of Dinosaurs. Booklet published in 1967, in Park Files, Dinosaur Valley State Park, Glen Rose, Texas.

Texas Good Roads Association. Newsletter. No. 68-9 (September 1968), Austin.

Texas State Library and Archives, Genealogy Department, Texas Death Index Records.

THC Marker Files. "Barnard's Mill." Texas Historical Commission Library, Austin.

_____. "Barnard's Trading Post No. 2." Texas Historical Commission Library, Austin.

_____. "Dinosaur Tracks." Texas Historical Commission Library, Austin.

_____. "Lanham Mill Community." Texas Historical Commission Library, Austin.

_____. "Snyder Sanitarium." Texas Historical Commission Library, Austin.

_____. "Somervell County." Texas Historical Commission Library, Austin.

_____. "Squaw Creek Indian Fight." Texas Historical Commission Library, Austin.

Thomas, David A. "Bird was Right! The Most Peculiar Trackway." Article in Research Files, Natural Resources Program, Texas Park and Wildlife Department, Austin.

Tour of Dinosaur Valley & Paluxy Town-Site. Sunday October 15, 1995, Booklet produced for National Trust for Historic Preservation, copy at the Texas State Archives, Austin.

Vertical Files. "Cities and Towns—Glen Rose." Texas State Library and Archives, Austin.

_____. "Dinosaurs." Center for American History, University of Texas at Austin.

_____. "Dinosaur Valley State Park." Center for American History, University of Texas at Austin.

_____. "Dinosaur Valley State Park." Texas Parks and Wildlife Department, Cultural Resources Program / Natural Resources Program, Austin.

_____. "Dinosaur Valley State Park." Texas State Library and Archives, Austin.

_____. "Evans, Glen L." Center for American History, University of Texas at Austin.

_____. "Glen Rose, Texas." Center for American History, University of Texas at Austin.

_____. "Paleontology." Texas State Library and Archives, Austin.

_____. "Paluxy River." Center for American History, University of Texas at Austin.

_____. "Somervell County, Texas." Center for American History, University of Texas at Austin.

WPA Archives. Somervell County. Center for American History, University of Texas at Austin.

Government Records

Somervell County Deed of Records. Somervell County Clerk's Office, Glen Rose, Texas.

Somervell County Deeds of Trust. Somervell County Clerk's Office, Glen Rose, Texas.

Somervell County Marriage Records. Somervell County Clerk's Office, Glen Rose, Texas.

Somervell County Probate Minutes. Somervell County Clerk's Office, Glen Rose, Texas.

Land Grant Records. Galveston County School Land Papers. File No. 632, Original Land
    Grant Collection, Archives and Records Division, Texas General Land Office, Austin.

Theses and Dissertations

Carroll, Horace Bailey. "The Route of the Texan Santa Fe Expedition." PhD
    diss., University of Texas, Austin, June 1935.

Hawthorne, J. Michael. "Stratigraphy and Depositional Environment of the Dinosaur
    Track-Bearing Glen Rose Limestone in the Paluxy Basin, Texas." BS Thesis,
    Baylor University, Waco, August 1983.

Parker, R. Jay. "The Geomorphic Evolution of the Glen Rose Prairie, North-Central
    Texas." BS Thesis, Baylor University, Waco, August 1980.

Internet Sites

"Creation Evidence Museum." Website. (http://www.creationevidence.org), accessed July
    12, 2007.

"Evolution of the Company Symbol." Sinclair Oil Corporation Website.
    (http://www.sinclairoil.com/sinclair_history/.htm), accessed January 26, 2007.

Kuban, Glen J. "The Paluxy Dinosaur/'Man Track' Controversy," 1996–2008. Website.
(http://paleo.cc/paluxy/paluxy.htm), accessed July 7, 2007.

Kuban, Glen J. "The Texas Dinosaur/'Man Track' Controversy." The TalkOrigins Archive
    Website. (http://www.talkorigins.org/faqs/paluxy.html), accessed July 5, 2007.

"Sinclair." Sinclair Oil Corporation Website.
    (http://www.sinclairoil.com/about_sinclair.htm), accessed December 1, 2007.

"Texas: Pleurocoelus (state dinosaur)." Website.
    (http://www.statefossils.com/tx/txdino.html), accessed July 13, 2007.

"Your Gemologist—Petrified Wood." Website.
        (http://www.yourgemologist.com/Kids/petrifiedwood/petrifiedwood.html),
        accessed July 5, 2007.

INDEX

Abell crossing, 22

Abell, Elmer Heyman "Jack," 23, 110

Abell, Emma, 23, 168n37

Abell, George, 22, 27, 168n37

Abell, J.B., 93, 110, 168n39, 178n10

Abell, Mathias A. "Matt," 22, 25, 42, 93, 168n37, 168n39;
house, 22-23, 52, 110, 168n38;
house—illustration, 23

Abell, Ora, 23, 42

Abell, Tony, 23

Acrocanthosaurus, 130, 188n17;
description of, 5;
excavation of skeleton (1992), 147, 188n17;
illustration of, 3;
tracks of, 5, 130;
See also dinosaur tracks, theropods

Adams, Delila, 21, 168n33

Adams, Ernest Tolbert "Bull," 65-66, 177n33

Adams, Ester, 21, 168n33

Adams, George, 36-38, 59, 65, 66

Adams, Samuel, 21, 168n33

Adamson, Hans Christian, 63, 67, 174n11

African American population, 19, 167n24

agriculturalists, 7

agriculture, 30;
stock raising, 19, 52, 92
See also farming, Paluxy River Valley (farming), Somervell County (agriculture statistics)

Albuquerque, New Mexico, 132

Alexander, R. McNeill, 185n42

Allen, Bob, 124, 126

Allosaurus, 102

American Journal of Science, 39

American Museum of Natural History, New York, 39, 55, 62, 63, 67, 71, 114, 118, 134, 174n11;
and Paluxy River dinosaur tracks, 72, 77, 83, 88;
quarried Paluxy River dinosaur trackway—photo, 89

Ankylosaurus, 180n41

Apaches, 7, 8, 163n19

Apatosaurus, 72, 187n4

Archaeopteryx, 112, 113
archeology (North Central Texas), 6, 163n15

Arizona, 56, 163n16

artesian wells. *See* wells and water

Atlantic Richfield Company, 112, 113, 117, 118

Atomic Energy Commission, 124

Austin American-Statesman, 152

Austin, Moses, 11

Austin, Stephen F., 11, 14;
map of Texas, 11

Austin, Texas, 14, 88, 97, 99, 113, 149, 151

Baker, Billy Paul, 126-127, 131, 144, 145, 148, 152;
photos of, 127, 144;
testimony against proposed Paluxy reservoir, 135-138

Ball, Neva, 179n13, 181n9

Ball, Roland, 110, 179n13, 181n9

Bandera County, 74, 75, 76

bandstand, Glen Rose. *See* courthouse square—Glen Rose

Barnard, Charles, 15, 17, 18, 19, 165n9, 167n27;
attitude towards Indians, 167n27;
founding of Barnard's Mill (Glen Rose), 15, 18

Barnard, George, 15, 17, 18, 165n9

Barnard's Mill, 18, 19. *See also* Glen Rose

Barnum, P.T., 63

Bartholomew, Tim, 127

Bates, Susan, 170n7

Baugh, Carl, 129

Baylor University, 83

Beck, Carl (in photo), 81

Beck, Cassie Florence, 23, 168n39

Beck, Charlie Walton "Buck," 82, 176n28, 178n10

Beck, James, 23, 168n39

Beck, Johnny, 81, 82, 176n28, (in photo) 81

Beck, Nip (in photo), 81

Beck, Walter, 110, 168n39, 178n10

Bee Mountain, 165n5

Beleni, 17

Bessant, Geo. P, 38

Big Bend, 27

Big Town, 104, 180n46

Biloxi Indians, 166n18

Bird, Alice, 77

Bird, Harriet, 62

Bird, Hazel Russell 114, 182n24

Bird, Henry "Pater," 62, 75-76

Bird, Roland T.:
arrival in Glen Rose, 64;
assembling dinosaur trackway, 88;
and Buick, 62, 64, 66, 68, 70, 76, 79, 80, 85, 86, 87, 88, 116;
and "Bull" Adams, 65-66, 177n33;
Dallas Morning News article, 71-72;
death of, 131-132;
description of excavated trackway, 88;
description of sauropod tracks, 67, 70-72;
description of theropod tracks, 77, 79;
description of Tommy Pendley photo, 84;
description of WPA work crew, 76-77, 87-88, 175-176n11;
and Dillard Wilson, 62, 66, 79, 82, 83, 114-115, 117;
as dinosaur hunter, 62-63, 173n12;
early life, 62, 77;
and elongated (or "man") tracks, 63, 94-96, 128, 179n16, 179n20;
flooding, comments on, 79-80, 86, 87;
fossil bone exploration (Somervell County), 176n19;
fossil discovery in Arizona, 62;
health of, 62, 88, 114, 115, 174n3;
letter to Glen Rose citizens, 117-118;
letter to Hans Christian Adamson, 63-64, 67;
letter to Henry Bird, 75-76;
letters to Barnum Brown, 63, 66, 70, 76, 77, 79, 80, 86, 87, 88, 177n34;
letters to Novella Wilson, 84, 114-115, 118-119, 182n27;
meeting Wilson family, 62, 66;
memoir, 145, 182n24;
Paluxy excavation site (1970)—photo, 115;
at park dedication, 114-115, 117-118;
photos of, 72, 81, 116;
publicity of 1940 track excavation, 80-82, 177n33;
quarrying Paluxy trackway, 70, 75-89;

retirement of, 88;
return to Paluxy River (1970), 114-119;
return to Paluxy River (1970)—photo, 116;
and sauropod track discovery, 64-68, 70-72, 74-75;
and sauropod tracks, 130;
Sinclair dinosaurs (comments on), 102, 115;
sketches of sauropod tracks, 70, 71;
sketches of theropod tracks, 71;
theory of dinosaur attack, 83-84, 130, 134, 188n20;
Tyrannosaurus jaw, 148, 188n22;
at work in Paluxy quarry—photo, 81

"bird tracks" (dinosaur tracks), 39, 56

Black-capped Vireo, 137, 142

Blairsville, Georgia, 42

Blue Hole, 22, 32, 44, 58, 94, 98, 112, 123, 124, 131, 137, 144, 154, 182n14;
photo of, 22

Blum, Texas, 10

bones. *See* fossils

Bones for Barnum Brown: Adventures of a Dinosaur Hunter, 82, 145

Booker, Moody, 179n13

Booth, Frank, 137, 138, 187n71

bootlegging:
in Somervell County, 44-46, 50, 53, 57, 64, 153, 171n39, 171n40, 171-172n41;
photos, 45, 46;
Texas Ranger raid, 46

Bosque County, 11, 122, 165n5

Bosque (River), 14

Brazos Reservation, 18, 166n18, 166-167n19;
and trading post, 18

Brazos River, 6, 8, 9, 10, 14, 15, 17, 18, 19, 164n30, 165n4, 165n5, 165n11, 166n17

British Broadcasting Corporation, 148

Bring 'em Back Petrified, 63

Bronto egg, 112, 113, 182n19, 183n15

Brontopodus birdi, 88, 130, 178n50, 185n40

brontosaur, 5, 88, 100, 112, 114, 115

Brontosaurus, 72, 102, 112;
Sinclair dinosaur model ("Bronto"), 104, 112-114, 115, 142, 180n41, 187n4;
Sinclair dinosaur model ("Bronto")—photos of, 103, 104,

113, 117, 140;
Sinclair promotional brontosaur, 113;
Sinclair promotional brontosaur—photos of, 103, 147

Brooklyn College, 83, 177n34

Brown, Barnum, 56, 76, 77, 79, 80, 86, 87, 88, 102, 174n5, 177n33;
at American Museum of Natural History, 55, 62-63, 70, 71, 173n12;
career as dinosaur hunter, 63;
and Sinclair Refining Company, 72-74, 95

Bruseth, James, 164n30

Buckeye Creek, 142

buffalo, 4, 6, 10;
hides, 7, 8, 15;
hunting, 6, 8;
illustrations, 4, 7

Buffalo Gap, Texas, 126

Buick, 62, 64, 66, 68, 70, 76, 80, 116;
hauling track quarry, 79, 85, 88;
and lightning, 86-87;
photo of, 86

Burdick, Clifford, 95, 179n19

Busch, Curtis, 125-126, 184n20

Buster the dog (in photo), 58

Cabeza de Vaca, Alvar Núñez, 9, 164n29

Caddos, 17, 18, 19, 167n19;
"Dorf d. Caddoes," 165n11;
and trade, 7, 15, 17;
village, 15, 17, 165-166n11

Camarasaurus, 187n4

Carnegie Museum (Pittsburgh), 39

Catholic missionaries, 9, 164n30

Catskills, 62, 132

Cavasos, Juana Josefina, 165n9

cedar, 44, 52, 92, 94, 122, 142;
cedar chopping, 57-58, 154;
cedar posts, 57-58, 92

Cedar Point, 21

Cedral Creek, 11

cellars, 31, 52

Cemetery crossing (sixth crossing), 35

chalybeate, 26

Chariots of the Gods? Unsolved Mysteries of the Past, 184n28

Cherokees, 17

Chisolm Trail, 24, 168n40

Civil War, 19, 26, 31

Clay County, 74

Clear Fork of the Brazos, 18

Cleburne–Glen Rose Road, 47;
bridge on, 47;
postcard of, 47

Cleburne, Texas, 25, 34, 46, 70, 76

Coahuila, 11

Colbert, E.H., 88

College of Wooster (Ohio), 127

colonization in Texas, 10-12, 14;
land empresarios, 11;
National Colonization Law of August 18, 1824, 11;
State Colonization Law of March 24, 1825, 11

Colorado River, 14

Comal County, 185n40

Comanche County, 26

Comanche Peak:
council of Indian groups, 15, 17;
description of, 9, 14;
and exploring parties, 165n4, 165n5, 166n11;
illustration, 7;
on maps, 9, 11;
as observation point, 9;
as strategic point, 9, 126;
trading post, 15, 17, 18

Comanche Peak Steam Electric Generating Station, 124-126, 149, 189n23;
and dinosaur tracks, 125-126, 184n20

Comanche Reservation, 18, 166-167n19

Comanches:
and buffalo, 8;
and Comanche Peak, 7, 9, 17;
Comanche Reservation, 18, 166-167n19;
diet of, 8;
migration of, 7-8;
organization—individual bands, 8;
Penatekas ("Honey-Eaters," "Wasps"), 8, 166n19;
raids in Somervell County, 19;
in Somervell County, 8;
and trade, 10, 15;
and warfare, 8, 163n19;
wintering ground, 8

Comanche, Texas, 26

Comanche Trail, 9

Committee on Interior and Insular Affairs, 105, 181n47

Connally, Eugene, 97, 98 99

Connally, John (Governor), 105, 106

Connecticut, 96

Connecticut River Valley, 39, 170n20

"Connie" Award, 123

contrabandistas, 10

corn, 24, 27, 42, 66, 92

Cornell University, 26

Corythosaurus, 180n41

cottage industries:
animal pelts, 57;
bootlegging, 44-46, 50, 53, 57, 64;
cedar chopping, 57-58, 64;
quarrying dinosaur tracks, 58-59;
petrified wood, 47, 57

cotton, 27, 66, 92;
cotton harvest, 24;
prices, 24, 44, 52

cotton gin, 20;
description of cotton harvest, 24;
Tidwell gin, 30-31

cottonmouth moccasins, 143

Coue, Emile, 171n33

courthouse square—Glen Rose, 28, 96;
bandstand track, 54-55, 64, 148-149, 173n8;
bandstand track—photo of, 55;
construction of, 20;
and duckbilled dinosaur silhouette ("Tex"), 101, 188-189n23;
and duckbilled dinosaur silhouette ("Tex")—postcard of, 101

Cox, V.M., 31

Creation Evidence Museum, 129

creationists, 95, 127-129;
and dinosaur tracks, 184-185n31;
and Earth's age, 95, 179n19;
and "man" tracks, 95, 179n19;
and Paluxy River, 95, 184n28, 185n36

Cretaceous Period, 4-5

Cretaceous rock, 5, 15, 27, 36, 129, 132, 145, 169n50

Creuzbaur, Robert, 18

crossings. See Paluxy River crossings

Cross Timbers, 3, 14, 46

Crump, George, 187n71

Dallas Morning News, 55, 64, 71, 72, 80, 96, 126, 173n11, 180n46

dam, proposed on Paluxy River, 135-138

Dallas, Texas, 19, 39, 44, 48, 64, 87, 92, 96, 103, 104, 105, 115, 119, 124, 134, 180n46

Daniel, Gabriel T., 31

Daniel, Joe, 31

Daniel, Mary Ann, 31

Davis, Charlidell, 80, 82, 94;
observations of Paluxy River track quarry, 80, 82;
photos of, 81, 154

Davis, Coll and Lois (in photo), 81

Davis, Larry (in photo), 81

Davis, Paul R. (Judge), 138

De Cordova, Jacob, 14, 18

Delawares, 17, 18, 167n19

Denio Branch, 142

Depression (Great), 52, 59, 62, 66;
and agriculture, 52, 66;
and bootlegging, 46, 57;
and crop prices, 52;
and natural resources, 56-59

De Soto, Hernando, 9

Diffily, James, 145-146

"Dino" (Sinclair trademark), 72-74, 104, 182n16;
ads—images, 73

"Dinoland," 102, 103, 104, 112;
types of dinosaur models, 180n41

Dinosaur Attack!, 148, 188n20

dinosaur hunting licenses, 101-102, 103;
illustration of, 102

Dinosaur Park Country Estates, 123

Dinosaur Park Option Fund, 108

dinosaurs:
in ad campaigns, 72-74, 104;
fossil hunting, 27, 39, 56;
name—origin, 39;
reptilian birds, 39;
and tourism, 48-50, 64, 97-98, 100-102

dinosaurs in Texas, 5;
first discoveries of fossils, 27, 169n50;
fossil remains, 5, 145-147, 162n10, 188n17;
illustrations, 3, 134;
sketch of, 48;
state dinosaur, 147;
trackways, 5, 162n10;
See also dinosaur tracks, ornithopods, sauropods, theropods

The Dinosaurs of Dinosaur Valley State Park, 145

dinosaur tracks:
age of, 4, 48, 161n6, 172n50;
amusing observations, 79, 131;
bandstand at Glen Rose, 54-56, 64, 148-149, 173n8;
bandstand at Glen Rose—photo of, 55;
carving of, 59, 173n20;
at Comanche Peak Steam Electric Generating Station, 125-126, 184n20;

in Connecticut River Valley, 39, 170n20;
damage from floods, 56, 67, 68, 79-80, 149;
damage from frost, 135, 136;
dinosaur attack theory, 83-84, 130, 134, 188n20;
dinosaur attack theory—painting of, 134;
elongated tracks, 41, 64, 94-96, 128, 132, 150;
and erosion, 56, 135-136, 149-150;
and erosion—photos of, 149;
excavation in 1940, 75-88;
excavation in 1940—American Museum trackway photo, 89;
excavation in 1940—description of quarried trackway, 88;
excavation in 1940—film of flooding, 87, 177n43;
excavation in 1940—photos of, 78, 81, 85;
excavation in 1940—publicity, 80-82;
excavation in 1940—right-of-way schemes, 82;
experimental test pit (1974), 124, 143, 150;
experimental test pit (1974)—photo and sketch, 125;
Farlow (James) studies, 129-131, 150, 134, 148;
first discovery (Somervell County), 36-41;
First International Symposium on Dinosaur Tracks and Traces, 132-133, 177n37;
gimmicks—Somervell County, 64, 101-102;
and Indian groups, 6, 163n16, 166n18;
Kuban (Glen) studies, 127-129, 150;
and locomotion, 128, 130;
making of, 4-5, 79, 162n8;
map of, 150;
mapping of, 149-150;
Natural Landmark status, 109-117;
ornithopods, 5;
in Paluxy River, 3, 41, 54-57, 64-68, 70-72, 75-88; 96-98;
protection of, 96-97, 98, 105;
quarrying and Texas state law, 96-97;
sales of, 49, 58-59, 64-65, 96;
sales of—photo, 65;
sauropods, 5;
sauropods—in Bandera County, 74, 75;
sauropods—in Colorado, 175n23;
sauropods—descriptions of trackway by R.T. Bird, 67, 70-72, 88;
sauropods—discovery in Paluxy River (R.T. Bird), 64-68, 70-72;
sauropods—discovery in Paluxy River (Moss brothers), 56, 57, 173n14, 171n25;
sauropods—evidence regarding their walking, 68, 71;
sauropods—*Paluxysaurus*, 5;
sauropods—photo of 1934, 57;
sauropods—photo with Charlie Moss, 110;
sauropods—sketches by R.T. Bird, 70, 71;
sauropods—and Toddler photo, 132;
sauropods—and Tommy Pendley

photo, 84;
sauropods—use for local farmers, 56, 70;
and speed, 130, 185n42;
study of—Paluxy River (Ellis Shuler), 54-56, 173n9;
study of—Wheeler Branch, 38-41, 170n23;
and tail furrows, 70;
theropods, 5;
theropods—*Acrocanthosaurus*, 5, 54-56;
theropods—*Acrocanthosaurus*, photos of, 40, 55, 65;
theropods—photo of 1929, 50;
theropods—descriptions of trackway by R.T. Bird, 77, 79;
theropods—sketches by R.T. Bird, 71;
and tourism, 47-50, 64, 97-98, 100-101;
trackways on Paluxy (1978)—photo, 131;
in United States, 39;
in Wheeler Branch (measurements), 40;
in Wheeler Branch—postcard, 40

Dinosaur Tracks and Traces, 133

"Dinosaur Trail," 98, 100, 101

Dinosaur Trail National Monument, 100, 105, 110

Dinosaur Valley State Park:
    acquisition of land tracts, 108-109, 110, 123, 124, 140, 181n6, 181n7, 183n10, 187n1;
    acreage, 3, 140;
    amphitheater, 124;
    and Blue Hole, 22, 32, 58, 112, 123, 124, 131, 137, 144, 154, 182n14;
    climate, 3;
    Cretaceous Period landscape, 4, 145-147;
    dedication, 114, 117-118;
    dedication—photos, 117, 118;
    development/construction of, 111-114, 122-124, 126, 133;
    dinosaur track maintenance/preservation, 111, 124, 144-145, 149-150;
    dinosaur track research, 145, 149-150;
    dinosaur trackways (1978)—photo, 131;
    early settlement, 20-21;
    establishment of—bond issue, 106, 108, 109, 181n4;
    establishment of—early support, 98-106, 110;
    establishment of—land option, 99-100, 105-106, 108;
    establishment of—Texas Parks & Wildlife preliminary report, 105;
    experimental test pit (1974), 124, 143, 150;
    experimental test pit (1974)—photo and sketch, 125;
    facilities, 122, 123, 140-142;
    Farlow (James) studies, 129-131, 134, 148, 150;
    fishing, 144;
    and flooding, 124, 136, 137, 145, 146, 188n11;
    and flooding—photo, 146;
    headquarters, 32, 122, 127, 133, 134, 149, 186n54;
    headquarters—photo, 133;
    "Images of Dinosaurs" exhibit, 134;
    "Images of Dinosaurs" exhibit—mural, 134;
    international media attention, 145, 147-148;
    interpretive museum plans, 124;
    interpretive programs, 144-145;
    Kuban (Glen) studies, 127-129, 150;
    landowners. See landowners (Dinosaur Valley State Park);
    Lanham Mill School site, 53, 124, 153;
    LDL Friends of Dinosaur Valley State Park, 152-153;
    location, 2;
    Longhorn herd, 112, 123, 142, 182n15;
    maps of, 2, 33, 43, 141;
    as National Monument, 88, 100, 105, 181n47;
    Park Road No. 59, 183n10;
    park superintendents:
        Bob Allen, 124, 126;
        Billy Paul Baker, 126-127, 131, 135-138, 144-145, 148, 152;
        Lester Galbreath, 111-112, 113, 114, 122, 142, 181n10, 182n13, 182n14, 182n19, 183n2;
        Richard Tafoya, 126;
        Loyan Walker, 113, 122, 124;
    park store, 32, 142, 152;
    and proposed Paluxy Reservoir, 135-138;
    real estate tracts map, 160;
    River Ecology Trail, 153;
    Sinclair dinosaur models, 122, 142;
    Sinclair dinosaur models—acquisition, 103, 112, 117;
    Sinclair dinosaur models—installation, 112-114;
    Sinclair dinosaur models—installation (photo), 113;
    staff of, 109, 140;
    track excavation in 1940, 75-89;
    Track Site 2 (Main Track Site), 131, 143, 153, 168n33;
    Track Site 2 (Main Track Site)—erosion photos, 149;
    Track Site 2 (Main Track Site)—map of, 150;
    Track Site 2 (Main Track Site)—painting, 111, 119;
    Track Site 2 (Main Track Site)—photo by R. T. Bird (1970), 115;
    Track Site 2 (Main Track Site)—photos, 150;
    Track Site 3, 143, 144;
    trails, 141, 142;
    trees in, 3, 126, 137, 143;
    visitation, 122, 123, 124, 135, 140, 187n2;
    weather, 3;
    wildlife, 137, 142

"Dinosaur Waltz"—drawing by Novella Wilson, 156

Diplodocus, 187n4

Discovery Channel, 148

Dismukes, Zula, 94

Dixon, Jeanne, 179n20

dogtrot house, 21, 42, 52, 171n29

Dougherty, Cecil, 127, 179n19

Douglas, William O. (Associate Supreme Court Justice), 101

drought, 3;
    1950s, 92-93, 94

duckbilled dinosaurs, 101, 176n19, 188-189n23

Duffie, Rhonda, 167n27

Eastern Cross Timbers, 3

elongated tracks, 41, 64, 94-96, 128, 132, 150
    See also "man" tracks
    See also footprints—human

Erath County, 19, 162n10, 166n15

Erath, George, 17, 165n4, 165n5, 166n15

Ernst, Walter, 99

Eubrontes? glenrosensis, 55, 173n10

Eubrontes? titanopelopatidus, 41

Eulogy, Texas, 122

Evans, Glen:
    early life, 74, 175n8;
    as field geologist, 74-75;
    and Paluxy River tracks, 79, 86, 154;
    photo of, 74

Ewell, Thomas T., 18

exploration—American:
    mapping of Texas, 10;
    Nolan, Philip, 10
exploration—European:
    Cabeza de Vaca, Alvar Núñez, 9, 164n29;
    Catholic missionaries, 9, 164n30;
    French traders, 9-10;
    Mares, José, 10;
    Mézières, Athanase de, 10;
    Moscoso Alvarado, Luis de, 9;
    Moscoso Expedition, 9;
    Roemer, Ferdinand, 15;
    Spanish explorers, 9-10, 164n30;
    Vial, Pedro, 10, 14

exploration—Texan:
    George Erath, 17, 165n4, 165n5;
    Texan Santa Fe Expedition, 14-15, 165n5

Fannin, Oliver W., Jr., 98, 123, 183n10, 183n11

Farlow, James, 132, 134, 135, 145, 161n6, 162n10, 177n37, 178n50, 185n40;
    Paluxy River track studies, 129-31, 148, 150, 185n42;
    photos of, 129, 149;
    quoted—amusing observations, 131;
    quoted—early career, 129-130, 185n38;
    quoted—theory of dinosaur attack, 130

farming:
    in Paluxy River Valley, 19, 24, 30, 52, 66, 92, 122;
    in Somervell County, 19, 24, 30, 52, 92, 122

Farm Road 205, 92, 93, 98, 123, 129

farm-to-market roads, 92

Federal Land and Water Conservation Act, 109

Fiedler, Albert G., 56-57, 92, 178n6

Films for Christ, 184n27

Finley, James Cyrus, 32, 36

First International Symposium on Dinosaur Tracks and Traces, 132-133, 177n37

Fishner, John, 142

Flemmons, Jerry, 108, 123

floods—Paluxy River Valley:
  1859, 18;
  1908, 34, 36, 38, 41;
  1918, 41;
  1935, 56;
  damage to dinosaur tracks, 56, 79-80;
  and dinosaur track excavation (1940), 79-80, 86, 87;
  film of, 87;
  and Paluxy River crossings, 32, 46, 80;
  R.T. Bird comments on, 79-80, 86, 87

Florida, 62, 114

footprints (human-like), 41, 63, 64, 94-96, 127-129, 171n25;
  carving of, 59, 173n20;
  and creationists, 95, 127-129, 179n19, 184n28;
  erosional features, 95-96, 128;
  photos (concrete fabrications), 95;
  studies by Glen Kuban, 127-129

Footprints in Stone, 127

Fort Belknap, 18, 164n30

Fort Griffin, 112, 142

Fort Worth Museum of Science and History, 145, 147, 152, 153

Fort Worth Press, 100

Fort Worth Star-Telegram, 105, 108, 123, 126

Fort Worth, Texas, 3, 44, 64, 87, 92, 98, 100, 103, 105, 124, 147, 149

fossils:
  marine, 4, 146;
  modern discoveries, 145, 147, 162n10, 188n17;
  in Texas, 5, 15, 27, 145, 147, 162n10, 169n50

Freas, Sam (on photo), 109

freestone water, 26, 27

French traders, 9-10

Fry, Ken, 165n5;
  art by, 4, 7

Gafford, William D. and Ethelene, 181n9

Galbreath, Lester, 111-112, 113-114, 122, 142, 181n10, 182n13, 182n14, 182n19, 183n2

Gallagher (diarist), 165n5

Gallup, New Mexico, 63

Galveston County School Land:
  first sales, 21;
  land grant, 17-18, 94, 166n17, 179n13;
  map of, 16;
  surveying of, 17-18

Garner, Roy "Bummy," 109

The Genesis Flood, 95

Geography and Geology of the Black and Grand Prairies, Texas, 27

Geological Society of America, 27

geology: See also Somervell County—geology of. See Hill, Robert T. See Roemer, Ferdinand
  studies in Somervell County, 25-27

Gibbs, Dorothy Lewis, 152

Gilmore, C. W. (Charles), 38, 39, 177n34

Glen Hotel, 50

Glen Rose:
  aerial view, 28;
  bandstand track, 54-55, 64, 148-149;
  Barnard's Mill, 18-19;
  boosterism, 25;
  bridge photo, 34;
  and "Connie" Award, 123;
  "courthouse senate," 96, 179n21;
  courthouse square, 20, 34, 101;
  and dinosaur tracks, 47-50, 64, 96, 97-98, 101-103, 105-106;
  early newspaper descriptions, 24-25;
  early travel, 25, 46-47;
  founding of, 18-20;
  gimmicks—dinosaurs, 64, 101-102, 148-149;
  as health resort, 25-27, 30, 44, 92;
  Heritage Park, 153, 154;
  naming of, 19, 167n27;
  Oakdale Park, 13, 117, 118, 119, 147, 180n44;
  as the "Petrified City," 47;
  population—1890, 25;
  population—1900, 169n2;
  population—1930, 172n1;
  population—1950, 92;
  population—2000, 149;
  railroad, lack of, 25, 27, 44, 88;
  as Tonkawa site, 6;
  tornado (1902), 31;
  town slogan, 45, 49, 52, 126;
  wells, 25-27

Glen Rose and Geo. P. Snyder..., 29, 44, 48

Glen Rose beds, 27, 169n50

Glen Rose Chamber of Commerce, 64, 122

Glen Rose Citizen, 24-25

Glen Rose Future Farmers of America, 101

Glen Rose Herald, 34, 38

Glen Rose Limestone, 5, 39, 55

Glen Rose–Paluxy Road, 32

Glen Rose Prairie, 161n2

Glen Rose Reporter, 98, 99, 102, 105, 108, 112, 134

Glen Rose School, 36

Glen Rose–Somervell County Chamber of Commerce, 98, 99, 103, 108, 113, 117

Glen Rose–Stephenville Road, 20

Golden-cheeked Warbler, 105, 137, 142

Good Roads Movement, 47

Gosdin, Betty, 167n27

Grahamsville, New York, 132

Granbury, Texas, 19, 24, 25, 46, 135

Grand Prairies region, 3

grasses:
  in Dinosaur Valley State Park, 143;
  prairie types, 6

Graves, John:
  as landowner, 94;
  quoted—Comanches, 8;
  quoted—descriptions of land, 3;
  quoted—drought of 1950s, 92-93;
  quoted—settlement of Somervell County, 18-19

Gravitt, C. W., 176n28

Green, George, 17

Guadalupe River, 9

Hamberlin family, 45

Hamberlin, John, 171n38

Hamberlin–Moss crossing (second crossing), 32, 35, 45, 154

Hamick, T.J., 20

Hard Scrabble: Observations on a Patch of Land, 3, 94

Hard Scrabble Ranch, 3, 94

Hartford, Connecticut, 15

Helton, Era Mae, 94

Hendrix, Martha A. (Blackstock), 21

Hendrix–Ramfield crossing (fourth crossing or Hendrix crossing), 21, 22,

32, 35, 54, 55, 56, 64, 92, 94, 111

Hendrix, Wiley, 21, 32

Henrietta, Texas, 74

Heritage Museum of the Texas Hill Country, 185n40

Hicks, Elijah, 15, 17

highways. See also roads:
Cleburne–Glen Rose Road, 47;
Cleburne–Glen Rose Road—postcard, 47;
Farm Road 205, 92, 93, 98, 123, 129;
farm-to-market roads, 92;
Glen Rose–Paluxy Road, 32;
Glen Rose–Stephenville Road, 20;
and Good Roads Movement, 47;
Highway 68, 47;
improvement, 46-47, 92;
Old San Antonio Road, 14;
scenic parkway, 98, 179n25;
and tourism, 46-47;
U.S. Highway 67, 47

Hill County, 10, 166n11

Hill, Jack, 63, 94, 179n16, 179n19

Hill, Robert T.:
column in Dallas Morning News, 55-56, 173n11;
dinosaur track studies (1934), 55-56;
geological studies, 26-27, 166n11, 169n50

Historic Lanham Mill Community and Cemetery, 24, 154

History of Hood County, 18

Hitchcock, Edward, 39

hoe beer, 45, 171n40

Holder, Johnny (in photo), 65

Holding, Earl, 182n16

Homestead, Florida, 114

"Honey-Eaters," 8

Hood County, 9, 17, 19, 20, 25, 135, 147, 162n10

Hope College (Holland, Michigan), 185n38

Hopkins, Paul, 137

horses, 10, 11

Houston, Sam, 15, 165n9

Howe Quarry site (Wyoming), 173n12

Hudson River, 102

Huffman, Clay, 179n13

ichnologists, 5

ichnology (resurgence in study), 129, 132, 133

iguanodonts, 162n11
I Married a Dinosaur, 63

Indiana University—Purdue University Fort Wayne, 129

Indian groups, 16-17;
Indian raids, 19, 167n26;
Indian reservations, 18, 166-167n19;
Thunderbird mythology, 163n16;
and trade, 9-10, 15
See also Caddos, Comanches, Tonkawas, and Wichitas

Indian Territory, 15, 18, 167n19

Irenesauripus glenrosensis, 130

Jackson, Earl, 99, 105

Jacobs, Louis, 4, 145, 147, 152, 161n6

Japan, 148

Johnson County, 19

Johnson, Early (on photo), 109

Johnson, Lady Bird, 101

Jonas, Louis Paul, 102, 114

Jones Ranch, 147, 162n10

Jones, W. D., 82, 93, 110, 176n28

Jones, William R., 147, 162,10

Jordan, Annie R. Lewis, 19, 167n27

Jordan, Maj. Tyler Calhoun, 19, 167n28

Jumanos, 164n30

Jurassic Park, 148

Kansas, 7

Keechis, 17

Kendall, George Wilkins, 14-15, 165n5

Kenmotsu, Nancy, 164n30

Kerr, John, 94, 140

Kickapoos, 17, 166n19

Kimball's Bend, 165n5

Kimmel crossing (seventh crossing), 35, 178n4

Korea, 147

Kuban, Glen, 127-129, 132, 150, 184-185n31;
quoted—elongated tracks, 128;
quoted—"man" tracks, 128;
quoted—track colorations, 128

Lake Granbury, 163n15

Lake Whitney, 163n15
Lamar, Mirabeau B., 14

Lampasas Cut Plain, 3, 27, 161n2

Lampasas (River), 14

land empresarios, 11

land grants (in North Central Texas), 16-18

landowners (Dinosaur Valley State Park):
Abell, Elmer, 23, 110;
Abell, J.B., 110, 168n39, 178n10;
Abell, Mathias A. "Matt," 22, 93, 168n37, 168n39;
Adams, Samuel, 21, 168n33;
Ball, Neva, 179n13, 181n9;
Ball, Roland, 110, 179n13, 181n9;
Beck, Charlie Walton, 82, 176n28, 178n10;
Beck, James, 23, 168n39;
Beck, Walter, 110, 168n39, 178n10;
Cox, V.M., 31;
Daniel, Gabriel T., 31;
Daniel, Joe, 31;
Daniel, Mary Ann, 31;
Dismukes, Zula, 94;
Fannin, Oliver W., Jr., 98, 123, 183n10;
Finley, James Cyrus, 32;
Gafford, William D. and Ethelene, 181n9;
Gravitt, C.W., 176n28;
Helton, Era Mae, 94;
Hendrix, Wiley, 21;
Huffman, Clay, 179n13;
Jones, W.D., 82, 93, 110, 176n28;
Kerr, John, 94, 140;
maps, 33, 43, 160;
Martin, Isaac Edgar, 32, 170n7, 171n36;
Martin, Jacob T., 31-32, 170n7;
Martin, Ollie Mae Lanham, 32;
McDonald, Dwight, 94, 179n13;
Muse, William E., 41-42, 58, 94;
Nix, Euella Marie Jones, 110;
Pair, I.C. "Charley," 21, 42, 168n33;
Pruitt, J.O., 94;
Ramfield, Michael T.W., 31, 41, 58, 94;
Rowland, Christopher Columbus, 42, 52, 94, 110;
Segelhurst, Anna, 176n28;
Segelhurst, G. E., 176n28;
Shults, Helen Lee Kerr, 140;
Stephens, E.L., 23;
Tidwell, Houston Obediah, 30, 169n3, 170n7;
Walton, Felix, 168n37;
West, Doyle, 94, 98;
West, Ella, 94, 98;
Whitaker, Earnest, 93;
Whitaker, Earnest Winston, 93, 98, 99, 108-109, 178n9;
Whitaker, Esquire, 93;
Whitaker, Julia, 93;
Whitaker, Martha, 98, 99, 108-109

Lane's Ford Agency and Garage, 47

Lane's Hotel, 77

Lane's swimming hole, 48;
photo of, 48

Langston, Wann, 105, 129, 130, 132, 134

Lanham crossing (fifth crossing), 20, 35

Lanham, Mary E. (illustration), 20

Lanham Mill, 30;
establishment of, 20, 24;
photo of, 21

Lanham Mill Cemetery, 21;
Lanham Mill Cemetery Association, 154;
photo, 21

Lanham Mill Community:
agriculture, 24, 30, 42, 44, 52, 66;
bootlegging, 44-46, 53, 57;
church gatherings, 22;
early settlement, 20-22;
flood of 1908, 36;
gins, 20-21, 24, 30-31;
historical marker, 154;
map, 93;
and proposed Paluxy reservoir, 135-138;
roads, 25, 46, 92, 93;
school. See Lanham Mill School;
tornado (1902), 31, 34;
tornado (1930), 52;
wheat harvest (photo), 30;
and World War II, 92, 93

Lanham Mill School, 65;
as community center, 32, 53-54;
consolidation/closing, 92, 93;
and Dinosaur Valley State Park, 124;
donation of land for (1903), 32, 170n9;
first schoolhouse (Cedar Point), 21-22;
photos of, 53, 153;
preservation of, 124, 153-154, 184n16;
and recreation, 52-54;
teachers, 32, 53, 168n35

Lanham, William, 20, 27, 32;
illustration, 20

LBJ Ranch, 101

LDL Foundation, 152

LDL Friends of Dinosaur Valley State Park, 152-153

Leach, Dorothy, 47-48, 99, 101, 105, 109;
photo of, 99

Leach, Maxie Parker, 47-48;
in photo, 48

Leon (River), 14

León, Diego, 164n30

Lewis, Ted, 179n25

lime mud strider, 41, 47

limestone, 3, 15, 40-41, 46, 58, 59, 79, 92, 94, 129, 145, 151, 162n8;
and fossil bones, 145-147

limy mud. See mud, limy

Lipans, 17

Lockley, Martin, 132

Loma Linda University, 184-185n31

Lone Star Dinosaurs, 4, 145

Longhorns, 112, 123, 142, 182n15

Louisiana sugar cane, 27

Lower Cretaceous Glen Rose Formation, 3, 27, 63

Lull, R. S. (Richard Swann), 39, 170n20

Lupton, New Mexico, 63

Maceo, Peggy, 132, 134, 149, 150, 151

magnetic healers, 44

Malony, Vance, 9, 164n30

"man" tracks, 41, 63, 171n25;
carving of, 59, 173n20;
and creationists, 95, 179n19, 184n28;
erosional features, 95-96;
photos of (concrete fabrications), 95;
and R.T. Bird, comments on, 63, 64, 94-96;
studies by Glen Kuban, 127-129

Map of the State of Texas (De Cordova), 18

maps:
by Austin, Stephen F., 11;
Dinosaur Valley State Park (park map), 141;
Dinosaur Valley State Park, Real Estate Tracts, 160;
Dinosaur Valley State Park and Vicinity, 2;
Galveston County School Land, 16;
geological map of Texas, 15;
Lanham Mill Community and Vicinity (ca. 1947), 93;
Major Owners of Future Parklands, early 1900s, 33;
Major Owners of Future Parklands, ca. 1920s and 1930s, 43;
Map of the State of Texas (De Cordova), 18;
by Philip Nolan, 10;
North Central Texas Wilderness (ca. 1830), 11;
Paluxy Valley River Crossings, 35;
Track Site 2 (Main Track Site)—Dinosaur Valley State Park, 150

Mares, José, 10

Marsh, O.C., 39

Martin, Elna, 29, 44, 172n56;
quoted on dinosaur tracks, 48-49;
quoted on tourism, 44, 46-47

Martin house, 32, 41, 82, 93, 109, 176n28, 182n13

Martin, Isaac Edgar, 32, 170n7, 171n36

Martin, Jacob (J.T.), 31, 170n7

Martin, Ollie Mae Lanham, 32

Martin's Park, 49

Maryland, 147, 162n10

Mask family, 104

Mask, Linda, 104

Matthews (WPA worker), 88

Matthews children, 84

Mauermann, Robert G., 108;
on photo, 109

May, Alton, 58, 180n44;
photo of, 58

May, Connie—photo of, 103

May, Daisy Ryals, 58-59
See also Ryals, Daisy

May, Dora Ramfield, 52, 111

May, George, 53

May, Marvin, 53

May, Mrs. Alton (Geneva "Pete"), 103, 180n44, 182n19

May, Newt, 172n4

May, Vivian, 32, 52, 57, 58, 92, 172n4;
farm, 52;
photo of, 58

Mayor, Adrienne, 163n16

McCamant–Booker crossing (first crossing), 35

McCarty, Dan, 99, 102, 105, 108, 112, 134

McCarty, Jack, 99, 100, 103, 112

McConnell, Joseph Carroll, 164n30

McCoy (WPA worker), 87

McDonald, Dwight, 94, 179n13

McDonald, Robert E. (quoted) 36-37

McFall, Elsie, 124

McFall, Emmett, 124, 127

McFall farm, 96, 101, 124, 129

McFall, Jacob, 96

McFall, Robert, 153, 154

Medina County, 75

Meridian, Texas, 117

Mesozoic Era, 4

Mexican independence, 10

Mexico, 9, 10, 19

Mexico City, 15

Mézières, Athanase de, 10

Milam County, 14, 164n2

Milam Land District, 17

Milam Municipality, 14

Millsap, Texas, 169n50

mineral waters, 44, 64

Missouri, Kansas and Texas Railway Company, 177n39

Model T, 53;
coupé, 49;
postcard, 47;
and roads, 46-47;
truck—photo of, 58

Monastir, Tunesia, 123

Montague County, 10

Montgomery, Nola (painting by), 134

Moody, Pliny, 39

Moon, 8

moonshine. See bootlegging

Morris, John, 127, 179n19, 184n28

Moscoso Alvarado, Luis de, 9

Moscoso Expedition, 9

Moss brothers (and sauropod tracks), 56, 57, 65, 171n25, 173n14

Moss, Charlie:
description of "human" tracks, 41, 171n25;
and dinosaur tracks, 41, 56, 57, 96, 97, 173n14, 181n52;
and moonshining, 45, 171n38, 171n39;
as park guide, 109, 110;
photo by (sauropod tracks, 1934), 57;
photo of, 110

Moss, Lallah Hamberlin, 171n38

Moss, William Boone, 171n38

Moss, William Boone "Grandy," 41, 45, 173n14

mud, limy:
making of dinosaur tracks, 4, 41, 55, 79, 88

Murphy crossing (third crossing), 35, 41, 52, 67, 75, 129, 171n38, 173n14;
photo of, 75

Muse, William, 41-42, 58, 94, 171n26;
photo of, 42

Nashville, Texas (Nashville-on-the-Brazos), 14, 164n2

Natchitoches, Louisiana, 10
National Colonization Law of August 18, 1824, 11

National Geographic, 84, 89, 94, 114;
R.T. Bird article "We Captured a 'Live' Brontosaur," 88

National Museum of Natural History, Smithsonian, 83

National Park Service, 88, 100, 109

Native Americans. See Indian groups

Natural History (R.T. Bird article "Thunder in His Footsteps"), 71, 94, 179n20

Navajos, 163n16

Navasota River, 14

New Braunfels, Texas, 49

Newcomb, William W. Jr., 7

New Mexico, 15, 63, 164n30

New York World's Fair (1964), 102, 104, 112, 115

Nix, Euella Marie Jones, 110

Nolan, Philip, 10

Nolan River, 165n5, 166n11

North American Archeologist, 164n30

North Central Texas:
archeological evidence, 6, 163n15;
climate, 3;
as coastal plain, 4-5, 145-147;
Cretaceous Period, 45, 145-147;
as crossroads of travel and culture, 3, 9;
dinosaurs in, 4-5;
early habitation, 6;
exploration of, 9-12, 15;
fossil remains in, 5, 145-147, 162n10;
geological observations, 15;
land grants, 17-18;
landscape—description, 3, 6;
landscape—illustrations of, 4, 7;
"layer cake" geology, 145-146;
on map, 11;
prairies, 3;
seas of, 4-5;
settlement of, 14-19;
trade in, 9-10, 15, 17;
trading posts, 15, 17, 63;
wildlife, 6

North Star, 8

Northern Hill Country, ix, 3, 12, 30, 49, 50, 142

nuclear power plant. See Comanche Peak Steam Electric Generating Station

Nunn, W.C., 6, 164n29, 164n30

Oakdale Park (Glen Rose), 113, 117, 118, 119, 147, 180n44

O'Brien, Mike, 149-150, 151, 152;
photo of, 152

Odom, Will, 99

Off the Beaten Trail, 97

Oklahoma (and fossil remains), 5, 188n16

Old San Antonio Road, 4

Open Meetings Act, 137-138

Opossum Branch, 85, 110, 142, 168n33

Ornitholestes, 180n41

ornithopods, 5, 162n11

Ortega, Fray Juan de, 164n30

Osages, 7

Ostrom, Dr. John H., 180n41, 185n38

Owen, Richard, 39

Oxford University, 65

Painted Bunting, 142

Pair, I.C. "Charley," 21, 42, 168n33

Palaeontologia Electronica, 147

paleontologists, 5, 27, 177n37;
American, 66;
debate over sauropods walking, 66-67;
fossil hunting, 27, 74-75;
German, 66

paleontology:
"Dark Age," 63, 174n6;
"Golden Age," 39, 63;
"Second Golden Age," 129, 132

Paluxy River:
See also Blue Hole;
bridge, 34, 36;
bridge—photo, 34;
crossings, 32, 46, 75, 82, 92, 154;
crossings—map, 35;
description of, 3, 6;
dinosaur tracks in, 3, 54-57, 64-68, 70-89, 96-98, 130;
flooding. See floods;
origin of name, 17-18, 166n18;
proposed reservoir, 135-138, 187n71, 187n74;
and recreation, 54

Paluxy River crossings:
Abell crossing, 22;
Cemetery crossing, 35;
and flooding, 32-33, 80 (See also floods);
Hamberlin–Moss crossing, 32, 35, 45, 154;
Hendrix–Ramfield crossing (Hendrix crossing), 21, 22, 32, 35, 54, 55, 56, 64, 92, 94, 111;
Kimmel crossing, 35, 178n4;
Lanham crossing, 20, 35, 92;
map, 35;
McCamant–Booker crossing, 35;
Murphy crossing, 35, 41, 52, 67, 75, 129, 171n38, 173n14;
Murphy crossing—photo of, 75

Paluxy River Valley:

absentee ownership, 93, 94;
archeological evidence, 6;
early habitation, 6, 9;
exploration of, 9-10, 165n5;
farming, 19, 24, 42, 44, 52, 66, 92, 122;
and Farm Road 205, 92, 93, 98 129;
first geological studies, 26-27;
floods, 18, 32, 34, 36, 87, 94, 124, 145, 146, 167n27;
landscape, description of, 3, 6, 25, 44;
making of, 5-6;
photo of, 154;
proposed reservoir, 135-138;
settlement of, 18-24;
surveying of, 17-18;
and tourism, 46-47, 97-98;
wildlife, 6;
and World War II, 92, 93

Paluxysaurus, 130;
description of, 5;
excavation of fossil remains (Jones Ranch), 147, 162n10;
illustration of, 3;
name proposed, 5, 147, 162n10;
tracks of, 5, 130

Paluxysaurus jonesi, 147, 162n10

Paluxy, Texas (Hood County), 20, 32, 36, 135, 147, 162n10, 172n48

Parker County, 147, 169n50, 188n16

Peabody Museum of Natural History, 180n41

peanut farming, 66, 92, 122

pelts, animal, 15, 57

Penatekas, 8, 18, 166n19;
wintering ground, 8

Pendley, Tom, 84

Pendley, Tommy, 132, 177n37;
description by R.T. Bird, 84;
photo of, 84

"Petrified City," 47

petrified wood, 15, 54, 148, 172n48;
buildings, 47, 64, 77;
buildings—photo of, 47;
making of, 6;
sale of, 47, 57

Phoenix Award, 183n7

Pleurocoelus, 147, 162n10

Poage, W.R. "Bob" (Congressman), 98, 99, 100, 105, 179n25

Popular Science Monthly, 39

Porter's Spring (Brazos River), 165n5

prairies:
fire, 14-15;
grasses, types of, 6;
illustration, 4, 7

Prohibition, 44, 57

pronghorn antelope, 6;
illustration, 4

Pruitt, J.O., 94

que-tah-to-yah, 9

railroad, 25, 27, 44, 88

Rainbow, Texas, 31

Ralph, Ron, 161n6

Ramfield, Chris, 32, 52

Ramfield, Michael T.W., 32, 36, 41, 58, 94

Rattlesnake Hollow, 143

Ravenel, W.A.C., 39

Red Oak, Texas, 111

Red River, 7, 10, 163n21

Reeder, William, 151

Relación, 9

The Resources, Soil, and Climate of Texas, 25

Rhodes, Billie Jean, 53

Ring Games, 54

Riskind, David, 132, 135

river crossings. See Paluxy River crossings

Riverside Park (New York), 115

roads:
Cleburne–Glen Rose Road, 47;
early maintenance, 25, 46;
Farm Road 205, 92, 93, 98, 123, 129;
farm-to-market roads, 92;
Glen Rose–Paluxy Road, 32;
Glen Rose–Stephenville Road, 20;
Hereford Street (Cyclone Street), 31;
Lanham Mill Road, 46;
Old San Antonio Road, 14;
overseers, 25;
Park Road No. 59, 183n10;
routes of early explorers, 14;
scenic parkway, 98, 179n25;
and tourism, 46-47;
troubles and travel, 25, 32, 46-47

Roden, Tom, 99

Roemer, Ferdinand, 15, 17, 165-166n11

Roming, Ralph, 137, 187n71

Rose, Peter, 147

Rowland, Christopher Columbus, 42, 52, 94, 110

Rowntree, Ralph S. (sketch by), 48

"rubbin' doctors," 44

Ryals, Daisy, 58-59;
observation of Paluxy River track quarry (1940), 82

Ryals, James (Jim), 84, 128;

photo of, 65;
quarrying dinosaur tracks, 58-59, 64-65, 82, 177n34

Rye, New York, 62

Salado (River), 14

Salas, Juan de, 164n30

San Antonio, 98;
route to Santa Fe, 10

Sanchez, Jason, 184n20

Sanders, Joe:
Glen Rose road trip 1929, ix, 49-50, 172n54;
photo by (theropod track), 50;
photos of, viii, 49

Sanders, Laurie:
Glen Rose road trip 1929, ix, 49-50, 172n54;
photos of, viii, 49;
quoted—dinosaur tracks, 49-50, 172n56

sandstone, 145, 146, 147

San Jacinto, 17

Santa Fe, 10, 14

Santa Fe train, 34

sauropods:
See also dinosaur tracks, sauropods;
Apatosaurus, 72;
Brontosaurus, 72, 102;
debate about their walking, 66-67, 68, 71, 83;
description of, 5;
excavation of fossil remains (Jones Ranch), 147, 162n10;
illustrations of, 3, 134;
Paluxysaurus, 5, 130, 147, 162n10;
Pleurocoelus, 147, 162n10;
postcard art by Novella Wilson, 148;
and Sinclair oil, 72-74;
track and Charlie Moss photo, 110;
track and toddler photo, 132;
track and Tom Pendley photo, 84;
tracks of—American Museum trackway photo, 89;
tracks of—Bandera County, 74, 75;
tracks of—Colorado, 175n23;
tracks of—discovery in Paluxy (Moss brothers), 56, 57, 171n25;
tracks of—experimental test pit (1974), 124-125;
tracks of—Paluxy River, 56, 57, 64-68, 70-72, 83, 84, 87, 88, 131, 177n34, 177n37;
tracks of—Paluxy trackway 1940 photo, 78;
tracks of—Paluxy trackway excavation 1940, 75-89;
tracks of—photo 1934, 57;
tracks of—R.T. Bird discovery, 64-68, 70-72;
tracks of—significant evidence about sauropods, 68, 83;
tracks of—sketches by R.T. Bird, 70, 71

Schreiber, V.T., 114, 182n24, 188n22

Scotland, 167n27

seas, 4, 41;
  inland sea (Cretaceous Period), 5

sedimentary rock, 3, 6

Segelhurst, Anna, 176n28

Segelhurst, G.E., 176n28

Sellards, E.H., 74, 75, 79, 80, 82, 175n8, 177n33, 177n34

Seminary South (Fort Worth), 103

shale, 126, 145, 146, 147, 162n8

Shawnees, 17, 18, 167n19

Sheppard, John Ben, 99

Sherrell, Liz, 152

Shuler, Ellis:
  dinosaur track studies—bandstand, Glen Rose, 54-55;
  dinosaur track studies—Paluxy River, 54-56, 173n9;
  dinosaur track studies—Wheeler Branch, 39-41, 170n23

Shuler Museum of Paleontology, 124, 145, 153

Shults, Helen Lee Kerr, 140, 187n1

Signs of the Times, 95

Sinclair dinosaur models, 102, 115, 122;
  acquisition for park, 112, 117, 180n44, 183n15;
  Brontosaurus ("Bronto"), 104, 112-114, 142, 187n4;
  Brontosaurus ("Bronto")—photos of, 103, 104, 113, 117, 140;
  installation in park, 112-114;
  installation in park—photo of, 113;
  promotional brontosaur, 113;
  promotional brontosaur—photos of, 103, 147;
  Tyrannosaurus ("Rex"), 104, 112-114, 142;
  Tyrannosaurus ("Rex")—photos of, 104, 113, 118, 140

Sinclair Dinosaur Show, 102-104;
  at Dallas, 104, 180n46;
  at Dallas—photo of, 104;
  at Fort Worth, 103, 180n44;
  at Fort Worth—photo of, 103

Sinclair, Harry, 95

Sinclair Oil Corporation, 105, 112, 134, 182n16

Sinclair Refining Company:
  ad campaigns, 72-74, 102, 104;
  ads—images, 73;
  and "Dinoland" (New York World's Fair), 102-103, 104, 112;
  merger with Atlantic Richfield Company, 112, 182n16;
  as patron of dinosaur expeditions, 72-74

The Sky, 174n11

Sky & Telescope, 174n11

Slaughter, Bob, 124

slave labor, 19

Smith, Preston (Governor), 112, 117;
  on photo, 118

Smithsonian Institute (Institution), 38, 39, 177n34;
  Division of Vertebrate Paleontology, 38;
  National Museum of Natural History, 38, 83

Snap, 54

Snyder, George P., 44, 171n33

Snyder Hotel, 44

Snyder Sanitarium, 44, 95

Society of American Travel Writers, 123, 183n7

Society of Vertebrate Paleontology, 71

Sogorka, Frank, 113, 117;
  on photo, 118

Somervell, Alexander, 19

Somervell County:
  African American population, 19, 167n24;
  agriculture statistics—1880 and 1890, 24;
  agriculture statistics and Depression, 52;
  boosterism, 25;
  and Civil War, 19;
  as Comanche wintering ground, 8;
  courthouse, 20;
  courthouse—postcard of, 101;
  and Depression, 52, 56-59;
  early travel, 25;
  establishment of, 19-20;
  exploration of, 9-10, 14;
  geological studies of (Hill), 26-27;
  geology of, 3, 26-27, 145, 146, 147;
  gimmicks—dinosaurs, 64, 101-102, 148;
  highway development, 46-47, 92 (See also roads, highways);
  Indian groups in. See Indian groups;
  Indian raids, 19, 167n26;
  land grants, 16, 17-18;
  maps of, 2;
  and moonshine, 44-46, 50, 53, 57, 171n40, 171-172n41;
  museum, 101;
  natural resources of, 24-25, 56-59, 122;
  nuclear power plant, 124-126;
  population statistics—1880 and 1890, 24, 167n24;
  population statistics—1900, 30;
  population statistics—1940 and 1950, 92;
  population statistics—1960 and 1970, 183n1;
  population statistics—1970 and 1980, 126;
  population statistics—2000, 149;
  prohibition of liquor sales, 44,
171n36;
  settlement of, 15-20;
  stock raising, 19, 24, 92, 122;
  topography, description, 3, 25;
  tornado (1902), 31, 34;
  and tourism, 46-50, 64, 97-98, 122, 126;
  and World War II, 92, 93

Somervell County Commissioners Court, 98, 123

Somervell County Historical Commission, 47, 99, 165n5, 177n43, 179n25

Somervell County Historical Society, 98, 101, 179n25

Somervell County Museum, 45, 101, 126, 148

Somervell Expedition, 19, 168n28

Somervell: Story of a Texas County, 164n29, 164n30

Southern Methodist University, 39, 54, 59, 83, 124, 145, 147, 177n34

South Hadley, Massachusetts, 39

Spaight, A.W., 25

Spanish Fort, Texas, 10

Spanish government (and Nolan expeditions), 10

Squaw Creek:
  and Comanche Peak Steam Electric Generating Station, 124, 125;
  flood, 18;
  Indian raid, 19

Squaw Creek Reservoir, 125, 163n16

State Colonization Law of March 24, 1825, 11

State Highway Department, 123

State Parks and Wildlife Commission, 99

Stegosaurus, 180n41

Stephens, Charlie Henry, 168n33

Stephens, E.L., 23

Stephens, Marion C.A., 168n33

Stephenville, Texas, 46, 135, 162n10, 176n19

stills, bootlegging, 45, 153;
  photo of, 45

The Story of Comanche Peak, Landmark of Hood County, Texas, 9, 164n30

Struthiomimus, 180n41

Styron, Charles (in photo), 81

Sulphur Springs (Somervell County), Texas, 168n28

sulphur water, 6, 25, 26, 27, 44, 97

Summer Tanager, 142

Summers, Temple, 98, 99

surveying (land grants), 14, 17-18

swimming holes:
Blue Hole, 22, 32, 44, 58, 94, 98, 112, 123, 124, 131, 137, 144, 154, 182n14;
Lane's, 48;
photos, 22, 48

Syers, Ed, 91, 97-98

Tafoya, Richard, 126

Tanner, H.S. (published 1830 Texas map), 11

Taovayas, 7, 10

Tawakonis (Tehuacanas), 7-8, 10, 17

Taylor, Stanley, 127, 184n27

Tehuacana Creek, 15, 165n11

Texan Santa Fe Expedition, 14-15, 165n5

Texas A&M College (Texas A&M University), 49, 172n51

Texas Cedar Oil Company, Inc., 183n1

Texas Central Railroad, 177n39

Texas Congress, 14

Texas General Land Office, 14, 17;
land grant map, 16;
maps from, 11, 16

Texas Hill Country, 3, 49, 185n40

Texas Legislature, 15, 19, 105, 147

Texas Memorial Museum, 75, 175n8;
and Paluxy River dinosaur tracks, 79, 88, 97, 150-152, 189n30;
WPA trackhouse, 88, 150-152;
WPA trackhouse—photo, 151

Texas Parks and Wildlife Department, 109, 110, 112, 113, 122, 123, 126, 132, 134, 140, 149, 150, 151, 152, 177n43;
lawsuit against proposed Paluxy reservoir, 135-138, 186n69, 187n71, 187n74

Texas Rangers, 45-46;
photo—bootlegging raid, 46

Texas Reptile Control Commission, 101, 102

Texas State Parks System, 3, 126, 140

Texas State-wide Paleontological Survey, 74

Texas Utilities Company, 124, 152
Texas Water Commission, 135, 137-138, 187n71

therapsids, 174n6
Theriot, Ed, 152

theropods:
See also dinosaur tracks—theropods;
Acrocanthosaurus, 5, 130, 188n16, 188n17;
description of, 5;
illustration of, 3, 48, 134;
track of—bandstand, Glen Rose, 54-55, 64, 148-149, 173n8;
tracks of—Comanche Peak Steam Electric Generating Station, 125-126, 184n20;
tracks of—Connecticut River Valley, 39;
tracks of—experimental test pit (1974), 124-125;
tracks of—Paluxy River, 54-56, 67, 77-78, 83, 84, 87, 88, 131;
tracks of—Paluxy trackway 1940 photo, 78;
tracks of—Wheeler Branch, 36-41, 47-50, 172n54, 172n56;
tracks of—photo 1929, 50;
tracks of—sketch by R.T. Bird, 71

Third District Court of Appeals, 138

Thomas, O.P. (on photo), 118

Throckmorton County, 18

Thunderbird, 163n16

"Tiddle Town," 30-31, 94, 140;
photo, 31

Tidwell, Elizabeth, 169n3

Tidwell, Henry A., 170n7

Tidwell, Houston Obediah, 30, 169n3, 170n7

Tidwell, Percy, 30, 31

Tolar, Texas, 24

Tolbert, Frank, 96

"Tonk Nation," 94

Tonkawas, 6-7, 17, 94;
attitudes of settlers and other Indian groups, 7, 163n19;
and cannibalism, 7;
descriptions of (clothing and decoration), 7;
diet, 6;
dwellings of, 7;
on Indian reservation, 18, 166-167n19;
name of, 6;
in Somervell County, 6, 19;
and trade network, 7, 15

tonkaweya, 6

tornado (1902), 31, 34;
(1930), 52

Torrey Brothers, 15

Torrey, David, 15

Torrey, James, 15
Torrey, John, 15

Torrey, Thomas, 15

tourism:
and the dinosaur, 48-50, 148;
Sanders 1929 road trip, 49-50;
in Somervell County, 30, 46-50;

Trachodon, 102, 180n41, 188-189n23

Tracking Those Incredible Dinosaurs...and the People Who Knew Them, 127, 179n19, 184n28

tracks. See dinosaur tracks

trade:
French, 9-10;
Indian groups, 9-10, 15, 17;
Texan Santa Fe Expedition, 14-15;
wild horses, 10;
See also trading posts

trading posts:
Barnard Brothers, 15, 165n9;
Brazos Reservation, 18;
at Comanche Peak, 15, 17, 166n13;
establishment of, 15;
in Gallup, New Mexico, 63;
Tehuacana Trading Post, 15, 165n9, 166n11;
Torrey Brothers, 15, 165n9;
Trading Post No. 2, 15

Travis County, 138

trees:
landscape, historic, 3, 6, 17;
petrified wood, 6;
prehistoric forest, 4

Triassic rocks, 39

Triceratops, 180n41

Trimble, Olive Fay (photo of), 53

Trinity Group, 161n2

Trinity reservoir, 27

Trinity River, 9, 10

Tucker, Jim, 180n41

turkeys, 6, 53, 142;
illustration, 4

Turner, Janette, 170n7

tyrannosaur, 100, 112

Tyrannosaurus, 5;
jaw by R.T. Bird, 148, 188n22;
Sinclair dinosaur model ("Rex"), 104, 112-114, 142, 180n41;
Sinclair dinosaur model ("Rex")—photos of, 104, 113, 118, 140

United States Geological Survey, 26-27, 39, 169n49

University of Texas at Austin, 74, 75, 77, 79, 83, 105, 129, 132, 150, 151

U. S. Department of the Interior, 109

U. S. Highway 67, 47;
bridge constructed, 47

Valley of the Giants, 127, 179n19, 184n28

vara, 17

Veteran's Land Board, 94

Vial, Pedro, 10, 14

von Däniken, Erich, 127, 184n28

Waco News-Tribune, 122, 123

Waco, Texas, 10, 15, 98, 100

Wacos, 7-8, 14, 17, 165n11

Walker, Loyan, 113, 122, 124

Wall Manufacturing Company, 183n1

Walnut Springs, Texas, 46, 85, 168n33, 177n39

Walton, Felix, 168n37

Ward, J.E. (Representative), 99, 100, 105, 117;
on photos, 109, 118

Washington, DC., 38

"Wasps" (wintering ground), 8

water:
artesian wells, 25-27, 44, 56-57, 92, 153, 169n48;
drought of 1950s, 92-93, 94;
irrigation, 27, 56;
sulphur water, 6, 25, 26, 27, 44, 97;
usage (statistics, 1934), 56-57, 173n16;
and wasteful practices, 56-57, 92, 173n16, 178n6

Weekly Enterprise (Cleburne), 34, 36, 38

wells, artesian, 25-27, 36, 44, 56-57, 92, 153, 169n48;
and bootlegging, 44-45, 53, 57;
domestic use, 27, 56-57, 173n16;
drilling, 25-26, 56, 123;
postcard, 26

West, Doyle, 94, 98

West, Ed, 109

West, Ella, 94, 98

Western Cross Timbers, 3, 14, 165n5

Western Diamondback rattlesnake, 142-143

West Texas Chamber of Commerce, 99, 122

The West Texas Frontier, 164n30

wheat harvest (photo), 30

Wheeler Branch:
dinosaur tracks in, 36-41, 47-48, 54, 65, 88, 154, 172n54, 172n56;
dinosaur tracks in—photo, 40;
dinosaur tracks in—1929 photo, 50;
Lane's swimming hole, 48;
Lane's swimming hole—photo, 48;
photo of, 37;

picnics, 47-48

Whitaker, Earnest, 93

Whitaker, Earnest Winston, 93, 98, 99, 108, 109, 178n9;
on photo, 109

Whitaker, Esquire, 93

Whitaker, Julia, 93

Whitaker, Martha, 98, 99, 108-109;
on photo, 109

White Bluff Branch (Creek), 20, 94

White, Kay, 118

Wichitas, 7-8, 17, 18, 163n19;
belief system, 8;
crops of, 8;
division of labor, 8;
dwellings of, 8;
language, 7;
major groups, 7;
migration of, 7, 163n21;
and trade, 10, 15;
and treaties, 10;
villages, 8

Wildcat Hollow, 110, 142

Wilkins, Zollie, 109

Williams, John, 133, 135

William's Mill, 20

Williams, Samuel May, 14

Wilson, Charlidell, 80, 81, 82, 94;
photos of, 81, 154;
See also Davis, Charlidell

Wilson, Doyle, 94;
childhood, 53, 59;
Dillard Wilson and Roland T. Bird, comments on, 79, 82, 117;
and Dinosaur Valley State Park, 110;
meeting Roland T. Bird, 62, 68;
observations of Paluxy River track excavation, 77, 79, 80, 85, 154;
observations of Dillard Wilson, 66;
and Paluxy tracks, 154, 189n24;
photos of, 77, 154;
sale of pelts, 57

Wilson, Fern, 52

Wilson, George Eugene, 171n28

Wilson house, 110, 111, 122, 181n9, 182n13

Wilson, Jerdon Dillard Bismark (Dillard Wilson), 42, 52, 57, 58, 92;
and farming, 42, 44, 66;
leaving Paluxy Valley farm, 94;
meeting Roland T. Bird, 62, 66, 68;
as musician, 54;
photo of, 83;
and Roland T. Bird, 79, 80, 82, 83, 117

Wilson, John, 42, 45, 52, 57, 58, 59, 82, 85, 92, 154, 173n21, 189n40;
photo of, 58

Wilson, Murry, 52

Wilson, Ora Helen Abell, 42, 45, 94

Wilson, Novella, 103;
childhood, 52-54, 59, 154;
and dinosaur tracks, 58-59;
drawing—"The Dinosaur Waltz," 156;
as historian, 154;
observation of Paluxy River tracks quarry and work, 82, 85;
paintings by, 23, 110, 181n11;
Paluxy River tracks painting, 110-111, 119;
photo of, 52;
postcard art of sauropods, 148;
quoted—Abell house description, 23;
quoted—cedar chopping, 57-58;
quoted—childhood games and recreation, 52-54;
quoted—cotton harvest, 24;
quoted—flooded crossing, 32,34;
quoted—rattlesnakes, 143;
quoted—turkey thief, 53;
and Roland T. Bird, 114-119

Wood, Andy, 109

Word, J.P. (State Senator), 99, 105, 112, 117;
on photos, 117, 118

Works Projects Administration, 74, 80;
crew at Paluxy River, 76-77, 84, 85, 87-88, 123, 175-176n11;
work crew—photos of, 78, 85

Wright, Jim (U.S. Representative), 100, 109

Wyoming, 56, 173n12

Yarborough, Ralph (Senator), 109

Yellow-billed Cuckoo, 142

Yocham, Leta, 152

Young County, 18, 164n30

YWCA, 82

Zappler, George, 133